WINTERS
IN THE
WORLD

WINTERS
IN THE
WORLD

A JOURNEY THROUGH THE
ANGLO-SAXON YEAR

ELEANOR PARKER

REAKTION BOOKS

For my parents

Published by
REAKTION BOOKS LTD
Unit 32, Waterside
44–48 Wharf Road
London N1 7UX, UK

www.reaktionbooks.co.uk

First published 2022
Copyright © Eleanor Parker 2022

Printed and bound in Great Britain
by TJ Books Ltd, Padstow, Cornwall

A catalogue record for this book is available from the British Library
ISBN 978 1 78914 672 1

CONTENTS

PREFACE

This book is a guide and introduction to the Anglo-Saxon year, and my hope is that it will also serve as an introduction to the immensely rich and creative literature of Anglo-Saxon England – a treasury of poetry and thought, profoundly rewarding to explore but not easy for many people to access today. Quotations and references have all been chosen with this purpose in mind, prioritizing what will be most useful for the general reader. For reasons of space, it hasn't been possible to give every quotation in the original Old English as well as in translation, but for selected short quotations I've included the original text too, to allow interested readers to get a flavour of the language. Many Old English words can be readily recognizable for speakers of Modern English, especially once you know that the unfamiliar letters þ (thorn) and ð (eth) are both pronounced 'th'. Unless otherwise noted all translations are my own, so not every poem quoted is referenced in the endnotes, but all can be found in the 'Further Reading' section of the Bibliography.

A famous preface from Anglo-Saxon literature, introducing one of the books which formed part of Alfred the Great's programme for rebuilding education among the English in the late ninth century, compares the act of translation to going into the woods to collect timber, gathering materials for building and coming back laden with branches. The translator collected as much as he could carry from the original texts, he says, but still wished he could have brought more: 'in every tree I saw something I needed at home.' So he recommends every reader to go to the woods – the forest of books – and gather for themselves:

> I advise everyone who is able and has many wagons to make his way to that same wood where I cut these posts, and gather more for himself and load up his wagons with fine timbers, so that he may weave many elegant walls, and establish many a noble house, and build a fine homestead, and there dwell in happiness and peace both summer and winter.

I've tried to make it possible for every reader of this book to do the same.

INTRODUCTION:
THE ANGLO-SAXON YEAR

Winter byð cealdost,
lencten hrimigost – he byð lengest ceald;
sumor sunwlitegost – swegel byð hatost;
hærfest hreðeadegost; hæleðum bringeð
geres wæstmas, þa þe him God sendeð.

Winter is coldest,
spring frostiest – it is longest cold;
summer sun-brightest – the sun is hottest;
harvest most glory-blessed; it brings to men
the year's fruits, which God sends them.

These lines are from an Anglo-Saxon poem called *Maxims II*, sketching a word-portrait of the cycle of the year. The four seasons are given the very briefest of descriptions, and each has one superlative, summing up its essential characteristic in a single word. Though they might sound like obvious statements, they're not as straightforward as they seem. The cold of winter, the brightness of summer, the abundance of autumn, all immediately make sense – but is *frostiest* really the first thing that leaps to mind when you think of spring, the season of daffodils, blossom and baby lambs? Perhaps not. These lines offer a picture of a cycle we know by heart, and even some familiar words: *winter, sumor, sun*. But this is not quite our year, and the round of seasons this poet knew was both like and unlike our own.

In this book, we'll explore how poets like the anonymous author of *Maxims II* and the writers of other works from Anglo-Saxon England – histories, scientific texts, sermons and many more – thought about the cycle of the seasons. We'll look at the festivals and traditions they associated with particular times of year, considering how the changing seasons affected patterns of work and religious custom, as well as investigating the language these English writers used to describe their experience of the year. The six centuries we today call the Anglo-Saxon period – six hundred summers and winters – were a formative time for English society, in which many things first took shape which, after the passage of centuries, are still to some degree recognizable as those the Anglo-Saxons knew: the English language; the settlement and naming of most of our cities, towns and villages; the monarchy; the national church; and England itself. Among the most enduring aspects of English life that evolved in the Anglo-Saxon period was the cycle of the year that we'll be exploring in this book. Through the four seasons described by *Maxims II*, weaving in and out of the circling months, there developed a yearly round of feasts and festivals, celebrations and customs, which still forms the basis of our own seasonal cycle. Christmas and Easter, Candlemas and Whitsun, Michaelmas, Lent and Lammas – all these first began to be celebrated in this country during the Anglo-Saxon period and owe their names to the Anglo-Saxons. The later Middle Ages added more festivals to the calendar, the Reformation swept many away, but through more than a thousand years of religious, political and social upheaval the basic pattern of the festival year remained a stable part of life. Well into the twentieth century, it provided the shared cycle of high days and holidays, as well as all the common waymarkers in the agricultural, legal and educational year.

Over the past hundred years, it has grown increasingly unfamiliar: many of us have lost touch with the agricultural calendars that determined these cycles of feast and fast, and in modern secular Britain we now celebrate a wide and diverse range of festivals alongside these older feasts. Even if the calendar is changing, though, our year is still shaped by the rhythms of the seasons, and as we go on our journey through the Anglo-Saxon year we'll encounter some familiar sights: poets finding ways to capture in words the beauty of glittering ice, blossom and birdsong, green summer meadows or the falling leaves of autumn. There are also aspects of their year which can seem strange to modern eyes, and intriguingly so. We'll see writers imagining the calendar imbued with divine power, as if time itself can be sacred; we'll hear them explaining the close kinship between humans and the natural world, recognizing our own experiences of growth and decay reflected in the cycles of the sun and moon and the waxing and waning of plants and trees. We'll explore an understanding of the world in which human life as lived through the seasons was one part of an organic whole, inseparable from the patterns of nature, where the natural, the human and the holy were interrelated in the most essential ways.

THE MONTHS OF THE ENGLISH

Let's start by thinking about time. In modern Britain, the calendar in most widespread use is the Gregorian calendar, which, though devised in the late sixteenth century, has its origins in the Julian calendar used in the Roman Empire. It's a solar calendar, following the cycle of the sun rather than the moon, and it has twelve months, whose names in Modern English also derive ultimately from the Latin month-names of the Roman calendar. We have four seasons in a year, though ideas about when they begin vary. While the Gregorian calendar is our common standard, though, many people live simultaneously according to other calendars too: different religious calendars, solar and lunar, which determine the dates of fasts and festivals, the calendars that structure school and university terms, the legal calendar, the tax year. Even the football season has a fixed calendar by which many people track the passage of time. All this may seem self-evident, but as we'll see, the seasons of the Anglo-Saxon year don't map directly onto any modern pattern – so it's helpful to start by recognizing that our own calendar is a human construction, like any other, and not the only or the obvious way to organize the passage of time.[1]

When considering Anglo-Saxon England, we should also think of a diversity of calendars, used by different groups in society for varying purposes. Farmers and monks, kings and labourers, would all have experienced the seasons in different ways, depending on the patterns of work that gave shape to their months and years. Nonetheless, there were some calendars that affected everyone. In the Middle Ages, the agricultural year was much more fundamental to most people's lives than it is today, and some awareness of it would have been general. Even kings had to know how the harvest was going and order their plans by it; at times when labourers were needed for the harvest, they weren't available to fight in their kings' wars. For the majority of the Anglo-Saxon period, the liturgical year of the Christian calendar was also observed by society in common. Everyone kept the same seasons of fasting or observed religious holidays at the same time, since these dates were not a matter of personal choice but enforced by royal decree. When we talk about the agricultural and church calendars in a medieval context, we're talking about communal structures of time that were shared across society.[2]

Agricultural cycles were a constant, but when it came to the religious calendar, the Anglo-Saxon period witnessed a radical shift in the reckoning of time. At the start of this period in the fifth century, the peoples of Anglo-Saxon England were predominantly pagan; over the course of the seventh century they converted to Christianity, and with the new religion came an entirely new calendar. All our surviving written sources on this subject date from after the conversion, so it's difficult to get a clear picture of what the structure of the year might have been like beforehand. For that we're largely dependent on one important source, a short chapter in a work by the Anglo-Saxon historian Bede. Around 725, Bede wrote a book called *De temporum ratione* (The Reckoning of Time), a learned discussion of the calendar and the principles by which time was calculated in the medieval church.[3] In the early Middle Ages, this was the science of *computus*, a source of endless fascination to mathematically minded medieval scholars. *Computus* was important because it taught you how to calculate the date of Easter – crucial for working out the dates of other key festivals in the church year – but there were many other aspects to this study too. It involved understanding the cycles of the moon; calculating leap years; knowing the proper dates of the months, seasons, equinoxes and solstices; and measuring periods of time from the briefest to the longest, the instant to the aeon.

All these topics are explored in Bede's *De temporum ratione*. One purpose of his text is to explain that there are many different ways of reckoning these things across different cultures; his discussion shows that calendars are the product of convention and human reasoning, so they're culturally determined and prone to change, error and correction. But for Bede, as for other medieval scholars, the study of time was not just a human science, but a sacred pursuit. In their eyes, the structure of the year reflected profound truths about the nature of the universe, planned and created by God, which found expression in every detail of the calendar. Time was part of God's creation; to study it was to learn something about the mind of its divine creator.

In discussing the year's structure in different cultures, Bede lists the month-names of the Hebrew, Roman, Greek and Egyptian calendars and adds a brief chapter about the 'months of the English' in ancient times, before the Anglo-Saxon conversion to Christianity. 'It did not seem fitting,' he says, 'that I should speak of other nations' observance of the year and yet be silent about my own.'[4] What he tells us about the pre-conversion calendar is a tiny part of a lengthy work, and it doesn't take long to summarize. Before the conversion, he suggests, the Anglo-Saxons used a lunisolar calendar and divided the year into two seasons, summer and winter. Winter began on the full moon of the month roughly equivalent to October in the Julian calendar, which for this reason was called *Winterfylleð*. The two months around each solstice shared a name, suggesting that these were important turning points of the year, and Bede says that the year began on 25 December (that is, probably the winter solstice), which was called *Modraniht*, 'mothers' night'. He then lists the names of the months in English and offers an explanation for each name. As the calendar was lunisolar, these wouldn't be exactly equivalent with the months in the Julian calendar to which Bede matches them, but from his information we can construct a list (see table).

We'll explore the names he provides in more detail as we go on. Some of Bede's suggested etymologies are convincing, but others, as we'll see, have been challenged by modern scholars.[5] Most likely Bede wasn't relying on personal knowledge but was using a written source for the month-names and adding his own speculations about their meaning – and in some cases he may just have been guessing. This means that although this is a very useful and interesting list, it has to be taken with some caution. These names don't seem to have been in widespread use in Anglo-Saxon England, at least after the seventh century; Bede implies they had already fallen out of use by the time he was writing, and in our surviving written sources they have been replaced for most practical purposes with the Latin month-names from the Julian calendar. When writers do use the Old English names recorded by Bede, it's typically as a kind of scholarly curiosity. They appear alongside the Latin names in English calendars as late as the twelfth century, sometimes with month-names in Hebrew and Greek too, for those who really wanted to show off their calendrical learning. But the people who wrote those calendars were usually copying from Bede, so these sources don't tell us that the names were actually in

Latin month	English name	Bede's interpretation
December and January	Geola	named after the winter solstice
February	Solmonað	'month of cakes, which they offered to their gods in that month'
March	Hreðmonað	named for a goddess, Hreða, 'to whom they sacrificed at this time'
April	Eastermonað	named for a goddess, Eostre, 'in whose honour feasts were celebrated in that month'
May	Þrymilce	'because in that month cattle were milked three times a day'
June and July	Liða	'gentle' or 'navigable', because calm weather made these months good for sailing
August	Weodmonað	'month of weeds, because they are very plentiful then'
September	Haligmonað	'month of sacred rites'
October	Winterfylleð	because winter began on the full moon of this month
November	Blotmonað	'month of sacrifices', because cattle slaughtered then were consecrated to the gods

general use in Anglo-Saxon England, any more than the Hebrew and Greek ones were.

What's more, though Bede presents this list as 'the months of the English', it's likely that there was originally a fair amount of diversity in month-names, rather than one unified system. Each region of Anglo-Saxon England (in Bede's day, a group of separate kingdoms) spoke its own dialect of Old English, and Bede's list may well record a system used in only one area. Some alternative Old English month-names are recorded in other sources, including *Hlyda* (March), *Rugern* (August) and *Hærfestmonað* (September), which seem to have been in use in other parts of the country.

We should conclude, perhaps, that Bede isn't describing to us *the* Anglo-Saxon year, but only one version of it, and there may have been other calendars of which we now have no record.

Nonetheless, Bede's evidence is very helpful, since some aspects of the system he describes seem to have endured for centuries – long after the Anglo-Saxons adopted Christianity, and with it the Julian calendar. He appears to be right, for instance, when he says that the Anglo-Saxons originally had a two-season year, summer and winter, which was replaced with the four-season structure with which we're now familiar. This four-season pattern is used in a number of Anglo-Saxon texts (like *Maxims II*, the poem with which we began), and where these specify dates for the seasons, the transition usually occurs roughly halfway between the solstices and the equinoxes: winter starts on 7 November, spring on 7 February, summer on 9 May and autumn on 7 August. This means that the solstices and equinoxes fall at the middle or height of each season, rather than (as often today) marking the beginning. Bede discusses alternative systems for dating the seasons in *De temporum ratione*, but recommends this structure, which he attributes to 'the Greeks and Romans'.[6] Following his lead, calendars in Anglo-Saxon manuscripts frequently use these dates to mark the beginnings of the seasons. Some poems employ this system too, especially those most influenced by Christian learning and the liturgical calendar.

In other contexts, however, many Anglo-Saxon writers still seem to think in terms of a two-season year, with the solstices, often called 'Midwinter' and 'Midsummer', falling halfway through each season.[7] The dark, cold half of the year is universally called *winter* in Old English, and the other half-year may be called *sumor*, 'summer', or, more rarely, *gear*, the origin of our word 'year'. Though *gear* in Old English can simply mean 'year' as we would understand it, a period of twelve months, in poetry it often seems to have a more specialized meaning: 'the season of growth and light', including both spring and harvest, the whole warm half of the year. It's common in Old English to count time by 'winters' – to speak, for instance, of someone having lived a certain number of 'winters in the world' – and we'll see that winter is a season which looms large in Anglo-Saxon poetry. The other season, *sumor*, was not so often used to measure time in this way, but *gear* was, and that's why we count time in 'years'.

In this two-season structure, what we'd think of as spring was part of summer, and the months we'd consider autumn fall partly at the end of summer (in harvest), partly in winter. This probably explains why words for spring and autumn have fluctuated much more in the history of English than the names for summer and winter. Though the words 'summer' and 'winter' go back to very similar Anglo-Saxon names, 'spring' and 'autumn' are much later additions to the language.[8] In Old English, spring is called *lencten*, a word which derives from the same Germanic root as 'long' and 'lengthen', denoting the season when the days are growing longer. After the conversion, *lencten* also came to be used for the season of fasting before Easter, and so became the origin of the word 'Lent'. Right through the Anglo-Saxon period and well into the fourteenth century, the word continued to have both meanings – the season of spring and the season of fasting, which of course always falls in spring. In the centuries after the Norman Conquest other alternatives also came into use, such as *ver*, borrowed into Middle English from French. It was only in the late medieval period that 'spring' began to be used as a season-name, *ver* fell out of use and 'Lent' narrowed its meaning to refer only to the pre-Easter fast.

Similarly, the word 'autumn' – another borrowing from French, though like *ver* ultimately deriving from Latin – only appeared in English at the end of the fourteenth century. Before that, the season was *hærfest*, the origin of Modern English 'harvest'. With this season, too, there was variety in naming right through the later Middle Ages and the early modern period: 'harvest' persisted alongside 'autumn' and another term, 'fall', first recorded in the mid-sixteenth century. At the time when British and American English began to diverge, the alternatives 'autumn' and 'fall' predominated in the two varieties of the language, and are still distinct today. Meanwhile 'harvest', like 'Lent', survived, but in a more specialized sense than its Old English meaning; gradually it came to mean not one of the four seasons of the year, but only the period when crops and fruits are gathered in. All this suggests that in popular understanding of the year both these transitional seasons have been more fluid, while the core pairing of summer and winter remained basically unchanged. The older way of thinking about the seasonal pattern, which Bede ascribes to the Anglo-Saxon calendar before the conversion to Christianity, persisted for many centuries.

A NEW RELIGION AND A NEW CALENDAR

In most other ways, however, the calendar that arrived with the conversion set down firm roots in the English festival year. By the time the Anglo-Saxons converted to Christianity, the essential structure of the Christian liturgical calendar was already well established. It had developed as the product of a long process of negotiation and adjustment in the first centuries of the church's history, in order to find a way of reconciling the Jewish calendar – crucial to dating festivals based in the Gospel narratives of the life of Christ – with the calendars used in the Roman Empire and other parts of the church.[9] At the time of the Anglo-Saxon conversion, the most important aspects of this process were complete. Nonetheless, the calendar did not remain static, but continued to grow and develop as more feasts and observances were added, spreading through international networks of cultural exchange in which the new Anglo-Saxon church soon began to play its part.

While Christianity might have been new to the Anglo-Saxons in the seventh century, it was not, of course, new to Britain. Present in Roman Britain in the third and fourth centuries, after the departure of the Roman armies it continued to flourish in Wales and other parts of western Britain; it's likely that some form of Romano-British Christianity survived in England into the Anglo-Saxon period, though the evidence is patchy.[10] British and Irish Christianity exerted an important influence in the early years of the Anglo-Saxon church, especially in Northumbria – sometimes a controversial issue when it came to the calendar, as we'll see later. Nonetheless, the foundational narrative of Anglo-Saxon Christianity – as told most influentially by Bede – gave the prominent role in the conversion to the mission that arrived in Kent in 597, sent from Rome by Pope Gregory I. Æthelbert, king of Kent, agreed to accept baptism and supported the establishment of a new church, and the mission's leader, Augustine, became the first Archbishop of Canterbury, Æthelbert's royal city. From Kent, Augustine and his companions sent missionaries to convert the other Anglo-Saxon kingdoms, where they met with a more mixed reception; during the seventh century, however, one region after another gradually adopted the new religion.

In the early medieval period, religious conversion was frequently a collective rather than an individual process, and it marked a profound cultural shift. The introduction of a new shared festival calendar was an important part of this. In a letter of advice to the Augustinian mission, Gregory counselled them to treat conversion as a process of adaptation, telling them to offer the newly converted Anglo-Saxons Christian feasts in exchange for their existing festivals and to repurpose the sites of pagan shrines as Christian churches. The idea was that it would be easier for people to accept the new religion if they were allowed to keep aspects of their old festivals: 'while some outward rejoicings are preserved, they will be able more easily to share in inward rejoicings,' Gregory wrote.[11] This was a tried-and-tested practice in the early Middle Ages, and one there was no attempt to hide. Medieval historians were well aware that the church had frequently Christianized pagan festivals and customs, not only in the context of the Anglo-Saxon conversion, but – much more importantly, even in the eyes of medieval English historians

– in Rome. Bede, for instance, explains how the custom of processing with candles at the feast of the Purification of the Virgin Mary (2 February) was a Christianized version of a processional ritual of expiation, observed in pagan Rome and adopted by the early church.[12] Similar explanations are provided by Anglo-Saxon writers for the processions of Rogationtide, which we'll consider in detail later, and for the Ember Days, four periods of prayer and fasting corresponding to the four seasons of the year, which probably had their roots in pagan Roman rituals seeking the aid of the gods at different stages in the agricultural cycle. In writing about such customs, Anglo-Saxon historians show that they were fully aware that the Christian liturgical cycle borrowed in part from older customs, and that they understood how festivals and rituals could take on new forms and meanings as the result of religious change.

In the case of Anglo-Saxon England, Gregory's advice on adapting existing festivals must have been only the beginning. Developing a festival calendar for the new English church meant harmonizing a religion which had its origins in the Middle East and the Mediterranean world with the seasonal and agricultural calendar of a country on the edge of northern Europe, and that was a complex process of synthesis. It was not simply a matter of laying one calendar on top of another, or celebrating old festivals under new names; it must have involved a considerable amount of negotiation and adaptation on both sides. It's a common claim in popular accounts of the festival year that remnants of Anglo-Saxon pagan belief long survived after the conversion and had an important influence on later English customs, festivals and folklore. As we look at the surviving sources, we'll be able to test in more detail, case by case, how far this claim can be substantiated. Our priority, however, will be studying the evidence we have rather than speculating about pagan festivals which are almost entirely unrecorded in surviving Anglo-Saxon sources. In some cases, we can look to comparative cultures for suggestive parallels: early medieval England and Scandinavia, for instance, had close cultural affinities, and Old Norse paganism is much better attested than pre-Christian belief from Anglo-Saxon England. However, it would be a mistake to draw too direct lines of comparison between early Anglo-Saxon paganism and the Old Norse evidence, which in most cases dates from centuries later. It's best not to worry too much about labelling certain practices as remnants of ancient paganism, unless they were clearly perceived in that way in the Anglo-Saxon period; what we want is to try and understand Anglo-Saxon culture on its own terms, and that's often more fluid and more interesting than modern labels allow room for.

To a large degree, the details of the process by which the Anglo-Saxons adopted a new cycle of Christian festivals are lost to us. But the outcome of that process was the calendar we'll be exploring in this book, which proved remarkably durable, lasting – not unaltered, but essentially stable – for many hundreds of years. It was a strength of this calendar that it was, at one and the same time, firmly rooted in Anglo-Saxon culture and fully part of the wider international church. A key attraction of Christianity to early Anglo-Saxon kings was that it offered an opportunity to join the mainstream of European culture, becoming part of a network of Christian rulers, and throughout the Anglo-Saxon period the English church was in constant communication with churches across Europe and beyond. Anglo-Saxon monks and nuns travelled and studied abroad, foreign scholars came to live in England, and for Anglo-Saxon pilgrims the route to Rome was already a well-trodden path. Two of the most significant leaders in the early Anglo-Saxon church, whose influence can hardly be overstated, were Theodore, a scholar from Tarsus in Cilicia, a Greek-speaking province of the Byzantine Empire, who was appointed Archbishop of Canterbury in 668, and Hadrian, an African-born monk who at the same time became abbot of the monastery of St Augustine's, Canterbury. Working together, these men established an unparalleled centre of learning in Canterbury which introduced new forms of scholarship to England from much further afield than Rome – the learning of Antioch and Constantinople, Syria and Libya. Their great learning included, Bede tells us, scholarship on the calculation of the calendar, and they attracted many eager pupils; 'never had there been such happy times since the English first came to Britain,' Bede comments with enthusiastic praise.[13]

Such international links meant that as new festivals sprang up in other parts of the church, they were soon adopted in England. At the same time, over the centuries the Anglo-Saxon church developed its own feasts, saints and customs, and grew into a thoroughly vernacular form of English Christianity, with its own characteristic habits of prayer, devotion and scholarship. That culture was not unchanging or monolithic. The six centuries of Anglo-Saxon history saw huge political and cultural change – new waves of immigration from Scandinavia, the birth of a single kingdom of England, war, invasion, conquest.[14] New festivals became fashionable and new customs were introduced. But some things remained constant. The year turned from Midwinter to Midsummer; the length of the days waxed and waned; fields were sown and harvested. Scholars found methods for reckoning the passing of years, poets found words to praise it, and everyone lived through the cycle together in their different ways, year by year.

WRITING THE YEARS

In this book we'll explore sources from across the Anglo-Saxon period which deal in different ways with the seasons and festivals of the year: histories and sermons, scientific and medical texts, calendars and saints' lives, and poems of many kinds. Before we begin, let's meet some of these texts and their authors. We've already encountered Bede, and we'll look at his writings several times over the course of this book – not only *De temporum ratione*, our most important source for the structure of the year in the pre-conversion period, but his *Historia ecclesiastica gentis Anglorum* (Ecclesiastical

History of the English People). Born around 673, Bede was just seven years old when he entered the twinned monasteries of Wearmouth–Jarrow, near the River Tyne in Northumbria, where he spent the rest of his life. At the end of the *Historia ecclesiastica*, he tells us that the guiding principle of his life was his love of learning: 'it has always been my delight to learn or to teach or to write,' he says.[15] This scholarly delight led him to write on many topics in addition to the reckoning of time and the history of his own people: he composed numerous biblical commentaries, poems, hymns, saints' lives and a translation – sadly lost – of the Gospel of John into English. The *Historia ecclesiastica*, written around 731, is an invaluable source of information about the early Anglo-Saxon kingdoms and the establishment of the English church, and it had a huge and lasting impact on the Anglo-Saxon church's understanding of its own history. Bede was influential in popularizing the idea that there was a single 'people of the English', sharing a common culture, language and religion, centuries before England became a political reality.[16]

Bede wrote mostly in Latin, as did other early Anglo-Saxon writers, since this enabled them to communicate with readers and scholars across Europe. In time, however, Anglo-Saxon England also developed a very rich and diverse vernacular literature. Writing in English especially flourished between the ninth and eleventh centuries, and in this period the English language could be used to write just about any kind of text you can think of, whatever its subject or intended audience. After the Norman Conquest, that would change radically: French became the language of high-status literature, law, politics and bureaucracy, while learned technical or specialist topics – history, science or theology – were largely discussed in Latin. But in Anglo-Saxon England all those subjects could be written about in English, and even the most arcane and erudite topics find expression in the common tongue. This includes many different kinds of writing about the calendar and the seasons.

There are, for instance, reference works such as the encyclopaedic *Old English Martyrology*, a ninth-century compilation with a short entry for each day of the year which provides bite-size information about the festival or saint commemorated on that date.[17] Practical knowledge of the calendar crops up in Old English medical texts, which often advise on the best season – and sometimes specific days – for administering remedies most effectively. From the late Anglo-Saxon period, we have some descriptions of the day-to-day administration of farming estates, outlining the duties and rights of different groups of labourers: they stipulate, for instance, how many extra days a peasant might be called upon to work during harvest and when he should pay his taxes (ten pennies at Michaelmas, a quantity of barley at Martinmas), but also what a shepherd should receive in return for his work (a portion of dung at Midwinter, a lamb and a ram's fleece in the spring, a bowl of whey all through the summer). An Old English text known as *Gerefa*, 'Reeve', advises the overseer of an estate about the jobs he needs to keep track of at different seasons in the year, from setting hedges and making sheepfolds in the summer to chopping timber in the winter frost.[18] At the other end of the social scale, the seasonal calendar also influenced when Anglo-Saxon kings would hold assemblies with their advisors,[19] and festivals regularly feature in royal laws and decrees: dates such as Easter or Martinmas were employed as fixed points of reference for the payment of taxes and tithes, and legislation laid down the amount of holiday to which workers were legally entitled at certain festivals. This pragmatic use of feast-days continued into the later medieval period and for many centuries afterwards. Festivals, especially the four quarter-days at Christmas, Lady Day, Midsummer and Michaelmas, have historically been used to set the dates when rents and payments were due and contracts and leases would begin or end. Remnants of this system still shape the legal, educational and parliamentary calendars in Britain; this explains, for instance, why the tax year starts in April, after 'Old Lady Day'.

All these different kinds of texts give us a fascinating insight into the Old English vocabulary of time-reckoning and the tasks or customs associated with particular seasons in Anglo-Saxon England. The calendar also features prominently in the *Anglo-Saxon Chronicle*, one of our best sources for England's early medieval history. The origins of the *Chronicle* lie at the court of Alfred the Great, king of Wessex from 871 to 899.[20] Ruling at a time when England had suffered decades of Viking attacks and the other Anglo-Saxon kingdoms had fallen under Scandinavian control, Alfred believed that learning among the English was in a dire state – a sad decline from the days of Bede. His solution was to invite foreign scholars to come and help him revive education in England, promoting the translation of a range of philosophical and historical texts into English so people could read them in their own language. The *Anglo-Saxon Chronicle* began as part of Alfred's project, but soon took on a life of its own. Kept up in different places over two or three hundred years, it's a year-by-year record of all the events that go to make up history: wars, plagues, invasions, political intrigues, the deaths of kings. It survives in several versions, which share common sources with each other but also incorporate different material, depending on the priorities of the people whose job it was to keep the annals up to date. As well as being a crucial historical source, the *Chronicle* is an excellent guide to the structure of the Anglo-Saxon year, because it usually dates the events it records by seasons and festivals, 'at Easter' or 'before Midsummer'. It tells us what people were doing at different times of the year, but also how they thought about and described the passage of time.

The vast majority of Old English texts are anonymous; we can deduce (sometimes) when and where they were written, but rarely know much about the people who wrote them. There are some important exceptions, though. These include two scholarly monks, writing in the decades around 1000, who in their different ways provide us with important information about the Anglo-Saxon calendar: Ælfric of Eynsham and Byrhtferth of Ramsey. They lived in tumultuous times. Ælfric was born around 955, Byrhtferth about fifteen years later, and both were educated in monasteries influenced by a spirit of renewal, often called the Benedictine Revival, which was energizing the tenth-century church. This was a time of relative peace in England, by now a single kingdom ruled by the descendants of Alfred the Great, with the Vikings kept temporarily at bay. But peace and prosperity did not last long. In the 980s Viking attacks resumed, posing not only a military danger but also a constant drain on the country's finances, as the king and his counsellors tried to pay ever-increasing sums of money in exchange for peace. Decades of warfare culminated in 1016 when England was conquered by the Danish king Cnut and became part of his Scandinavian empire – a precursor to the Norman Conquest which would follow fifty years later.

Ælfric and Byrhtferth lived much of their adult lives in a country falling apart under the pressure of war and political turmoil. Amid it all, these monks occupied themselves with the study of history, theology and time. Ælfric's life was spent at a succession of monasteries in Wessex: Winchester, Cerne Abbas in Dorset, then Eynsham in Oxfordshire. A prolific author, composing mostly sermons, translations and teaching texts, he's best known for his two great cycles of homilies and a large collection of saints' lives, which were intended to provide sermons for every significant feast and commemoration in the church year. These collections display the full range of Ælfric's talents as a communicator. Within his sermons he translates into English and explains for his listeners an impressive variety of biblical extracts, patristic texts, liturgical customs and historical and theological material. Almost all Ælfric's writing is educational or pastoral in its aims; he was a teacher to his fingertips, constantly engaged with the question of how best to explain complex and challenging ideas to his audiences. As well as his sermons, he also composed letters of pastoral guidance and works for use in the monastic classroom, including English textbooks on Latin grammar and science. Among these is a short text in English, *De temporibus anni*, which aims to be a more accessible, user-friendly introduction to the kind of material covered in Bede's *De temporum ratione*.[21] It summarizes scientific thinking on the structure of the year and the reckoning of time; the nature of the sun, moon and stars; and the operation of the winds and weather. It's a useful source for our purposes here, and so are Ælfric's sermons: though his primary focus is explaining the course of the church year, Ælfric was also interested in different systems of seasonal calculation, the connection between the liturgical cycle and the natural world, and how learned and popular understandings of the calendar coincide. From his writings we can get a sense of how beliefs about the cycle of the year and its religious significance were communicated to a wider audience in Anglo-Saxon England.

Byrhtferth, slightly younger than Ælfric, was a monk of Ramsey Abbey in what is now Cambridgeshire. Unlike Ælfric, he was primarily a historian – but since medieval historians were always thinking about time, how to calculate it and how to understand it, he wrote about the calendar too. Scientifically minded, Byrhtferth was as fascinated as Bede by the study of *computus*, and he had been trained at Ramsey under one of the leading tenth-century scholars of the subject, Abbo of Fleury. In 1011, Byrhtferth wrote a book which he called his *Enchiridion*, *Manualis* or *Handboc*, names which all mean 'hand-book', in Greek, Latin and English respectively. This was a guide to calendar calculation and *computus*, intended to help young monks learn about this complicated and technical subject. To aid his readers, Byrhtferth wrote in both Latin and English, switching between languages and incorporating many diagrams to help his pupils find their way through this maze. His book has some lovely moments, especially when he addresses his pupils with sympathy for their puzzlement at these complex topics, or when he imagines Bede, on whom he draws heavily as a source, turning up to talk to them as a kind of guest lecturer – coming to 'take his seat comfortably propped up on pillows, and declare to us with glad heart the things which are known to him'.[22] Though Bede had died nearly three hundred years earlier, Byrhtferth has a vivid sense of the older scholar's presence as he reads his works: 'we imagine that most learned of men sitting here now as we study his writings,' he says. The most impressive of Byrhtferth's virtuosic diagrams depicts a pattern of interlocking rings, designed to illustrate the interconnectedness of the universe. It shows parallels between significant sets of four and twelve, including the seasons, elements, months, winds, astrological signs and more. The seasons are aligned with the four ages of human life: spring with childhood, summer with adolescence, autumn with adulthood, winter with old age. The diagram is a work of art as well as a brilliant act of synthesis. Its purpose is to show that everything in the world has its correspondences in the heavens, the earth and the passage of time; nothing is random, and human existence is part of a great pattern as huge as the universe.

WYRD AND WISDOM

The decades around 1000, when Ælfric and Byrhtferth were writing, were also the period in which our most important sources for Anglo-Saxon poetry were recorded. Almost all surviving Old English poetry is preserved in just four priceless manuscripts, which were compiled around this time, though many of the poems in them may be much older. Most Anglo-Saxon poetry is anonymous, and it's generally difficult to be sure when or where individual poems were written; we do at least have the evidence of the manuscripts, though, which may be able to tell us when and where the poems were *read*. One of these four manuscripts contains *Beowulf*, along with other texts on marvellous creatures and distant lands; another consists of four long poems on biblical subjects; a third, the Vercelli Book, preserves *The Dream of the Rood* and poems about the lives of saints, as well as a collection of homilies. But it's the fourth manuscript we'll meet most often.

This is called the Exeter Book, because in the eleventh century it was given to the library of the monastery at Exeter Cathedral, where it's been ever since. It contains a miscellaneous collection of English poems on a very wide variety of subjects: poems of lament and love, wisdom poetry, allegories about the natural world, stories of saints, and a large collection of riddles that range from the erudite to the obscene. War, sex, animals, saints – Anglo-Saxon monks had eclectic literary tastes, and no subject is off-limits in these poems. We'll see poetic engagement with the seasons in many of these diverse contexts, as poets seek to describe natural cycles and landscapes both for their own sake and as reflections of human experience.

Only a handful of Old English poems survive outside these big compilations, but among them are two short, precious texts which are especially important in thinking about the Anglo-Saxon year. As we begin our journey through the seasons, let's take a moment to consider these two poems and what they can tell us about how Anglo-Saxon poets might imagine the passage of time. In the 1040s, scribes working at a monastery somewhere in the south of England – perhaps in Canterbury, or at Abingdon, near Oxford – copied out a manuscript of the *Anglo-Saxon Chronicle* and added as a preface two anonymous poems.[23] Though these poems are quite different from each other and from the *Chronicle*, the people who put them together must have seen a connection between them, an undercurrent of shared thought. All are linked by an interest in time and power, the cycle of the year, human experience of the seasons, and reflection on what it means to mark and record the passage of the years.

Like most Anglo-Saxon poems, these have no titles in the manuscript and have been given names by modern editors. They've been lumbered with rather dry titles, *The Menologium* and *Maxims II*, but if the titles are dry, the poems are not. *The Menologium* is a poem about the cycle of the year – a calendar in verse, time turned into poetry. It records the dates of feasts and festivals, the twelve months, the four seasons and the solstices and equinoxes, weaving them all together into a unified and beautiful picture of the whole year's course.[24] The poem could serve a practical function by reminding the reader of important dates in the calendar, but its purpose isn't solely functional. It uses the traditional language and imagery of Anglo-Saxon poetry to explore the relationship between all these aspects of the yearly cycle, between the seasons and sacred time. It begins:

> Crist wæs acennyd, cyninga wuldor,
> on midne winter, mære þeoden,
> ece ælmihtig, on þy eahteoðan dæg
> 'Hælend' gehaten, heofonrices weard.

> Christ was born, glory of kings,
> at Midwinter, marvellous prince,
> eternal Almighty, and on the eighth day
> named 'Healer', heaven's guardian.

At a basic level, these lines give you the date of Christmas and the year's first feast, Christ's circumcision and naming, celebrated on 1 January. (*Hælend*, which means 'healer, saviour', is the usual translation for the name 'Jesus' in Old English.) But they do this by employing the devices of poetry: alliteration, the building-block of Anglo-Saxon verse, and what's called 'variation', the use of a number of phrases denoting the same idea but with subtly different emphasis – here, four descriptors all referring to Christ. In Old English poetry alliteration links the key words within a line, drawing the listener's attention to the most important concepts and encouraging us to think about how they might be connected. Here, the first line's alliteration links 'Christ' and 'king' (*cyning*), which connects – but also perhaps contrasts – heavenly and earthly kingship. Importantly, it points us forwards to the subject-matter of the

Anglo-Saxon Chronicle, which records the failures and successes of many generations of kings. The poem also draws our notice to the link between Christ's birth and the season of Midwinter, as we'll consider in more detail later. In this poem the seasons are fundamental to the cycle of the year, but they aren't static – the passage of time is imagined as very active, very alive. As each month arrives, it's described as if it 'sweeps', 'glides' or 'travels' into our world, into the towns and villages where human beings dwell. As you read this poem you're taken on a journey through the year, but the year is moving too, carrying you along as it passes on its way.

Maxims II, the other poem chosen to preface the *Chronicle* in this manuscript, is also interested in the passage of time. Like *The Menologium*, it's a carefully structured poem, and its structure reflects a holistic view of the world as ordered and planned, arranged in every detail by a divine creator. Much of the poem deals with animals and the natural world, describing each with a brief statement assigning the creature to its proper place in the universe: 'a bird should be aloft, playing in the air'; 'a boar should be in the wood, strong with fixed tusks'; even 'a dragon should be in a barrow, old, proud in its treasures.'[25] Humans, like animals, have their habitat, their place in this ecosystem: 'a king should be in the hall, dealing out rings.' In this view of the world, everything belongs somewhere. The pattern of the seasons forms part of this ordered world. The poem opens, like *The Menologium*, with a reference to a king:

Cyning sceal rice healdan. Ceastra beoð feorran gesyne,
orðanc enta geweorc, þa þe on þysse eorðan syndon,
wrætlic weallstana geweorc. Wind byð on lyfte swiftust,
þunar byð þragum hludast. Þrymmas syndan Cristes myccle.
Wyrd byð swiðost.

A king should defend a kingdom. Cities are seen from afar,
the skilful work of giants, which are on this earth,

wondrous work of wall-stones. The wind in the sky is swiftest, thunder is loudest in season. Great are the powers of Christ. *Wyrd* is mightiest.

These lines are about power – mighty forces of the earth and sky. In a few swift phrases, the poet carries us on a journey through the universe, offering a series of quick, unconnected images: first a king, strong in his military defences; then a city-fortress, so cleverly built that it's imagined as 'the work of giants', *enta geweorc*; then we're swept up into the sky and battered by the wind and thunder, forces impossible for humans to control. The earthly power of kings and cities is dwarfed by the might of nature, and even more feeble when compared to the power of Christ and *wyrd*. The Old English word *wyrd* is usually translated as 'fate', but it often seems to mean something like 'the inevitable forward movement of time', which carries humans along on its course.

Then follows the brief sketch of the four seasons with which we began: *winter, lencten, sumor, hærfest*. The seasons represent another kind of power, the cycling year that keeps turning whether humans like it or not – another awesome and uncontrollable force, and the most visible manifestation of *wyrd*. But if we can't control the seasons, the poem implies, we can observe them, describe them and come to understand the place that they, like the bear, the king and the dragon, occupy in the world. The next lines hint at the benefits this kind of mindful observation can bring:

> Soð bið swicolost, sinc byð deorost,
> gold gumena gehwam, and gomol snoterost,
> fyrngearum frod, se þe ær feala gebideð.
> Wea bið wundrum clibbor. Wolcnu scriðað.

> Truth is most elusive, treasure is dearest,
> gold to every man, and an old one is sagest,

wise with by-gone years, he who has experienced much.
Sorrow is wondrously clinging. Clouds glide on.

Truth, treasure, wisdom: three precious things. The statements about truth and treasure could be taken literally, but are probably meant to point forwards to the next remark, implying that wisdom, the knowledge of truth, is another form of treasure. And what brings wisdom? The passage of 'by-gone years', like the cycle of the seasons described a few lines earlier. As the years pass, to live long is to experience many things, for good and ill. Sorrow may cling to the heart, but time keeps gliding on, like the clouds across the sky. The revolving years bring wisdom to the one who has 'experienced much', gathered many harvests and weathered many winters. If time can bring wisdom, then, let's see what we can glean as we go on our journey through the Anglo-Saxon year.

WINTER

1

FROM WINTER INTO WINTER

BEDE'S SPARROW

Around the year 624, a woman named Æthelburh left her home in Kent and travelled north to be married. She was the daughter of Æthelbert, king of Kent, the first Anglo-Saxon ruler to convert to Christianity, and his Frankish wife Bertha. Bertha was already a Christian when she married Æthelbert and she continued to practise her religion after her marriage, worshipping at St Martin's church in Canterbury. The Kentish king's marriage to a Christian princess must have been an important step in his willingness to accept her faith, and now their daughter was being sent to marry a pagan king, as her mother had been before her, in the hope that the marriage would further the spread of Christianity through the Anglo-Saxon kingdoms. With her went Paulinus, a monk from Rome who had been sent to England to join Augustine's mission and now accompanied Æthelburh to evangelize the north.

Æthelburh's new husband was Edwin, king of the Northumbrians, and he had already agreed in principle to consider accepting his wife's faith. He did not convert at once, however, but spent two or three years apparently weighing the implications of adopting the new religion before at last consenting to be baptized. Those years, as Bede records in his *Historia ecclesiastica*, were a turbulent and dramatic time. Edwin faced opposition in his kingdom, war with the West Saxons and an assassination attempt on the very night that Æthelburh gave birth to their first child.[1] While all this was happening, the king was in discussion with Paulinus about the idea of converting to Christianity. But whether the king should adopt a new religion was not only a personal choice; it was a matter that affected the whole kingdom, so Edwin held a council with his advisors and asked for their views. What did they make of the teaching Paulinus had brought?

Bede, writing around a century later, reports this crucial discussion in memorable detail, though some of what he says may come from his imagination – his own sense of what people might, or should, say in such a situation. First, he tells of the reaction of the chief priest, who swiftly abandons his old gods, reasoning that if the gods were truly powerful they would have rewarded him better in return for his devotion. Then follows another contribution to the debate, by a nameless counsellor to the king whose speech takes us to the heart of this chapter's theme: the Anglo-Saxon winter. This is what the anonymous counsellor says:

> O king, the present life of men on earth seems to me, in comparison to the time which is unknown to us, as if you are sitting at dinner with your men and counsellors in the wintertime, with a good fire kindled on the hearth in the midst of the hall and all inside well warmed, while outside storms of winter rain and snow are raging. A sparrow comes swiftly flying through the hall; it enters at one door, and soon goes out through the other. During the time it is inside, the storms of winter cannot touch it; but after the briefest moment of calm weather, it vanishes from your sight, quickly returning from winter into winter. In the same way, this life of men appears for a brief moment; what went before, or what will come after, we do not know at all. If, therefore, this new teaching offers something more certain, it seems worthy to be followed.

This story encapsulates both the best and worst of winter: the hostile weather and darkness outside, but also the pleasure of gathering inside with warmth and company to keep the winter away. In this speech, winter represents the vast unknowable beyond lying outside human perception. All we know in life is within the hall, and our experience of it is as transitory as the flight of the sparrow – one moment of light, preceded and followed by utter darkness. The appeal of Christianity, to this speaker, is that it offers a glimpse into that mysterious darkness, some knowledge of 'the time which is unknown to us'. It allows us to look outside the brief moment that is our life on earth, into eternity. Without that, we, like the sparrow, travel 'from winter into winter'.

In its literary heritage, this story exemplifies just the kind of cross-cultural dialogue in which Edwin, Paulinus and the counsellors were engaged during this momentous discussion. It's both deeply Christian and thoroughly Anglo-Saxon. In choosing a sparrow to represent the soul, it draws on a biblical tradition of using the little sparrow to evoke the frailty of human life, watched over by God's all-knowing providence.[2] In the Gospels, for instance, Jesus tells his disciples not to fear persecution because 'Are not two sparrows sold for a penny? And not one of them will fall to the ground without your Father's will. But even the hairs of your head are all numbered' (Matthew 10:29–30). Bede's story places the sparrow, resonant with these biblical associations, within the distinctly medieval setting of a royal mead-hall. King Edwin is invited to imagine himself within a scene he must often have experienced, feasting with his friends and counsellors in the hall while winter rages outside. In Anglo-Saxon poetry, the mead-hall is often used as a microcosm of human society, a symbol of fellowship and community. We see this for instance in *Beowulf*, where the hero's first battle is to defend the royal hall of the Danes from night-time attack by the monster Grendel. An assault on the hall represents a terrible threat to the peace and security of the king and his people. In that poem, the hall is not just a place of feasting but also where the king sits in counsel with his advisors and receives his guests – a seat of government and royal authority. That makes it a meaningful setting in which to locate this parable, as Edwin is asked to make a crucial decision on behalf of all his people.

In drawing on both these literary traditions, the story reveals how carefully it has been constructed. As a result, we may suspect that it doesn't really reflect what Edwin's counsellors might have argued as they debated whether or not to accept Christianity. It's a reminder of how difficult it can be for us to get a reliable sense of Anglo-Saxon beliefs before the conversion: in this speech we have what purport to be the views of a pagan on his own belief-system and his reasons for accepting a new religion, but we're surely hearing the thoughts of Bede, not Edwin's counsellors.[3] When the advisor talks of his uncertainty about what comes before life and after death, of an ignorance as profound as winter darkness about these key questions of human existence, he's articulating a Christian perspective on the limitations of non-Christian belief. It's hard to imagine that whatever Edwin's people believed before they accepted Paulinus' teaching, it didn't offer some form of answers to these questions – where do we come from, what happens to us when we die? Perhaps Bede didn't know what those answers were, or didn't want to repeat them. Either way, we are the ones left in the dark.

Nonetheless, this episode does reflect something important about what winter could mean for Bede and his Anglo-Saxon readers. In this, as in the metaphor of the hall, it draws on imagery found throughout the corpus of Anglo-Saxon literature. In the early days of the English church, missionaries like Paulinus and Christian writers like Bede found ways of exploring the new faith through language, symbols and stories that held meaning in Anglo-Saxon culture and literary tradition. One of those deep-rooted ideas was the threat of winter – and as we look at how winter is imagined by Anglo-Saxon poets, we'll start to see why the thought of life running 'from winter into winter' evoked such potent dread.

THE FROST'S FETTERS

Anglo-Saxon poetry is full of winters. Snow, hail, frost and ice beset the characters of many Old English poems, and it's clear that this season appealed strongly to the imaginations of Anglo-Saxon writers. The poetic language and imagery of winter exhibit many consistent features that recur again and again, in very different stories and contexts. Let's start with *The Menologium*, the calendar poem which moves through the cycles of the natural and liturgical year. According to the system of reckoning used in this poem, winter runs from 7 November to 6 February, from a few days after All Saints' Day until just after Candlemas. The first day of winter has its own name, *wintres dæg*, 'Winter's Day', and its arrival is described in language we'll start to recognize as characteristic of Anglo-Saxon poetry of winter.

> Syþþan wintres dæg wide gangeð,
> on syx nihtum, sigelbeortne genimð
> hærfest mid herige hrimes and snawes,
> forste gefeterad be Frean hæse,
> þæt us wunian ne moton wangas grene,
> foldan frætuwe.

> After [All Saints' Day] comes Winter's Day, far and wide,
> six nights later, and seizes sun-bright autumn
> with its army of ice and snow,
> fettered with frost by the Lord's command,
> so that the green fields may no longer stay with us,
> the ornaments of the earth.

The description of winter in this poem, brief as it is, has remarkable force. Winter is imagined as an invading warrior, a conquering king who sweeps through the earth with the fierce blasts of his snow-army and takes the earth prisoner in his fetters of frost. This is a poem which finds beauty in almost everything about the turning year, and we'll see later how it extols the exuberance of spring, the warmth of summer, the plenty of autumn. But here all the beauty belongs to what's lost when winter takes hold. We have a last glimpse of the loveliness of the abundant harvest, *sigelbeortne hærfest*, 'sun-bright autumn'; then winter violently seizes it and puts the earth in chains. The poet plays with the mournful contrast between two similar-sounding words, *frætuwe* and *gefeterad*, contrasting the green summer fields adorned ('fretted') with beauty and the winter 'fetters' of frost.

Imagery of winter imprisoning or chaining the earth appears across the Old English poetic corpus, and it's a way of thinking that shapes not only the poets' imagination of winter but also their descriptions of the coming of spring, when these chains are loosed and the earth is set free. As earth is trapped by winter, so are human beings. This metaphorical language of imprisonment partly evokes the literal restraints winter imposes on human and natural activity: winter weather keeps people indoors and stops them from travelling, and plants can't grow. But in many poems this language is also used to explore other forms of constraint and oppression, psychological as well as physical. We see this, for instance, in the poem *Andreas*, which includes a short but powerful passage describing a winter snowstorm. This poem, preserved in the Vercelli Book, is based on a Latin apocryphal narrative about the apostles St Andrew and St Matthew and their adventures among a race of cannibals; in its heroic style and idiom, however, it seems to have been directly inspired by *Beowulf*. The moment in question occurs when Andrew has been taken prisoner. As he languishes in jail, a storm assails the world outside:

> Snow bound the earth
> in winter-tumults. The skies grew cold

with hard hail-showers, and ice and frost,
hoary battle-marchers, locked up the homeland of men,
the dwellings of the people. The lands were frozen
with cold and chilly icicles; the force of the waters was
    shrunken.
Across the river-currents ice built a bridge,
a dark sea-road.

This is the Anglo-Saxon poet's addition to his Latin source, and
you'll see at once the parallels with the language and imagery in
The Menologium. Again, winter is imagined locking and binding
the earth, but here that also reflects the straits of the poem's hero:
Andrew's imprisonment, through which he bears up courageously
all the long winter night, is mirrored in the way winter is binding
the world around him. In the heroic style of this poem (as often
in Anglo-Saxon adaptations of biblical and apocryphal material),
Andrew is presented in traditional language as a warrior, brave and
fearless as he endures torments – and here winter is a warrior too. Ice
and frost are described, wonderfully, as *hare hildstapan*, 'hoary battle-
marchers'. The word *har* is a colour, white or grey, so a good word
for ice and frost; it's from this that we get the term 'hoar-frost'. But
because *har* could be used of grey-haired people as well, it had already
in Old English also come to mean 'aged, venerable, experienced', a
word used of tried-and-tested warriors and wise old men. This means
that the 'hoary' ice and frost are being imagined as grizzled warriors,
personifying the forces who have taken the land prisoner.

There's something in all this about the overwhelming power of
winter and the helplessness of humans to do anything more than
patiently endure it. That meant winter was a metaphor to which
an Anglo-Saxon poet might turn when trying to evoke a mood of
powerlessness, the sense of being trapped by forces beyond one's
control. In a moving poem called *Deor*, a poet suffering loss in his
own life tries to find consolation in his troubles by looking to past

stories of suffering, the tragedies and griefs of famous men and women from Anglo-Saxon heroic legend. One story he tells is that of Weland, a mighty smith of superhuman power and skill. Legend has it that Weland was trapped on an island by a cruel king who wanted to exploit his gifts, forcing him to make weapons and treasures. His hamstrings cut, Weland could not escape, until he constructed a magical suit of wings he used to fly away, exacting terrible revenge on his captor as he went. During his time of imprisonment, *Deor* says, Weland endured *wintercealde wræce*, 'winter-cold misery'. At the literal level, Weland's suffering had nothing to do with winter, and yet the phrase 'winter-cold misery' calls the reader's mind to this familiar association between winter and imprisonment. Weland's lonely, bitter life in captivity is a winter of the spirit. The only consolation *Deor* can offer is its refrain, repeated after each story of suffering: *Þæs ofereode, þisses swa mæg*, 'That passed away; so can this.' Perhaps that's all that can be hoped for in winter too: that with the passage of time, its hardships will come to an end.

There are many more examples we could look at – far more than there's space to discuss here. An especially interesting one features in a poem called *Solomon and Saturn*, which imagines a debate between a pagan named Saturn and wise King Solomon. It's a kind of riddle contest, in which Saturn challenges Solomon with a series of questions about the nature of the world and Solomon provides cryptic and often puzzling answers. The text is difficult and obscure, but by any standard Saturn's questions are unanswerable: why are earthly goods distributed unequally? Why do sorrow and laughter live so close together? Even when the questions are about nature, they reflect this sense that the world is a mysterious and unfathomable place governed by forces beyond human control. At one point, Saturn questions his wise interlocutor about a strange and terrible force of chaos: a mighty creature who travels through the world, destroying and devouring, causing grief wherever it goes. All things are helpless before it, and every year it consumes thousands of living creatures. This horror, Solomon answers, is *yldo*, 'age', which 'has power over everything on earth'. He elaborates on its destructive power, describing age as if it is a giantess on a rampage: she uproots trees and smashes branches, gobbles up birds, gnaws iron with corrosive rust. And, Solomon concludes after this catalogue of devastation, she consumes humans too: 'she does the same to us.'

This riddling speech figures the passage of time and the process of ageing as universally destructive, so it seems natural that Saturn's next question should be about another oppressive force closely linked to time: winter.

> But why does the snow fall, hide the ground,
> conceal the shoots of plants, bind up fruits,
> crush and repress them, so that they are for a time
> shrivelled with cold? Very often too he puts
> many wild beasts to the test. He builds a bridge over
>   the water,
> breaks the city-gate, proceeds boldly on,
> plunders . . .

At this point a large portion of text is lost in the manuscript, so if Solomon was able to give an answer to this question about winter, it's been lost. Snow and ice, like age, are personified as violent forces of destruction, and once again the image is of winter as an invading warrior, subduing the earth to his power. Ice (as in *Andreas*) 'builds a bridge' over the water, and it's as if winter, attacking the earth, is besieging a fortified city: it breaches the moat of the fortress with its causeway of ice, breaking through the walls and bursting in, stealing and plundering at will.

Winter is imagined as crushing and repressing the life within the earth, painfully forcing back any shoots of growth. That sense of oppression is echoed by several Old English poems which use winter to explore human grief and sorrow, reflecting on how suffering can have a numbing effect on the spirit, like snow on the frozen earth. Perhaps the most poignant instance is a poem in the Exeter Book called *The Wanderer*, in which an exile, mourning the loss of home and friends, is trapped in a winter which is his own grief:

> There is now none living
> to whom I dare openly speak
> the thoughts of my mind. I truly know
> it is a noble virtue among warriors
> for a man to bind his spirit-chest fast,
> conceal his heart, whatever he may think.
> The weary mind cannot withstand *wyrd*,
> nor the troubled heart provide help.
> So those eager for glory often
> bind fast sorrowful thoughts in their breasts,
> and I have had to keep my mind –
> often wretched, deprived of homeland,
> far from kinsmen – fastened in fetters,
> since long ago I buried my lord
> in the darkness of the earth, and from there
> journeyed, winter-sorrowful, over the binding waves . . .
> He who has experienced it knows
> how cruel sorrow is as a companion
> for him who has few beloved friends.
> The path of exile holds him, not twisted gold;
> a frozen spirit, not the glory of the earth.

In this poem, winter gets into your very heart. Deprived of his lord and home, the lonely speaker describes himself as *wintercearig*, 'winter-sorrowful', 'as desolate as winter', and he has a 'frozen spirit'. Though not literal imprisonment like that of Weland and St Andrew, it's a painful, claustrophobic enclosure; the earth trapped beneath its winter covering is like the aching heart concealed in the grieving warrior's breast, which strains at its enforced silence.

This is what it's like to face winter alone, without the consolations of Bede's mead-hall; it's exactly that kind of convivial society, and the company and protection it offers, for which this speaker is mourning. He describes journeying alone across the icy sea, falling asleep and waking to the cries of seabirds, which for a moment he mistakes for the voices of his lost friends. The winter landscape reflects the agonizing stasis of his emotional condition: though he travels, he doesn't seem able to hope for change or improvement, or the coming of spring. All he can feel, in the midst of his grief, is the pain of what he has lost.

This is winter chill numbing and enervating, forcing back even the expression of emotion – freezing the spirit. It's echoed by another poetic link between winter and suppressed human emotion that features memorably in *Beowulf*, in a short narrative recounted within the main story.[4] A distinctive feature of *Beowulf* is that it contains many allusions to other legends of kings and heroes from early medieval northern Europe, which are woven into the story around the main narrative strand of Beowulf's adventures. At one point, Beowulf and his men listen in the mead-hall as a poet sings the tragic story of a long-ago feud between Frisians and Danes. It begins with Hildeburh, a Danish woman married to Finn, king of the Frisians, who becomes caught in the middle of conflict between her husband and her brother, Hnæf. While Hnæf and his Danish companions are visiting Finn and Hildeburh at their home, Finnsburh, they're set upon by the Frisians, and in the battle that follows Hnæf and Finn's son are both killed. Hildeburh has to lay her brother and son together on the same funeral pyre, her ties to both sides of the feud bringing her double grief. After Hnæf's death, command of the Danes passes to a man named Hengest. War-weary and depleted on both sides, the Frisians and Danes make peace, swearing oaths that they will not seek vengeance for past injuries. But the truce cannot last. The feud breaks out again, Hengest avenges Hnæf by killing Finn, and the mourning Hildeburh is carried back to her homeland.

The audience of *Beowulf* might have known this story well, since Hengest may be the man identified in legend as the founder, with his brother Horsa, of the Jutish kingdom of Kent – according to medieval tradition, one of the first Anglo-Saxon settlers in Britain (and an ancestor of Æthelbert of Kent and his daughter Æthelburh, with whom we began).[5] If there's any truth in that, it would situate the events of this story around the middle of the fifth century. In *Beowulf*, the story provides the context for an incredibly claustrophobic winter scene, set in the weeks after Hnæf's death. Hengest and other survivors of the battle are still staying with Finn, choosing not to leave as winter weather comes on. As part of the peace treaty they have all sworn oaths not even to speak of the recent conflict, but beneath their silence the memory is fresh. It is a *wælfagne winter*, a 'slaughter-stained winter', and the turmoil of the weather reflects Hengest's tormented mind:

> Still Hengest
> stayed with Finn that slaughter-stained winter,
> ill-fated. He brooded on his homeland,
> though he could not drive on the sea
> his ring-prowed ship. The ocean seethed with storms,
> battled against the wind; winter locked the waves
> in icy bonds, until another spring came
> to the dwellings, just as it does now still,
> the gloriously bright weathers which unchangingly
> follow their appointed seasons. Then winter was past,
> fair the face of the earth. The exile was anxious to go,
> the guest out of those dwellings. He thought more readily
> of avenging his wrongs than of the sea-voyage,
> and whether he could find some occasion for violence.

As in other poems we've looked at, Hengest's freedom of action is constrained by winter, but the constraint is internal as much as external. The stormy seas and raging winds seem to imprison him temporarily at Finnsburh, but they also mirror his surging grief and aching desire for vengeance, seething away beneath the silence imposed by the truce. If he had got away from Finnsburh at once, perhaps the frail peace could have held, but the enforced inaction of winter gives him time to brood on his wrongs. By the time spring comes and he's free to go, the longing for vengeance has taken control of him: he stays, and bloodshed breaks out again. There's an extraordinary emotional intensity to Hengest's conflicted feelings here: his eagerness to escape from the place where he has fought and suffered contends with the brooding anger that is gaining mastery over him. Though the poet tells the story in a brief, elliptical way, what comes across powerfully is the push and pull of Hengest's warring impulses, buffeting against each other with the force of clashing waves in a winter sea.

The poet sets all that turbulent human emotion in juxtaposition with something very different: the ordered, impassive changing of the seasons. This is one of a number of moments in *Beowulf* where the poet turns to the seasons to explore some of the more abstract philosophical concerns of the poem, including an interest in power, history and God's interventions in the world. Here, as we'll see again later, the turning of the seasons acts as a reminder that even in this poem about mighty heroes and kings, there are many things in the world that humans just can't control. The great warrior Hengest may be striving to take command of his emotions, but he can't influence the weather, the seas or the passage of time; they follow their own courses, and constrain his actions in ways he can't escape. The seasonal setting is also a means of exploring continuity between past and present, thinking about time on a big scale. To the Anglo-Saxon poet the world of Beowulf is already far in the distant past, and the time of Hengest is even further back in history, the subject of legend for Beowulf and his contemporaries, just as Beowulf is for the poet and his audience. But one thing that connects them all – and links them with us – is the passage of the seasons. The cycling seasons the poet imagines Hengest living through, impatient and restless, are the same as in his own time: as winter passes, *oþer com gear in geardas, swa nu gyt deð*, 'another spring came to the dwellings, just as it does now still.' The language moves into the present tense, and Hengest's world seems suddenly less distant. In Hengest's day, in Beowulf's and in ours, the seasons are a constant: whatever else changes – whatever humans may be suffering in any particular winter – the year keeps turning.

WINTER WONDERS

The idea of winter that emerges from all these disparate poems is remarkably consistent: this season oppresses and constrains human beings in mind and body, with a power almost too much for the *wintercearig* heart to bear. Not all characterizations of winter in Anglo-Saxon poetry are so negative, though. Winter may offer evocative ways of thinking about human suffering, providing metaphorical language with which to evoke the storms of emotional turmoil or the chilling stasis of grief. But it offers other things too, and Anglo-Saxon poets were not incapable of seeing beauty in winter. It can be a time of transformation, when a familiar landscape may be rendered suddenly alien by a blanket of snow, a flooded field can be turned into a spreading lake, or a flowing river can change its nature and become frozen and immobile. These transformations are deeply strange, and in their suddenness they may seem something more than natural – more like a miracle than a simple process of the weather. The wisdom poem *Maxims I*, from the Exeter Book, muses on some of these transformations:

Forst sceal freosan, fyr wudu meltan,
eorþe growan, is brycgian,
wæter helm wegan, wundrum lucan
eorþan ciþas. An sceal inbindan
forstes fetre: felameahtig God.
Winter sceal geweorpan, weder eft cuman,
sumor swegle hat.

Frost must freeze, fire burn up wood,
the earth grow, ice build bridges,
water wear a helmet, wondrously locking up
shoots in the earth. One alone shall unbind
the frost's fetters: God most mighty.
Winter must pass, good weather come again,
summer bright and hot.

There's the familiar image of the 'frost's fetters', but nonetheless this is a more positive image of winter than we've seen so far. It not only promises that the season will – must – end, turning again as everything in the year turns, but also finds something wondrous in winter itself. These lines describe a range of natural processes, showing how elements act out their nature and fill their place in the divinely ordained structure of things. Like *Maxims II*, with its catalogue of animals in the habitats where they belong, this kind of wisdom poetry seeks to understand the world as ordered and patterned. Everything has a place and function, including frost and fire.

But there's also an interest and delight in mutability and change – how winter turns the natural world into something unlike its usual self. Ice becomes an engineer, building bridges where none have been before; water wears a new 'helmet', as if temporarily in disguise (*helm* can mean a war-helmet or any other kind of head-covering, like a crown). Here, the conventional image of the chaining of the earth seems less like a threat than another marvel. It's as if the conceal-ment of growing plants within the ground is a magic trick, a token of unseen creative power. The shoots are hidden for a while, like a rabbit in a hat, but they'll spring forth again in time as if they had never been gone. Winter is full of surprises. God is in command of it all, the poem suggests, and since he can be trusted to set the earth free from imprisonment in time, it's possible to marvel at these wonders without fearing that winter will never end.

This is not the only poem to explore winter's marvels. 'Water wears a helmet' could almost be a riddle, with the solution 'ice' – so it's not surprising that among the collection of riddles in the Exeter Book, there should be one that plays with the relationship between water and ice.

Wundor wearð on wege: wæter wearð to bane.

There was a wonder on the wave: water turned to bone.

The solution to this riddle must be some kind of ice, though it's debatable precisely what form is being imagined: 'iceberg' or 'icicle' both seem possible answers. The comparison between ice and bone conveys the whiteness and smooth texture of ice, as well as its para-doxical combination of toughness and fragility. Ice is hard, but also – like the bones of the human body – all too easily broken.

The word *wundor* in this one-line poem is crucial to what such riddles seek to do: they aim to awaken a sense of wonder by making the familiar unfamiliar, leading us to see objects we know with fresh eyes, just as winter does when it transforms the landscape. More riddle-like wonders of winter are found in a text known as *The Old English Rune Poem*. This is a catalogue poem, which devotes a short verse to each of the 29 characters in the Anglo-Saxon runic alpha-bet. Though most Anglo-Saxon literature is written in the Latin alphabet, runes had been used for writing Old English before that alphabet was adopted in England, and they still occasionally appear in manuscripts and inscriptions right through the Anglo-Saxon period.[6] Some runic letters also continued in use for sounds not found in the Latin alphabet, such as the 'th' sound, for which the rune þ (thorn) was often employed. Poets and scholars kept up an antiquarian interest in the runic alphabet, as *The Old English Rune Poem* exemplifies. Because the runes have names – they're not just letters, but also represent words – each verse of this poem provides a riddling description of the idea denoted by the rune. Many of these relate to the natural world (sea, sun, horse), while others are objects used in human society (bow, gift, torch) or more abstract concepts (necessity, joy). A number are named for trees, including the oak, ash and thorn. Two are about winter weather, describing the runes *Hægl* and *Is*:

Hægl byþ hwitust corna. Hwyrft hit of heofones lyfte,
wealcaþ hit windes scura; weorþeþ hit to wætere syððan.

Is byþ oferceald, ungemetum slidor,
glisnaþ glæshluttur, gimmum gelicust,
flor forste geworuht, fæger ansyne.

Hail is the whitest of grains. It whirls down from the air
   of the sky,
gusts of wind toss it about; afterwards it turns into water.

Ice is very cold, immensely slippery;
it glistens glass-clear, most like a gem,
a floor wrought by frost, fair to behold.

In its concise, tightly packed language and imagery, the *Rune Poem* has affinities with Old English wisdom poetry like *Maxims I* and the riddles; it also shares their delight in polysemy and shape-shifting, seeing familiar objects through new eyes. The image of a hailstone as *hwitust corna*, 'the whitest of grains', plays with the likeness and unlikeness between hailstones and grains or seeds. Any little round hard thing could be called a *corn* in Old English (a usage we preserve in 'peppercorn' and the 'corns' of the feet), and it's obviously appropriate for the shape and size of hailstones. But it also evokes what the hail *isn't*, since this is a seed from which no plant will grow, and its hardness is deceptive, because it will soon melt into water. The hail's descent is described with verbs that are dynamic and full of energy, imagining it in constant movement. It *hwyrft*, 'whirls', down from the sky, is tossed about by blasts of wind and then very abruptly, suddenly, transforms into water, melting away as quickly as it appeared.

The ice verse, too, is about swift transformations, and it sees definite beauties in winter weather. With the phrase *glisnaþ glæshluttur*, 'glistens, glass-clear', the poet conjures up the blinding whiteness of winter sunlight glinting off an icy path, as well as the fragile, glass-like quality of ice – smooth and clear, but easily shattered. The description of the 'floor wrought by frost' of course refers to the new coverings of ground and water that can spring up overnight on an icy morning. But *flor* in Old English often suggests specifically a constructed floor, as in a house or ship – something that has been designed and built, perhaps even decorated. In *Beowulf* a 'fair floor' is part of the beautifully adorned royal hall of the Danes, and in that context might refer to patterned carpeting or woodwork; we also know that Anglo-Saxon churches had decorative floor-tiles.[7] This suggests that the use of the word here might especially evoke the *patterns* of an icy floor, 'fair to behold'. As in *Maxims I*, where ice builds bridges, the ice seems to have power and agency over its own workings. It's a clever engineer, even an artist, with marvellous skills of construction and decoration. But it's not, perhaps, to be trusted. We might suspect that the word *slidor*, 'slidey', hints that ice is slippery in a metaphorical as well as a literal sense, like a shape-shifter or a trickster. Within two lines here it's likened to three different things – glass, a gem, a decorated floor – yet it's none of those things, only *like* them, and more transient than any. What these little verses show is that even amid the threat and danger of winter, there are marvels and beauties to be found.

2

MIDWINTER LIGHT

In the second half of *The Wanderer*, after the lonely exile laments the icy sea-journey which has frozen his grieving heart, the poem turns its attention to a different kind of winter scene. Now the focus widens from this speaker's individual sorrow to a more universal experience of loss:

> And so I cannot think, for the world,
> why my spirit does not grow dark
> when I consider all the life of men:
> how they suddenly left the hall,
> brave young warriors. Just so this earth
> every day declines and decays,
> and so a man cannot grow wise before he has had
> his share of winters in the world.

On one level, this phrase 'share of winters', *wintra dæl*, refers to the years of a person's life. (The word *dæl* is related to Modern English 'dole', an individual portion of something.) Since in Old English 'winters' can be a way of counting years, this echoes the link between old age and wisdom which we saw earlier in *Maxims II*. But when we take into account all that winter means in this poem and the others we've looked at, there's more to it than that. The implication is that wisdom is hard-won: it comes not only through living for a long time, but through experiencing a portion of suffering and trouble. That suffering is shared by all human beings, as well as the earth itself. Like the ageing human body, the world is declining day by day. The verbs *dreoseð ond feallep*, 'declines and decays', have autumnal connotations, and are also used in poetry of fruit and falling leaves. The progression of time, season by season, brings decay and death to all living things.

The exile in this poem has told us about his own winter of sorrow, and now goes on to share with us the wisdom it has taught him. To become wise, to learn from winter, means coming to accept that everything on earth is transient and temporary. Musing on this, *The Wanderer* doesn't only remain in the present, describing the world's current state of decline; it projects the imagination forwards into the future, and encourages every wise person to do the same.

> The wise hero must perceive how terrible it will be
> when all this world's wealth lies waste,
> as now in various places throughout this earth
> walls stand blown by the wind,
> covered with frost, buildings snow-swept.
> The halls decay, the ruler lies
> deprived of joys, the troop all dead . . .
> Thus the Creator of men destroyed this dwelling-place,
> until, deprived of its citizens' revelry,
> the ancient work of giants stood empty.

Autumnal decay may be the present state of the world, but winter is its future. This kind of description of a ruined city, battered by winter weather, is found elsewhere in Old English poetry, and may have been inspired by the Roman ruins Anglo-Saxon poets would have seen around them in the English landscape – massive standing remains of stone walls and fortresses, which must have seemed the work of a great civilization now vanished from the earth. Calling these ruins 'the ancient work of giants' is meant to evoke that sense of scale and power. Ozymandias-like, they are reminders of the limits of even mighty humans in the face of the much greater forces of time and decay.[1]

In Anglo-Saxon poetry such images of ruin are often linked to meditations on history and *wyrd*, the inevitable forward movement of time. Here that movement sweeps the mind onwards into the future, to imagine what it will be like when the whole world is as desolate as this ruined city. It's an apocalyptic scene. Picture a disaster movie: a character awakes after some terrible catastrophe and wanders alone through London or New York, picking their way across deserted streets, awestruck at seeing skyscrapers which were once full of people, now standing empty and beginning to collapse. Emptiness and desolation in places that should be full of human life are deeply uncanny, the sign of something horribly wrong, and that's exactly the sort of eerie landscape this poem is imagining. The Anglo-Saxon poet here speaks to the fears of the nuclear age as much as those of his own time: this could be a kind of nuclear winter, where wind, frost and snow have taken possession of the ruins and are breaking them down. The poem laments those who are gone:

> Where is the horse? Where is the young warrior? Where is
> the treasure-giver?
> Where are the seats of feasting? Where are the joys of
> the hall?
> Alas, the bright cup! Alas, the mailed warrior!
> Alas, the glory of the prince! How that time has passed
> away,
> grown dark under the cover of night, as if it had never
> been.
> There stands now in the tracks of the dear troop a wall,
> wondrously high, decorated with serpents.
> The warriors were taken away by the power of spears,

weapons greedy for slaughter, *wyrd* the famous;
and storms batter those rocky cliffs,
snow falling fetters the earth,
the tumult of winter. Then dark comes,
night-shadows deepen; from the north descends
a fierce hailstorm hostile to men.
All is full of hardship in this earthly realm,
the course of *wyrd* changes the world under the heavens.
Here wealth is fleeting, here friend is fleeting,
here man is fleeting, here kinsman is fleeting,
all the foundation of this world turns to waste.

From this picture of growing darkness, turbulent storms and falling snow (again imagined as 'fettering' the earth), the poem draws the lesson that everything in the world is under threat from winter, and all winter represents. Every aspect of human society is *læne*, a word which implies 'fleeting, transitory', but literally means 'on loan': friends, wealth, family have been lent to us for a while, but can be taken away at any time. The only place to seek stability, the poem concludes, is with God, eternal and unchanging. Its last lines offer the prospect of finding 'comfort from the Father in heaven, where for us all permanence stands'.

This way of reflecting on mortality and social collapse by picturing a ruined city under siege from winter seems to have appealed to Anglo-Saxon poets. Along with *The Wanderer*, the best-known example is *The Ruin*, another poem in the Exeter Book. This is a particularly evocative version of the theme, because this poem is itself a kind of ruin. The Exeter Book, though so precious and irreplaceable as a record of Old English poetry, has not always been treated well over the years: the manuscript bears scars of fire, water damage, even cuts from knives, as if at one time it was used as a chopping-board. As a result, *The Ruin* is fragmentary and many of its lines are past reconstruction. The match between the theme of the poem and its physical state is irresistible; it's as if the poem embodies the decay on which it reflects. Its opening lines, relatively undamaged, give us a picture of what's being described:

> Wondrously adorned is this wall-stone, destroyed by *wyrd*.
> The town buildings are shattered, the work of giants
>   crumbles.
> The roofs are fallen, the towers ruinous,
> the frosty gates caved in – frost on mortar –
> scarred rain-shelters cut down, ruined,
> age-eaten from below. Earth's grasp holds
> the mighty builders, rotted, deceased,
> in the ground's hard grip, while a hundred generations
> of humanity have come and gone. Often this wall,
> lichen-grey and red-stained, outlasted one reign after
>   another,
> standing in the storms. The high wide gate has collapsed.

This is less overtly wintry than the passage on the same theme in *The Wanderer*, with no mention of snow and falling darkness. Yet a winter scene it certainly is, as we learn from the phrase *hrim on lime*, 'frost on mortar'. This little phrase is telling. Since frost is so often imagined in Old English poetry as a chaining or imprisoning force, these are two materials of binding, substances which knit objects together and hold them fast. But everything here is crumbling and falling apart; neither frost nor mortar will hold these buildings together much longer, as age and time eat away at them.

These buildings have often been interpreted as the ruins of a Romano-British city – possibly Bath, since the poem goes on to describe hot springs and baths surrounded by impressive stone walls. The warmth and energy of the surging waters contrasts with the cold decay of the buildings and the utter absence of human life. As in *The Wanderer*, these halls are called 'the work of giants', remains of a mighty people whose buildings have outlasted them. They stand as a testament to the achievements of their civilization, awe-inspiring even as they crumble away. Transient as they are, subject to the forces of time, they are still much more enduring than the humans who built them – the builders were powerful, but only mortal nonetheless.

Though the poem trails away into ruin before offering any explicit comment on the meaning of the scene it describes, the message is probably similar to that of *The Wanderer*: every city in the world will be like this one day. Many of the Roman ruins these Anglo-Saxon poets saw still stand in the British landscape, despite the passage of another thousand winters. For us, as for the Anglo-Saxons, they are tangible and evocative relics of the ancient past – and the future these poets imagined, the time when the whole human world will stand waste and empty, is still in our future too.

ADVENT AND APOCALYPSE

This imaginative link between winter and scenes of an apocalyptic future seems to underlie numerous descriptions of this season in Anglo-Saxon poetry. Thinking of the end of the world in seasonal terms, as if the earth is in an autumnal state of decline, is far from unique to Old English literature, and is widespread in early medieval Christian writing. In one of his homilies for Advent, Ælfric translates for his Anglo-Saxon audience an expression of this idea in a sermon by Gregory the Great. It's prompted by Christ's words in Luke 21:29–33, where he tells his disciples that, as they know summer is coming when trees begin to sprout leaves, so they will be able to see from the signs of the times when the kingdom of God is at hand. Ælfric says:

> By these words it is shown that the fruit of this world is falling. It grows so it may fall; it sprouts up so it may destroy

with pestilence what had previously sprouted. This world is like a man grown old. In youth the body is thriving, with a powerful chest, with strong and healthy limbs; but in old age this man's growth is bowed down, his neck grows slack, his face is wrinkled, his limbs all made weak. His breast is oppressed with sighs, and between words his breath fails him; though sickness may not afflict him, yet very often health is like a sickness to him. So it is with this world. In the beginning it was thriving as in its youth, growing in bodily health, getting fat on the abundance of plenty, with a long time to live and dwelling in lasting peace. But now it is oppressed by old age, as if by its frequent troubles it is afflicted unto death.[2]

Such thinking may lie behind *The Wanderer*'s link between the decay of the world and the ageing human body, and we'll come back to this kind of autumnal imagery later. But it's winter, not autumn, to which Anglo-Saxon poets most often turn when they want to explore this idea – they're more interested in what *The Wanderer* calls 'the tumult of winter' than the slow decay of falling leaves.

Descriptions of winter are so prevalent in Old English poetry, so widespread and so consistent across different texts, that they suggest the season had profound meaning in Anglo-Saxon culture. When you read such descriptions of apocalyptic winter, they seem to echo the fears expressed by a powerful story from Old Norse mythology: *fimbulvetr*, the 'mighty winter' that will precede the coming of Ragnarök, the doom of the gods. According to Old Norse writers, this will be a terrible and protracted winter – three years of it, with no summer in between.[3] There will be snow from all directions, harsh frosts and sharp winds, and among humans all social bonds will break down into violence. Then the end will come: wolves will swallow the sun and moon, earthquakes and floods will overwhelm the land, and monsters will destroy the gods themselves. There may or may not be a direct connection between this Scandinavian myth and the dread of winter which appears so often in Anglo-Saxon poetry, and you don't necessarily need a mythological explanation to imagine what a terrible fear a hard winter was for these northern cultures; the prospect of unending cold, famine and darkness constitutes an obvious threat to human health and happiness. But precisely because it was such a deep-seated fear, it seems to have provided a potent way of thinking about other existential fears too: death, ecocatastrophe, societal collapse.

In the Christian era, the association between winter and apocalypse was made explicit through the season of Advent. It was in the early part of winter, the weeks leading up to the solstice, that the church directed medieval Christians to think about the Apocalypse, because Advent, as well as a season of preparation for celebrating Christ's first coming into the world at Christmas, is also a time for looking to his second coming at the end of the world. Advent and Apocalypse are closely entwined in medieval Christian writing. Again, this is explained in an Anglo-Saxon context by Ælfric, in one of the sermons he wrote for Advent. He tells his congregation, 'This season until Midwinter is called *Adventus Domini*, that is, "the coming of the Lord"', and he explains why it's a time for readings from the prophets, who 'foretold both the first coming in his birth, and also the second at the great judgement':

> We too, God's servants, strengthen our faith by the services of this season, because in our hymns we confess our redemption through his first coming, and we remind ourselves that we should be ready for his second coming, so we may follow him from that judgement to the eternal life.[4]

By 'Midwinter' Ælfric means Christmas, and he's explaining to his congregation that the preparation for Christmas involves thinking simultaneously about two frames of time. Through the use of prophetic texts, they're encouraged to imagine themselves back into a time when the birth of Christ was still in the future, the subject of prophecies but not yet of reality; at the same time, they were also meant to use Advent to look towards the eventual future, the Apocalypse. Christ's first coming into the world was his entry as a man into human time; his second coming will bring an end to time itself.

Keeping Advent, reflecting concurrently on these moments in the past, present and future of salvation history, involves some complex engagements with different moods of anticipation, hope and desire. In Anglo-Saxon literature these moods are most fully and sensitively explored through a sequence of poems in the Exeter Book, an extended meditation on Advent texts and themes. This sequence is usually called the *Advent Lyrics* or *Christ I*, and it's followed in the manuscript by two poems known as *Christ II* and *Christ III*, probably by different authors. The second poem deals with Christ's Ascension, the third with the second coming. Though the titles are modern, the threefold arrangement seems deliberate on the part of the compiler of the manuscript, leading the reader from Advent to Apocalypse.

The *Advent Lyrics* contain twelve sections, each based on a different liturgical antiphon. The principal sources are the 'O Antiphons', a group of texts used in the week leading up to Christmas. Sung at Vespers, in the early dusk of a midwinter evening, these antiphons address Christ by a series of allusive titles and appeal to him: *Veni*, 'Come'. These texts are best known today as the basis of the popular Advent hymn 'O Come, O Come Emmanuel', and many of the images that inspired the Anglo-Saxon poet are part of that hymn too: Christ is called 'Key of David', 'Emmanuel', 'Dayspring'. The *Advent Lyrics* are a good example of how a skilful Anglo-Saxon poet could combine the traditions of Old English verse with liturgical and biblical source material, finding a harmonious way of blending the two.[5] Each antiphon is only a few lines long, but the poems based on them can be as long as sixty or seventy lines, bringing in a wide range of additional material from the Bible as well as the antiphons. At the same time, the lyrics draw on the familiar language of Old English poetry, and since they're preserved in the Exeter Book, like many of the poems we've looked at so far, we can easily imagine an Anglo-Saxon reader 'reading across' from one to another and reflecting on what they have in common, how these different voices can speak to each other. The *Advent Lyrics* are theologically sophisticated texts, but – like the antiphons which inspired them – they're far from dry, and not solely meditative or reflective either: they have an urgent, eager tone, expressing a startling emotional intensity and a powerful sense of longing. They speak as if on behalf of the whole world, calling out for aid and comfort, light and liberation. 'Help the heart-sore,' cries one, 'have mercy on your servants and think on our sorrows, how we stumble on, weak at heart, wandering hopelessly.' These are songs of yearning desire, and it's no coincidence that they were sung at midwinter, in the darkest time of the year.

There's only space here for a few short extracts from these marvellous poems, but let's consider two examples that seem to respond to the fears articulated by texts we've already looked at. The first poem in the sequence speaks directly to the apocalyptic images of ruined buildings found in *The Ruin* and *The Wanderer*. Like *The Ruin*, this poem is itself in a semi-ruinous state, with a damaged opening. We can tell it's based on the antiphon 'O Rex Gentium' (O King of the Nations), but it begins mid-sentence:

> ... the king.
> You are the cornerstone which the builders long ago
> rejected from the building. It is well-fitting for you
> that you become the headstone of the glorious hall,
> and bring together the wide walls
> with bonds fixed fast, stone unbroken,
> so that throughout the cities of earth the sight of all eyes
> may marvel forever at the Lord of glory.

Reveal now through skilful craft your own work,
steadfast in truth, victory-bright, and at once let
wall stand against wall. Now is it needful for this work
that the Craftsman come, and the King himself,
and mend what is now in ruins,
the house beneath its roof. He created that body,
the limbs made of clay; now shall the Lord of life
save the weary multitude from its enemies,
the wretched ones from terror, as he has often done.

This is based on a much shorter Latin antiphon: 'O King of the nations, and their desire, the cornerstone who makes both one, come and save the human race which you fashioned from clay.' The first lines of the Old English poem pick up the antiphon's allusion to Psalm 118, interpreted in medieval Christian tradition as referring to Christ: 'the stone which the builders rejected has become the cornerstone.' But the idea is then developed within the context of Anglo-Saxon poetic tradition. If *The Wanderer* and *The Ruin* describe the windswept ruins of a great city as a symbol of decay and destruction in the transient human world, this poem offers the opposite: Christ is a craftsman who will repair the ruins, building them into a firm-fixed hall, with himself as the cornerstone.

We've seen how for Anglo-Saxon writers the hall can stand for all that's good about human society, representing community and a beacon of warmth and companionship amid the vast darkness of winter. So it is in this poem, where the hall is the community of the church, but it's something else too: the human body. The poet plays with words that can apply to both buildings and bodies, such as *heafod*, which means both 'headstone' and 'head', or the phrase 'the house beneath its roof' – easily transferable to the body, since in Old English the body is often described with such building metaphors as *feorhhus*, 'spirit-house'. The 'weary multitude' to be saved is called a *heap*, which means a crowd of people, but also what modern 'heap' does, a pile of stones. When the Craftsman comes the human body, reduced to rubble, is to be built up into a glorious and unassailable hall – an answer to the apocalyptic images in *The Wanderer* and *The Ruin*, where buildings and the people who inhabit them seem destined to crumble and perish together. In the final lines we're shown Christ defending the hall he has built, like Beowulf keeping night-watch in the hall of the Danes while Grendel stalks the moors outside.

Another of the *Advent Lyrics* closely echoes a phrase and metaphor from *The Wanderer* – and once again, it takes imagery which in *The Wanderer* is deeply melancholy and offers a more hopeful alternative. This section is based on the antiphon 'O Jerusalem', and concludes:

> Now that child is come,
> born to relieve the sufferings of the Hebrews.
> He brings joy to you, unlooses the bonds
> fastened by evil. The terrible need he knows,
> how the wretched have to wait for mercy.

These last words, *are gebidan*, use the same phrase as the first line of *The Wanderer*: 'Often the solitary one waits for mercy' as he travels on his journey across the winter sea. The translation 'wait for mercy' doesn't quite capture its full range of meaning, because *gebidan* can mean both 'wait for' and 'experience'; it expresses, perhaps, a state of hopeful waiting, not quite certainty, but trust. It's an apt characterization of the season of Advent, a time of waiting for something that has already happened but is still intensely desired. In *The Wanderer*, the statement that the solitary person 'waits for mercy' introduces a poem which movingly traces the difficulty of waiting for comfort, of coping with loss and loneliness amid the constraints of winter. Here, the imagery of binding and constraint recurs: Christ's coming 'unlooses the bonds fastened by evil'. But in this case the image concludes a poem confident that comfort and joy will come, that the chains will be loosened and the world's 'terrible need' will be met.

MODRANIHT, MIDWINTER AND YULE

In the depth of midwinter, when the days are shortest and the shadows longest, comes the winter solstice: the return of the sun. Centuries before the Anglo-Saxons converted to Christianity, 25 December – at that time the date of the winter solstice in the Julian calendar – had been chosen as the day on which to commemorate the birth of Christ, and a festival on this date is first recorded at Rome in 336.[6] This date was probably chosen not primarily because it was the solstice, but because it fell nine months after the spring equinox (25 March in the Roman calendar), which had perhaps already gained acceptance, as we'll see later, as the date of Christ's conception. But the winter solstice was of course a meaningful day on which to celebrate the birth of the creator of light. Bede explains this in *De temporum ratione*, articulating the widespread medieval understanding of the relationship between the church year and the solar cycle:

> very many of the Church's teachers recount ... that our Lord was conceived and suffered on the 8th kalends of April [25 March], at the spring equinox, and that he was born at the winter solstice on the 8th kalends of January [25 December]. And again, that the Lord's blessed precursor and Baptist was conceived at the autumn equinox on the 8th kalends of October [24 September] and born at the summer solstice on the 8th kalends of July [24 June]. To this they add the explanation that it was fitting that the Creator of eternal light should be conceived and born along with the increase of temporal light, and that the herald of penance, who must

decrease, should be engendered and born at a time when the light is diminishing.[7]

Bede himself thought that the solstice should more accurately be dated a few days earlier than this, on 21 December, but he doesn't dispute the central point of the symbolism: the birth of Christ is celebrated in midwinter, when the sun's light is reborn, because he is the source of light itself.

As Christianity took root in Anglo-Saxon England, this festival must have offered something powerful to a culture in which winter represented such a terrible threat. Living in northern Europe, where midwinter is the bleakest, darkest time of year, the Anglo-Saxons surely already celebrated some kind of midwinter festival before their conversion to Christianity – possibly a variety of different festivals. One is mentioned by Bede, who says that the pagan Anglo-Saxons

> began the year on the 8th kalends of January [25 December], when we celebrate the birth of the Lord. That night, which we now hold so holy, they used then to call by the pagan word *Modraniht*, that is, 'mothers' night', because, we suspect, of the rituals they performed through that night.[8]

This is the only surviving reference to 'Mothers' Night' from Anglo-Saxon England or anywhere else. As often when Bede comments on such matters, his knowledge seems limited, and here he admits he's speculating ('we suspect'). However, it's been suggested that he may be describing some form of survival of the Romano-British veneration of groups of mother goddesses, which is well attested in the first half of the first millennium.[9] If a form of such veneration survived somewhere in early Anglo-Saxon England, late enough for Bede to have heard about it in the eighth century, that's remarkably interesting. However, it can't have lasted much longer than this, as there are no later records of 'Mothers' Night'.

Another pre-conversion Anglo-Saxon midwinter festival may have been *Geola*, 'Yule'. Instead of being connected with a deity, this seems to be linked to the solstice. It gave its name – again according to Bede – to the months corresponding to December and January in the Julian calendar, 'the earlier *Geola*' and 'the later *Geola*'. The etymology of *Geola* is unclear, and we have no information to tell us how it might have been celebrated in Anglo-Saxon England. Unlike *Modraniht*, however, it was a word that survived into the Christian period, and it was adopted as a name for Christmas. It's used in this way in some Christian sources from the early Anglo-Saxon period, though it's not common, and from the ninth century onwards, with Scandinavian migration into northern and eastern England, it was reinforced by the related Old Norse name for the midwinter festival, *Jól*.[10] The Viking settlers swiftly converted to Christianity, but seem to have held on to their name for the festival. As a result, 'Yule' continued to be another name for Christmas into the later medieval period and long afterwards, especially in the north of England and in Scotland, areas where Scandinavian settlement had a deep and lasting impact on the local dialect.

In Old English, the name *Cristesmæsse*, 'Christmas', appears in the recorded sources surprisingly late, not until the first decades of the eleventh century – at least four centuries after the festival began to be celebrated in Anglo-Saxon England. This may be partly an accident of survival in the written sources, but it may also be because there was already a well-established name for Christmas – another which probably has pre-conversion origins but developed, like 'Yule', a new Christian meaning. That was *middewinter*, 'Midwinter', a term more prevalent in Anglo-Saxon sources than either *Cristesmæsse* or *Geola*. This name could refer to the whole Christmas season but was also frequently used for Christmas Day, *middewintres mæsse dæg*, 'Midwinter's mass-day'. It's used in this way, for instance, in the first lines of *The Menologium*, which begins 'Christ was born at Midwinter', and Ælfric tells in one of his sermons how after Mary conceived Christ she 'carried him until Midwinter's mass-day, and then gave birth to him'.[11] 'Midwinter' is also often used to mean 'Christmas Day' in the *Anglo-Saxon Chronicle*. At the end of 1066, when William the Conqueror was crowned king at Westminster on Christmas Day, one version of the *Chronicle* records that it took place *on midwintres dæg*.[12] This name too survived well into the later medieval period, both as a name for the Christmas season and for Christmas Day.

'Midwinter' was probably the name for this season long before the Anglo-Saxon conversion to Christianity; like 'Midsummer' (also a very long-enduring name), it reflected the older two-season pattern of the year and the importance of the solstices in the seasonal cycle. However, the name lasted because it was very much in harmony with the Christian feast as it developed in the Anglo-Saxon festival calendar, and for medieval English writers it must have made a powerful link between feast and season, evoking what it meant for Christ to be born into the very darkest time of winter. In the *Advent Lyrics*, the birth of the sun is associated with the antiphon 'O Oriens' (O Dayspring), sung on the evening of the winter solstice, the longest night of the year. The Old English poem based on this antiphon is a beautiful meditation on longing for the return of light:

O *Earendel*, brightest of angels,
sent to mankind across the earth,
and righteous radiance of the sun,
splendid above all stars, by your own self
you ever enlighten every age.
As you, God born of God long ago,
Son of the true Father, eternally existed
without beginning in the glory of heaven,
so your own creation cries with confidence
to you now for their needs, that you send
that bright sun to us, and come yourself
to lighten those who long have lived

surrounded by shadows and darkness, here
in everlasting night, who, shrouded by sins,
have had to endure death's dark shadow.

The opening address of this poem, *Earendel*, is a rare word, but its cognates in other Germanic languages suggest that it may originally have been the name of a mythological figure, perhaps a personification of a star or the dawn.[13] It was adopted into Anglo-Saxon Christian writing and is here transferred to Christ, the radiance of the eternal Father, sent to earth to bring light and comfort. Christ is imagined as the sun that dawns in the time of greatest darkness, in midwinter and in *deorc deaþes sceadu*, 'death's dark shadow'.

This image of Christ as the sun is one of the most familiar in Christian tradition – biblical in origin and immensely common in early medieval Christian writing. But it works in English (and other Germanic languages) in a different way from the Latin sources in which Anglo-Saxon writers would have encountered it, because of the verbal similarity between two English words, *sunne*, 'sun', and *sunu*, 'son', which are almost identical in Old English. That means that in this poem Christ can be called the Son/sun in two senses: he is both *soðfæsta sunnan leoma*, 'radiance of the true sun', and *sunu soþan fæder*, 'Son of the true Father'. To a medieval way of thinking, such a linguistic echo was not just coincidence but a potential revelation of truth; like the birth of Christ falling at the solstice, it pointed to the pattern and design underlying the whole created world. The 'sun' image was a metaphor that could bear a distinctive meaning for speakers of the English language – just as a midwinter festival like Christmas, though first celebrated in Rome, might come to develop its own meaning for a people living in northern Europe. At the time when Christianity began to influence Anglo-Saxon culture, winter may have already been associated with ideas and images like those we've seen repeated across the poetry – a natural product, perhaps, of the dark and cold of a northern winter. But it was reinterpreted in a Christian context, and *Middewinter* came to mean 'Christmas', with all that signified. For Anglo-Saxon writers, adopting terms like *Earendel*, *Middewinter* or *Geola* into Christian vocabulary was a way of interpreting their own culture and environment in the light of their Christian faith, finding in these terms a new meaning that was, in their eyes, more true and powerful.

It's surprisingly difficult to get a sense of what people actually did to celebrate Christmas in Anglo-Saxon England, beyond a general impression that it was a time for acts of religious devotion, such as almsgiving and attendance at church.[14] From at least the ninth century, a holiday at this season of the year was enjoined by law; Alfred the Great, for instance, ordered that people must be given a holiday for the whole Twelve Days of Christmas.[15] In one of his sermons for Christmas, Ælfric takes the opportunity to warn against 'overeating and excess drinking', so perhaps that gives us an idea of how *he* thought some people might be celebrating the Nativity.[16] Though we have little evidence for specific customs, we should surely imagine people feasting and enjoying convivial entertainment, driving away the winter cold as King Edwin and his counsellors are imagined doing in Bede's story of the sparrow.

In the centuries after the Norman Conquest, the three recorded Anglo-Saxon names for the festival – Midwinter, Yule and Christmas – were joined by other additions, such as the French borrowing *noël*. Today, although 'Christmas' is by far the most common name for the festival, 'Yule', 'Noël' and even 'Midwinter' are still words that belong to the familiar vocabulary of the season – fossilized in carols, if not in active use. This diversity of names, reflecting waves of Anglo-Saxon, Viking and Norman settlement, testifies to a festival that has grown and adapted, like the English language itself, with the introduction of new cultural influences. It seems likely that whatever people called the season, what they did to celebrate it has never changed all that much: at heart it has always been what it is today, a festival to brighten the darkest time of the year.

3

NEW YEAR TO CANDLEMAS

'YEAR'S DAY'

In the Anglo-Saxon period, there were different ways of reckoning the beginning of the new year. Bede says that before converting to Christianity the Anglo-Saxons began their year on 25 December, but afterwards, along with the new religion, they adopted the Roman practice of beginning the year on 1 January.[1] Calendars in Anglo-Saxon manuscripts conventionally begin with January, but alternative ways of thinking about the new year nonetheless persisted throughout the period. Different systems of reckoning could co-exist even within the same text: the *Old English Martyrology*, for instance, opens with Christmas, calling 25 December 'the first day of the year', but refers to January as 'the first month of the year'.[2] *The Menologium* does something similar, calling January 'the first month' but beginning and ending its cycle of festivals with the birth of Christ. The different versions of the *Anglo-Saxon Chronicle* show a range of options: they often start the year at Christmas, but entries may also begin in early January (after the Twelve Days of Christmas), around 25 March (the Feast of the Annunciation) or even in September (following a system derived from the Roman indiction, a cycle used for assessing taxation).[3] Meanwhile the church year began with Advent, so manuscripts of texts arranged by the liturgical cycle, such as collections of blessings, may open with the First Sunday in Advent. It was evidently possible for people to switch between different ways of thinking about the year depending on context.

For many people in Anglo-Saxon England, who did not govern their lives by written calendars, the question of when the year began wouldn't have made much difference; probably most were content to take the season around Midwinter as the beginning of a new year, without worrying too much about fixing an exact day. But it was more complicated for those who lived by the liturgical calendar – especially monks and nuns, who had to reconcile a number of disparate ways of marking time. To some monastic writers, this made the idea of keeping 1 January as the new year seem illogical and almost random. Why observe that date, which has no intrinsic significance? This is a question raised by Ælfric in a sermon he wrote for the feast of Christ's circumcision, observed on 1 January. He acknowledges that some people call this day 'Year's Day' (*geares dæg*); if this was a common Anglo-Saxon name for the first day of the year, it parallels *The Menologium's* use of 'Winter's Day' to describe the first day of winter. But Ælfric was well aware that different cultures had alternative dates for beginning the new year, and this makes him sceptical of attaching any meaning to 1 January.

We have often heard that people call this day 'year's day', as the first day in the course of the year, but we do not find any explanation in Christian books as to why this day should be appointed the beginning of the year. The ancient Romans, in pagan days, began the calendar of the year on this day; the Jewish people began it at the spring equinox, the Greeks at the summer solstice, and the Egyptians began the reckoning of their year in harvest. Now our calendar begins on this day, according to the Roman practice, not for any holy reason, but because of ancient custom. Some of our service books begin at the Advent of the Lord, but nonetheless that is not the beginning of our year. There is no reason for it being this day, although our calendars continue to put it in this place.[4]

Ælfric's comments here are a useful insight into his way of thinking about how time is, and should be, marked. For him, it just doesn't feel *right* to celebrate the new year on a day that has no spiritual meaning of its own, and it's not enough to say the practice is 'ancient custom' – there ought to be a better reason than that. Since time, like everything else, is governed by God, a date as important as the beginning of a new year ought to have sacred significance. It ought to mean something.

As an alternative, Ælfric proposes that it would make more sense to begin the new year at the spring equinox, 21 March. Unlike 1 January, he explains, this date does have a sacred meaning, in several different and important ways. First, it fits with his understanding of the instruction given by God to Moses about the first month of the year in the Jewish calendar (Exodus 12:1–2); this gives it biblical authority of a kind no other date can match. In early medieval reckoning 21 March was also, as we'll see later, thought to be the day on which time itself began, when God created the sun and moon on the fourth day of creation. There could be no better date to begin a new yearly cycle. Finally, Ælfric suggests that it's fitting to start the new year in the spring, rather than the bleak month of January, because 'the earth shows by the shoots which are then coming to life again that this is the time which should most rightly be the year's beginning, when the earth was created.' What season could be more suitable for the start of a new year than the spring, a time of birth, renewal and fresh growth? This final argument is an indication of how monastic writers like Ælfric sought to understand the cycle of the seasons: they wanted to read and interpret the natural world, to learn to recognize the meaning God had planted in it. They saw time and the seasons, from the very first day of the world, as carefully arranged by God with method and purpose – so they believed it should be possible to organize the calendar not according to the randomness of custom and inherited tradition, but in a way that reflected that divine plan.

In the later medieval period, 25 March became the beginning of the year in England and continued to be so until 1752, when Britain adopted the Gregorian calendar and formally changed the start of the year to 1 January.[5] Official practice and popular custom don't necessarily align, however. Although Ælfric disagreed with the significance attributed to 1 January, his sermon provides useful evidence for how other people in Anglo-Saxon England treated 'Year's Day'. In many cultures, the start of a new year is a popular time for predictions and good-luck customs, intended to ensure prosperity or foretell what might happen in the year ahead. In modern Britain, this is best known in the tradition of first-footing, an example of the widespread idea that the first thing you do on New Year's Day influences what you'll be doing for the rest of the year.[6] This belief that the character of New Year's Day predicts the year ahead was clearly popular in the Anglo-Saxon period, too. Ælfric mentions – and strongly criticizes – such means of trying to tell the year's future:

Now foolish men practise divination by many kinds of sorcery on this day, in great error, according to heathen customs contrary to their Christian faith, so they may prolong their lives or their health; but in doing that they anger the Almighty Creator. Many people are also so greatly wrapped in error that they plan their journeys according to the moon and their deeds by the days, and will not let blood on a Monday because it is the beginning of the week. But Monday is not the beginning of the week, it is the second day; Sunday is the first.

Ælfric calls these 'heathen customs', but we know from other sources that the people who engaged in such practices in Anglo-Saxon England were in fact most likely to be monks and clerics – especially because it required precise knowledge of the calendar, essentially a learned skill.[7] Bloodletting, for instance, was a standard part of medieval monastic medicine, and there's lots of detailed technical information in Anglo-Saxon manuscripts recommending the best dates on which to do it. It was necessary to choose the right phase of the moon, because its periods of waxing and waning were thought to correspond with strength in bodies on earth, and to identify the best season of the year; late summer was considered a bad time, but early spring was recommended, 'when trees and herbs first spring up'.[8] There was some reason in all this: the heat of summer would have been a dangerous time for cuts to become infected, while in spring, when people might have been showing signs of dietary deficiencies after the hard winter months, bloodletting may have seemed a timely remedy.[9] In late Anglo-Saxon England, this was the kind of pragmatic purpose for which it was necessary to have calendar-related information available in a monastic library – diagrams of the moon's phases, tables for calculating months and days, reminders of when seasons begin and end, and so on. Even Ælfric acknowledges that it's right to pay attention to natural cycles for some purposes: he goes on to say that it makes sense to cut trees at the full moon, because they're stronger and more durable then, and 'this is no sorcery, but a natural thing, through creation.' If that's simply recognizing God's creative power at work in natural cycles, then, it's not much of a step to try to harness that power to ensure health and prosperity at the start of the new year.

Other Anglo-Saxon monks had much more faith than Ælfric in 1 January as a significant date. From the tenth and eleventh centuries, many prognostics for the new year survive in manuscripts produced at the leading monasteries in England, which include various methods of predicting the course of the year from the conditions of New Year's Day or the Christmas season.[10] These predictions often relate to weather and agriculture, but they may also foretell times of peace or war, famine or sickness. For instance, one is based on observing whether the sun shines on each of the Twelve Days of Christmas: if it shines brightly on the fifth day of

Christmas, 'there will be abundant blossom and leaves that year'; on the tenth day, 'the sea and rivers will be full of fish'; on the second day, 'gold will be easy to obtain among the English.' (A useful one, that.) The day of the week on which the year begins can also be used for prediction. If 1 January falls on a Monday, 'it will be a stormy year, and there will be sickness'; on a Tuesday, 'it will be dangerous for ships, and kings and noblemen will die'; on a Wednesday, 'honey will not be plentiful.' The most auspicious day is Sunday, which heralds a year when peace and abundance will reign on earth, but Friday isn't bad either:

> If 1 January is on a Friday, there will be a variable winter, a good spring and a good summer, and much abundance, and sheep's eyes will be weak in that year.

Such a collection of disparate predictions may look strange to us, but it's important to remember that in the early medieval period texts like these were considered part of learned science, not popular folk-lore, and they're often transmitting information from Continental Latin sources.[11] Whatever Ælfric's opinion on divination, the monks who recorded these prognostics presumably wouldn't have thought of them as contrary to their Christian faith. Such predictions were another recognition of the interconnectedness of all created things, and they share with Ælfric's arguments about the new year a belief that the calendar itself had a sacred significance and potency. Learning to understand it could provide you with powerful and useful forms of knowledge.

WAKING THE CROPS

Although these texts mark the beginning of the year on 1 January, there's little evidence of New Year *celebrations* in Anglo-Saxon England on this day. For most people, the date would have been subsumed into the longer period of festivity of the Twelve Days of Christmas, which culminated on 5 January, the eve of the Epiphany. This is now known as 'Twelfth Night', but in the Anglo-Saxon period it was 'Twelfth Eve' (*twelftan æfen*), preceding 'Twelfth Day' (*twelftan dæg*) on 6 January. 'Twelfth Day' was commonly used as another name for the Epiphany, and it's sometimes even called 'Twelfthmas Day'.[12] This element 'mas', still found in many of our festival names, derives from the Old English *mæsse*, a borrowing into English from Latin *missa*. In Anglo-Saxon sources it means both 'mass', in the sense of a celebration of the Eucharist, and more generally 'festival, feast-day'. You could pretty much put *mæsse* on any word in Old English and make it a festival name: examples which go back to Anglo-Saxon usage include Christmas, Candlemas, Childermas (the feast of the Holy Innocents, 28 December), Lammas, Michaelmas and Martinmas.

In the English calendar, Twelfth Night was for many centuries a time of more riotous festivity than Christmas Day – a last hurrah of feasting before the return to work.[13] During the Middle Ages the Christmas season lasted forty days, until Candlemas on 2 February, and January was supposed to be a month of feasting, not fasting – the exact opposite of the modern 'Dry January'. But the period of actual holiday usually ended with Twelfth Night, and it was celebrated accordingly. This meant that for many people the days after 6 January were the time to get back to work. In Anglo-Saxon calendars which contain a sequence of 'Labours of the Months', images depicting the agricultural work associated with each month of the year, January is represented by ploughing – a scene of intensive labour as the farmer's year moves on. *Gerefa*, the text that outlines the tasks a reeve of an estate should oversee at different times of year, lists ploughing as the first job for both winter and spring.[14] In Ælfric's *Colloquy* – an imagined dialogue in which young monks adopt the roles of labourers and tradesmen from across Anglo-Saxon society – the ploughman laments that his work is very hard: however bitter the winter he has no choice but to go out into the fields, even when the boy who leads the oxen is hoarse with the cold.[15]

We can mark this point in the calendar by looking at a fascinating Old English text involving a plough – an agricultural ritual intended to ensure a good harvest. Known as *Æcerbot* (Field-Remedy), this text tells you what to do 'to make your fields better if they will not grow well, or if some troublesome thing has been done there through sorcery or witchcraft'. The ritual seeks to cure whatever might ail the land, whether natural or magical in origin, and it calls upon the powers of the earth and heaven, as well as a considerable amount of human labour, to assist in its work of healing.[16] This is one of a number of rituals preserved in Anglo-Saxon sources which aim to cure illness in humans or animals, ward off harm or ensure protection, and we'll look at some rituals linked to particular days in the year when we get to Midsummer and Lammas. *Æcerbot*, which survives in an eleventh-century manuscript, is an especially lengthy and complex example, involving a multi-stage process extending over several days. Passages of prose describing how to perform the ritual are interspersed with prescribed words, a mixture of Latin prayers and English poetry. It's a remarkable text, worth considering in detail.

The ritual is not tied to any specific time of year, but it begins at a particular time of day: the first step is to go out before dawn and cut four pieces of turf from the four sides of the land that needs to be cured. On these, you're told to drip a mixture of oil, honey, yeast, holy water, milk from every cow that grazes on the land and a portion of every tree and plant that grows there. As you drip this on the turf, you're to say, 'Grow and multiply and fill this earth, in the name of the Father and Son and Holy Spirit,' as well as the Pater Noster. The pieces of turf are then taken to church, where a priest sings four masses over them, and before sunset they are replaced in the field, with a cross, made of rowan-wood and inscribed with the names of the four evangelists, buried under each one. The person performing the ritual turns to the east, bows nine times and says:

Eastward I stand, for mercies I ask,
I ask the glorious Lord, I ask the great Ruler,
I ask the holy Guardian of the heavenly kingdom,
I ask the earth and the sky
and the true St Mary
and heaven's might and high hall,
that by the gift of the Lord I may open
this charm with my teeth through steadfast thought,
waken these crops for our worldly use,
fill this land with a fast faith,
beautify this grassy field; as the prophet said,
he would have mercy in the earthly kingdom
who gave alms wisely by the grace of the Lord.

This Old English verse is followed by Latin prayers taken from the texts of the liturgy, including the Sanctus and Magnificat and the Pater Noster again, with other prayers to Christ and the Virgin Mary. After that, it's time to bless the plough that will work the land. To do this, you're told to take some unknown seed from 'alms-men', beggars or people who live on charity, giving them back twice the amount of seed in return. You set this seed on your plough and say:

Erce, erce, erce, mother of earth,
may the All-wielder, the eternal Lord, grant you
fields growing and putting forth shoots,
increasing and becoming strong,
tall shafts, bright crops,
and the broad barley-crops
and the white wheat-crops
and all the crops of the earth.
May the eternal Lord and his holy ones
who are in heaven grant to him

that his field may be protected against every enemy,
and guarded against every evil
from poisons sown across the land.
Now I ask the Ruler who created this world
that there may be no talking woman nor cunning man
who is able to change the words thus spoken.

When you drive forth the plough and cut the first furrow, say:

Be well, earth, mother of mankind!
Be growing in the embrace of God,
filled with food for the use of all.

Then bake a loaf of bread kneaded with milk and holy water, lay it
under the first furrow and say:

Field full of food for human beings,
brightly flourishing, be blessed
in the holy name of the one who created the heavens
and the earth on which we live.
God, who made these grounds, grant us growing gifts,
that every grain may come to be of use.

More Latin prayers complete the process.

This ritual takes very seriously the power of words, both to curse
and to bless. The land is seen as vulnerable, at risk from enemies
who may harm it: the fear is that a 'talking woman' or 'cunning man'
might counteract these words of blessing with destructive speech,
presumably through witchcraft. To work against them, the ritual
uses the powerful words of the Latin liturgy and Christian prayer,
as well as some really lovely English poetry, to waken the field to life.
It's as if painting a word-picture of the beautiful crops might itself
have the power to bring them forth, 'bright-blooming'.

The actions that accompany the words have power too, paralleled in other rituals of this kind: taking turf from the four sides of the land and burying crosses at its edges mark out a hallowed space of ritual protection. It's evidently important to give back to the land more than you take from it, as it is to give the beggars more seed than you take from them, so that your use of these resources is generous rather than exploitative. If you want the earth to bear fruit for you, you have to treat her with respect, even veneration.

That veneration of the earth is the feature of this text which has attracted most attention: its address to earth as *fira modor*, 'mother of mankind', and the mysterious phrase *Erce, erce, erce, eorþan modor*, 'Erce, erce, erce, mother of earth'. No one knows for sure what *erce* means, since it's not recorded anywhere else, but it's often been interpreted as a name – possibly a name for Mother Earth herself. The idea of the earth as a fertile, life-giving mother is very clear in this ritual: it's implied in the description of the fields as *eacniendra*, which means 'increasing, growing big', but often specifically 'pregnant'. Is *Erce*, like *Earendel*, a name from pagan belief introduced into a Christian text? In all other ways the ritual is thoroughly Christian, involving the co-operation of a priest and making extensive use of Christian prayers, names and symbols. For Anglo-Saxon Christians, there was nothing unorthodox about a ritual like this: rituals for blessing fields and praying for a good harvest were an important part of the medieval church calendar, as we'll see later at Rogationtide. *Æcerbot* has sometimes been seen as a lightly Christianized relic of pagan belief, but it's unlikely the people who performed or recorded it thought of it as pagan; this was simply their form of Christianity, unfamiliar as it may be to modern eyes.[17]

There are two features of this intriguing text which seem to connect it with much later rituals for ensuring the health of crops. One is the salutation to the earth, 'be well', *hal wes þu*. In Old English this phrase was a common greeting, more usually found in the order *wes þu hal*, 'be thou well'. By the twelfth century, this phrase is recorded as a toast, used to wish someone health when presenting them with a cup of drink.[18] In time, it became contracted to *wassail*, and in Middle English it appears both as a toast and a general word for drinking and feasting. In medieval sources, wassailing has no connection to crops. From the sixteenth century onwards, however, there are records from across southern England of the custom of wassailing fruit-trees in the winter season, around Christmas or Twelfth Night, to ensure a good harvest of fruit in the coming year.[19] This often involved singing to the trees, beating them with sticks, toasting them with cider or putting pieces of cider-soaked bread in their roots or branches. More than five hundred years separate this Anglo-Saxon field-ritual from the first records of wassailing, so there may be no direct connection between the Old English text and the later custom. However, the use of the phrase *hal wes þu* as a salutation to the earth is a remarkable similarity, even if it's just coincidence. The ritual also uses strategies to 'waken the crops' that are paralleled in later wassailing customs: toasting apple-trees with cider reflects the same idea found in the ritual of giving back to the land the produce of its own crops – burying the loaf of bread – to encourage it to bear fruit next year.

The other notable parallel with later rituals of blessing is the role of the plough. From the fifteenth century onwards, the early days of January were marked in England by a variety of traditional customs involving a plough, usually on 'Plough Monday', the first Monday after Twelfth Night.[20] This might include, for instance, a plough being blessed in church, decorated and paraded around the village by ploughboys, who would dance, sing or perform plays as they went to collect money – originally to keep candles, 'plough lights', burning for them in church, and later, once the Reformation suppressed that practice, for their own purposes. These plough rituals provided an opportunity to seek God's blessing on the tools of daily life as the new year began, but doubtless also offered a way of making the post-Christmas return to work more palatable with some last festivity. Again, there's only a distant echo of the Anglo-Saxon field-remedy, but the central role given to the plough in each ritual suggests its enduring importance as both a tool and a symbol of agricultural labour.

In its complex use of word, gesture and symbol and its emphasis on a generous, appreciative attitude to the earth and its gifts, *Æcerbot* is a text of striking beauty. It contains some marvellous Old English poetry, calling up images of the bounty and loveliness of the longed-for harvest: especially beautiful is the copious alliteration of the penultimate line, *God, se þas grundas geworhte, geunne us growende gife*, 'God, who made these grounds, grant us growing gifts.'

WINTER CARRIED AWAY: CANDLEMAS

The Christmas season came to an end on 2 February, with Candlemas. Candlemas is the last feast of winter and the first feast of spring – a transitional festival, which looks back to Christmas and forwards to Easter. It commemorates an event from Christ's early childhood, narrated in the Gospel of Luke: forty days after his birth, Jesus was taken by his parents to the Temple in Jerusalem so that he might be presented, and his mother ritually purified, in accordance with Jewish law. In the Temple they were met by an elderly man and woman, Simeon and Anna, who recognized the baby as the Messiah for whom they had long been waiting. The aged Simeon took the child in his arms and spoke a prayer, the Nunc Dimittis, which became part of the daily cycle of Christian prayer, repeated night after night for many centuries: 'Lord, now let your servant depart in peace, according to your word; for my eyes have seen your salvation.' Anticipating his own peaceful death, Simeon also foretells the child's future suffering: 'a sword will pierce your soul,' he tells Mary, prophesying Christ's death and the grief his mother will endure for his sake.

This means that Candlemas is a festival which has at its heart a meeting between childhood and old age, birth and death, and winter and spring. The dating of the feast was fixed by its biblical origin, because the period of purification appointed in the law of Moses meant it must take place forty days after Christ's birth. However, 2 February coincided with a significant point in the solar year: midway between the winter solstice and the spring equinox, it's a time when the days are getting longer, daylight is growing stronger, and in northern Europe the earliest spring flowers are starting to appear. It was a natural time for a festival of light, and that was what Candlemas became.

Celebrated since the fourth century in the Eastern church, the seventh century in the West, this feast reached Anglo-Saxon England in the eighth century.[21] The English name *Candelmæsse* is first recorded in the late Anglo-Saxon period, and refers to the most distinctive custom of the feast: people would bring candles to church to be blessed, carry them in procession, then take them home and keep them all year. The association with light was inspired by the words of Simeon's prayer, which hails Christ as 'a light to lighten the Gentiles'. By bringing candles to church and taking them out into the world again, the congregation re-enacted the Gospel story of the presentation, each little candle flame representing the light of the baby Christ. Such forms of ritual re-enactment were a characteristic feature of early medieval liturgy, as we'll see again at Easter.

This custom of candle-blessing evidently captured the imagination of Anglo-Saxon writers, and it's described in numerous sources from medieval England. In his sermon for the day, Ælfric explains to his congregation how they are to walk in procession, carrying their candles and singing the appointed hymn, if they can sing – and 'though some people cannot sing, they can nevertheless bear the light in their hands, for on this day was the true Light, Christ, borne to the temple, who redeemed us from darkness and will bring us to the eternal light.'[22]

A miracle-story from the late Anglo-Saxon period illuminates for us an early English Candlemas. It's a story about St Dunstan, a leading figure in the tenth-century church – a scholar, influential royal counsellor and monastic reformer who served as Archbishop of Canterbury from 959 to 988 and became one of the most widely venerated saints in England. A lection written for Dunstan's feast a few decades after his death tells how his holiness was revealed, even before birth, by a miracle which took place at Candlemas in Glastonbury, around 910.[23] Dunstan's mother, Cynethryth, pregnant with the saint, had gone to church for the festival and was standing among the congregation with her lighted candle. During the service, it suddenly grew very dark and cold; all the candles went out, and everyone was struck by terror. Then, with a flash of blazing fire from heaven, Cynethryth's candle alone was miraculously re-lighted, revealing the sanctity of the child she carried. Prenatal miracles of this kind are common in medieval hagiography, but the connection between miracle and feast in this case is especially apt. It's a miniature Anglo-Saxon version of Christ's presentation in the temple: like Mary, Cynethryth carries her child to church with her offering, the glory of God is revealed in the sight of the people, and the future of the holy baby is prophetically made known. The miracle showed that, as one of Dunstan's later hagiographers put it, the child was to be 'a light to enlighten the land of the English'.[24]

The Menologium, a poem which may originally have been written under the influence of Dunstan's circle, refers to Candlemas in a way that makes clear its connection to the arrival of spring:

> we Marian mæssan healdað,
> cyninges modor, forþan heo Crist on þam dæge,
> bearn wealdendes, brohte to temple.
> Ðænne þæs emb fif niht þæt afered byð
> winter of wicum.

> [On 2 February] we keep the feast of Mary,
> mother of the King, because she on that day

brought Christ, the Ruler's child, to the temple.
Then after five nights winter is
carried out of the dwellings.

As Mary bears Christ to the temple, so winter is carried away, and
spring makes its entrance.

SPRING

4

THE COMING OF SPRING

'UNWINDING THE WATER'S CHAINS'

As we've seen, in Anglo-Saxon poetry winter is often imagined as a season when the earth and human beings are imprisoned, kept captive by the 'fetters of frost'. Naturally enough, then, spring is associated with images of liberation and freedom once those fetters are released. The end of winter is envisioned in terms of thawing snow: everything is free again, and the waters run.

There's a wonderful moment of this kind in *Beowulf* which imagines the passing of winter into spring. It comes at a crucial point in the poem, the climax of Beowulf's second fight with a monster.[1] After Beowulf mortally wounds Grendel in a fierce hand-to-hand struggle in the mead-hall, the Danes think they're safe, but they soon learn their troubles are not over: the monster's mother comes to avenge her son. To confront her, Beowulf has to venture into the cave where she lives, a grim place beneath a lake of dark and turbulent waters. There he meets Grendel's fearsome mother and has a hard battle with her, during which his sword fails him. Desperate, Beowulf grabs a giant sword lying in the cave, and with that he is finally able to kill the monster. Her blood surges up to the surface of the lake; Beowulf's friends, anxiously waiting for him, think it's his and begin to grieve for his death. But down in the underwater cave light has broken in, and the huge sword has begun to melt away at the touch of the monster's blood.

> Then that sword began
> to waste away because of the war-sweat,
> the blade into battle-icicles. That was a great wonder:
> it all melted, just like ice
> when the Father loosens the bonds of frost,
> unwinds the water's chains, he who has power
> over times and seasons. He is the true Measurer.

As the sword dissolves in the heat of the blood (the *heaþoswate*, 'war-sweat'), water and blood gush forth together, with the force of a spring thaw when the ice begins to melt. It's a great release, paralleling the relief from tension at this moment of victory: killing the monster has finally set the Danes free from the terror that has been assailing them. After their long misery, Beowulf has brought the spring.

There are similarities here with the *Beowulf* extract we looked at earlier, in which Hengest struggles to bear the enforced stasis of winter and the arrival of spring prompts him to exact vengeance on his enemy. In each case, the transition between seasons is used to mirror a decisive moment of change in the lives of the characters. Once again, the poet slips from the past tense into the present as he comments on the passage of the seasons, a deliberate reminder that what's being described is as much a feature of the poet's own world as of the days of these ancient heroes. The seasons are a point of connection between the familiar present and the strange and distant past. What could be further from the everyday world than a hero in a monster's underwater cave, fighting for his life with a giant's sword? But this metaphor of the thawing ice is drawn from our world, our time, our seasons.

As in the earlier passage, too, the poet connects the cycle of the seasons to the power of God, drawing an implicit contrast with the limitations of his human heroes. This scene is a display of super-human strength – Beowulf, we're repeatedly told, is the mightiest man in the world in his day, and he has used his physical power to release the Danes from the bonds of their suffering. But there's a strength far beyond his, of the one 'who has power over times and seasons' and can loosen the bonds of the frost. This divine governance is immeasurably greater than any power to which an earthly hero might aspire; it belongs only, the poet says, to the *soð Metod*, 'true Measurer'. *Metod* is a common epithet for God in Old English poetry, and it seems to mean something like 'the one who metes out' life, time or destiny – the one who governs times and seasons and the shape and duration of human lives.

The association *Beowulf* draws between God's supreme power and the spring thaw is also found in *Maxims I*, part of which we looked at earlier:

> One alone shall unbind
> the frost's fetters: God most mighty.
> Winter must pass, good weather come again,
> summer bright and hot. The never-resting sea,
> the deep way of the dead, will be longest hidden.

As in *Beowulf*, the unique nature of God's power is demonstrated by the passing of winter into spring: only he can set the world free from its captivity and bring the promise of summer to come. There's a further parallel with *Beowulf* in the reference to the turbulent sea, recalling the swirling waters of Grendel's lake and the flood that gushes from Beowulf's thawing sword. The poet doesn't explain what links the end of winter and 'the never-resting sea, the deep way of the dead'; as often in this type of wisdom poetry, the two phrases are brought together, but the connection between them is left for the reader to make. It must have something to do with the idea of waters thawing and moving, surging as they're set free from winter stasis. As the frost's chains are unwound, the sea swells and flows in its mysterious, restless depths.

If this is liberation from winter imprisonment, it's not of a gentle or tranquil kind – this is a mighty flood making its way through the world, a perilous freedom outside human control. But it's full of energy and vitality, possibility and promise. It recalls a simile used in Ælfric's *De temporibus anni*, as he explains how all the waters on earth are related:

> Every sea, however deep it may be, has its bottom on the earth, and the earth carries all the seas and the great ocean, and all wellsprings and rivers flow through it. Just as veins lie in a man's body, so these veins of water lie throughout this earth.[2]

If those veins of water carry the earth's blood, their freedom to run infuses all the world with life.

In texts like these, the coming of spring doesn't mean that the wildness of winter weather is over – if spring announces its arrival with the roar of floods, it's a noisy and turbulent season. That seems to be reflected in the Anglo-Saxon names for the months of February and March. The Old English name Bede records for February is *Solmonað*, and though the etymology of this word is uncertain, one plausible interpretation is 'mud-month' – an inevitable consequence of those spring floods. (Alternatively, Bede's theory is that it means 'month of cakes', because the pagan Anglo-Saxons offered cakes to their gods in that month; there's no other evidence to support this claim.) For March there are two recorded Old English names, *Hreðmonað* and *Hlyda*. For *Hreðmonað* too Bede proposes a religious explanation, suggesting that it was named for a goddess, 'to whom they sacrificed at this time', called Hreða (or Hreda).[3] But the other name, which he doesn't mention, probably derives from the weather: *Hlyda* means 'loud, noisy', and might well refer to the blustery winds of March.

Judging from the sources in which it's recorded, *Hlyda* may have been the West Saxon name for March (which might be why Bede didn't know it).⁴ It's unusual among Old English month-names because it survived in use after the end of the Anglo-Saxon period, long after the other Old English month-names had been replaced by the Latin-derived names we use today. As 'Lyde' or 'Lude', it's recorded in some Middle English texts, and in the southwest of England it endured even longer in dialect use. As late as the nineteenth century, the first Friday in March was known in Cornwall as 'Friday in Lide', and was kept as a holiday by tin-miners;⁵ 'Lide-lily' was an old name for the daffodil, and there was a proverb 'Ducks won't lay till they've drunk Lide water.'⁶ Centuries after the other Anglo-Saxon month-names had been forgotten, 'Lide' lived on in this part of the country.

March's association with stormy weather is also reflected in the description of the month's arrival in *The Menologium*:

> hrime gehyrsted, hagolscurum færð
> geond middangeard Martius reðe,
> Hlyda healic.

> adorned with frost, with hail-showers
> fierce March journeys through the earth,
> loud-voiced *Hlyda*.

March is imagined as savage with the last blasts of winter, and both Old English names for the month seem to be an influence here: though using the name *Hlyda*, the poem calls March *reðe*, 'fierce, wild', which might be an allusion to *Hreðmonað*. As well as this, however, the poet may also have known the history of the Latin name and its derivation from Mars, god of war. The Latin and English names seem to agree: whether it gets its name from a Roman god, an Anglo-Saxon goddess or just the loudness of its winds, March is the fiercest of months.

THE SPRING AND THE SEA

In medieval science, following classical tradition, the wind that makes the waters run in spring was identified as the west wind, Zephyrus: as Ælfric explains, this wind *blæwð westan, and ðurh his blæd acuciað ealle eorðlice blæda and blowað, and se wind towyrpð and ðawað ælcne winter*, 'blows from the west, and through its breath all earthly plants quicken and bloom, and that wind casts away and thaws every winter'.[7] At the breath of the wind, everything in the world 'quickens' with life – including human beings. This springtime energy is powerfully expressed in a poem from the Exeter Book known as *The Seafarer*, which links spring with an eager, restless longing to travel, to search for new things and a new life.

The Seafarer begins with a winter scene which will now be familiar from the poems we've already looked at, especially *The Wanderer*. The speaker has been out at sea, suffering from harsh weather, and he promises to tell us about the hardships he's encountered on his voyages:

> I can sing a true song about myself,
> speak of journeys, how I have often suffered
> in days of struggle times of hardship.
> Bitter heart-sorrow I have experienced,
> found in a ship many places of trouble,
> the terrible tossing of the waves, where often
> the anxious night-watch held me at the prow
> when it crashes by the cliffs.

From these first lines, it's already clear that his sea-journey is a metaphor for something more personal: the 'times of hardship' and 'places of trouble' he has found in his ship seem to be spaces within his own mind and heart, experiences into which life has carried him. His anxiety, as often in Old English, is described in physical terms

as *nearo*, 'narrow', as if it has a constricting effect on the body and
mind – a feeling of tightness and confinement, which is here set
against the wild freedom of the tossing waves. All the discomfort of
a winter journey is vividly described: his feet are frozen with frost,
he's beset by showers of hail, and he's so isolated that the only voices
he hears are those of seabirds.

> There I heard nothing but the roaring of the sea,
> the ice-cold wave. Sometimes the song of the swan
> became my pleasure, the cry of the gannet
> and voice of the curlew instead of the laughter of men,
> the singing of the seagull instead of mead-drinking.
> Storms beat the stony cliffs there, where the tern called,
> icy-feathered; very often the eagle cried back,
> feathers dripping.

He describes all these bird-voices calling to each other, but without
a human voice among them, the sailor is cut off from any company.

Unlike *The Wanderer*, however, this seafarer is neither aimlessly
drifting nor forced into solitude by events beyond his control. We
learn as the poem goes on that he has chosen this life – in fact, he
chooses it again and again, every year, as spring returns to the earth.
The force that compels him is described with extraordinary intensity:

> Now the thoughts of my heart
> clamour that I should strive myself with the high seas,
> the tossing of salty waves;
> my mind's hunger at all times urges
> my spirit to travel, that I, far from here,
> should seek the land of strangers.
> Indeed there is no man on earth so proud-hearted,
> so generous of his possessions, so keen in his youth,
> so brave in his deeds nor so loyal to his lord

that he does not always have anxiety in his sea-voyage
about how the Lord will treat him.
His mind is not on the harp, nor the giving of rings,
nor pleasure with a woman nor joy in the world,
nor anything at all but the tumult of the waves.
He always has a longing who sets out on the sea.

This longing is explicitly linked with the coming of spring:

The woods take on blossoms, towns become fair,
meadows grow beautiful, the world hastens on;
all these things urge the eager mind,
the spirit to the journey, in one who thinks to travel
far on the paths of the sea.
The cuckoo too gives warning with mournful voice,
summer's watchman sings, foretells sorrow,
bitter in the breast . . .
So now my spirit soars out of the confines of the heart,
my mind over the sea-flood;
it wheels wide over the whale's home,
the expanse of the earth, and comes back to me
eager and greedy; the lone flier cries,
incites the heart to the whale's way, irresistible,
across the ocean's floods. So to me
the joys of the Lord are warmer than this dead life,
lent on land.

Cold and desolate as life is at sea, he's irresistibly drawn back to it
– called back to it by the cuckoo's song in spring. Renouncing the
comforts of life on land, he voluntarily chooses the hardships of
a sea-journey and scorns those who stay at home. As the seafarer
describes the urgency of his desire, his 'longing' for the sea, the
language becomes intense, almost violent: his thoughts *cnyssað*,

'clamour, strike', a word earlier used of the beating of waves against the cliff, and *monað*, 'urge, cry', which a few lines later also describes the call of a bird. It's as if the crying birds and vigorous energy of the waves have got inside his own mind, and everything within and without is urging him to this journey. The cuckoo's voice is answered by a call in his own heart, and that internal call, the inciting spirit within him, is described as if also a bird: it's an *anfloga*, a 'lone flier', which soars out across the sea, far away from his physical body. The verb used of this bird-like spirit is *hweorfan*, 'to wheel about, wander', and it's called 'eager and greedy' (*gifre ond grædig*); it moves like a seagull soaring and turning through the air, with the complete freedom of a bird on the wing. The seafarer seems to have a ravenous hunger for something he can find out at sea, a desire calling him away from all that's safe and familiar and urging him out into the wilderness. The life he chooses may be dangerous and lonely, but he still prefers it to the sterile 'dead life' on land.

What's going on here? It's a kind of 'sea fever' – what a later poet of the sea would describe as 'a wild call and a clear call that may not be denied'. But in this poem, though the sea and the sailor's life are described with superb attention to natural detail, the sea is not only a literal environment; the journeys of this poem are mental and spiritual voyages, its waves and birds manifestations of yearnings and calls within the mind. What this seafarer desires are 'the joys of the Lord', and the hunger that calls him out to sea is a powerful longing for God.

The journey he chooses, it seems, is the life of the penitent Christian, renouncing the pleasures of the world to seek the joys of heaven. What he leaves behind, earthly comfort and human companionship, might seem to be happiness, but they won't endure: they are *læne*, just 'lent' to us during our short lives. Better to set your heart, the poem suggests, on something more lasting, on whatever lies beyond the sea of this world's troubles; best of all to seek out hardship or self-denial in this life if it brings you closer in spirit to that further shore. This poem doesn't present heaven as a haven from the discomforts of this world – what the seafarer is going towards is described as a place of heat and a 'land of strangers', and sounds far from cosy. It's not a refuge, but a place which offers something more vital, more truly alive than anything on earth.

In a poem where the natural world and the human mind are so closely interrelated as to be almost inseparable, it seems fitting that it's the coming of spring which calls the sailor back to sea. As the land awakens to life, he feels a quickening in his spirit; blossom makes the meadows beautiful, and 'all these things urge the eager mind, the spirit to the journey'. In this poem, as in many medieval poems of spring, the herald of the warm season is the cuckoo, called in Old English *geac*. The conventional association between the cuckoo and the spring was already a well-established trope. It appears, for instance, in the *Debate between Spring and Winter*, attributed to the Anglo-Saxon poet Alcuin (d. 804).[8] In this Latin dialogue, composed in a pastoral mode influenced by Virgil's *Eclogues*, personifications of winter and spring dispute whether or not they want the cuckoo to come, using the bird to represent spring itself. One of Winter's arguments may help to explain why the cuckoo's voice is, rather surprisingly, called a 'mournful' sound in *The Seafarer*, as in some other Old English poems. The cuckoo's coming heralds the joys of spring, but it also means (Winter argues) the end of the quiet peace of the winter months – spring can be a season of wars and disturbances, because it's a time when nothing is still. There's something bittersweet about it, and perhaps this fits with the sense in *The Seafarer* that spring's coming means time is hastening on: the world is full of life, but that's a reminder that existence on earth is not permanent, a spur to go in quest of something more lasting. As in the poems we looked at earlier, spring seems to be a restless season, turbulent as the sea – not a time of tranquillity but of movement, growth and change. In *The Seafarer*, that restless movement is valued above comfort and pleasure; true happiness, the real source of life, is found by contesting with the tossing waves. The coming of spring urges the seafarer not to rest on land and enjoy the beauties of the world, but to put out into deep waters and discover what can be found there.

There's another poem in the Exeter Book in which the cuckoo calls someone to a sea-journey, though its mood is quite different from *The Seafarer*. This is a short, fragmentary poem known as *The Husband's Message*, and it takes the form of a letter, which seems to be spoken by a piece of wood on which a nobleman has carved a message to his beloved. The lovers have been separated by feud and violence, and now he's urging her to come and join him again. He invites her, too, to listen for the cuckoo's voice and then set out on the sea:

> Now he has commanded me
> to joyfully tell you to take to the sea,
> after you have heard by the cliff's edge
> the mourning cuckoo sing in the woods.
> Do not then let any living man
> prevent your coming, hinder your journey.
> Begin to seek the sea, the gull's home,
> board an ocean-going ship, so that away to the south
> across the sea-track you will find the man,
> the place where your lord is waiting for you.

Here again the cuckoo plays the role of spring's herald, marking the approach of a season favourable for a sea-journey. This woman is urged to wait until the conditions are right, but then to be bold on her journey, hindered by no human being once the natural world is telling her to go. After this the poem becomes fragmented, and incorporates some runes whose interpretation is unclear, so scholars have disagreed about what it's all supposed to mean. It may simply be a love-poem, in which the desire for reunion between the lovers provides the urgency of the call to the journey. However, it's also been read as an allegory: an invitation from God to the soul, calling her to be joyously reunited with her lord and love.

The woman in this poem, like the seafarer, is to exchange the cuckoo for the cries of seabirds, out on the *mæwes eþel*, the 'gull's home'. The sea is often called by names like this in Anglo-Saxon poetry: 'whale's home', 'gannet's bath', 'seal's track', 'swan-road'. All these phrases emphasize that the sea is a space which belongs to wild creatures, not to human beings; they have roads, settlements and homes there, where they form societies and networks hidden from human eyes. A phrase like 'whale's way' suggests a web of invisible paths stretching under the sea, down in the dark abyss, while ships skim the surface above, unconscious of all that lives below. For humans, the sea is a place of travelling, never *home*, as it is to the gulls and whales.

As *The Seafarer* makes clear, though, earth is not our home either. That poem concludes by exhorting the reader, 'Let us consider where we have a home, and think how we may come there.' That home is heaven, because for the seafarer the end of the journey lies beyond this world. Perhaps that's the destination the woman in *The Husband's Message* is travelling towards, too – the place where her lord is waiting to greet her. But both poems have more to say about the journey, and the call that prompts it, than they do about the destination. Both urge the reader to *listen* – to be attentive to the voices of the natural world and the cry of the bird-like spirit within, and to reflect on what they might be calling you to do. Amid the tossing seas of the mind, and the heart's winter, there's a voice inside that may be the call of the spring.

GUTHLAC'S SPRING

In Anglo-Saxon society, the kind of challenging, self-denying life which the poet of *The Seafarer* had in mind might include the choice to be a hermit, monk or nun – to live apart from the world to follow the call of the voice within. In this section, we'll look at an Old

English poem about someone who made just that choice: the hermit St Guthlac of Crowland, in whose story the experience of spiritual renewal finds an echo in the rebirth of nature in spring.

Born in 674 into an aristocratic Mercian family, Guthlac became a warrior as a young man, but in his early twenties decided instead to follow the religious life. After spending time as a monk, he sought out the more demanding life of a hermit in the Lincolnshire Fens, arriving at Crowland in August 699 or 700. He established a hermitage for himself on the site of a prehistoric barrow-mound, where he lived until his death fifteen years later. Guthlac became a popular saint, and there are multiple accounts of his life surviving from medieval England. The first was written a few decades after his death by a monk named Felix, and there are also two poems in the Exeter Book (*Guthlac A* and *Guthlac B*) which explore his story in Old English verse.[9] Felix presented Guthlac as a hermit in the mould of the Desert Fathers, a holy man in a devil-haunted wilderness, assailed by demons but upheld by God and the power of his patron, the apostle St Bartholomew. This focus on Guthlac's hermit life as a form of spiritual combat is especially appropriate given the saint's own military background and the etymology of his name, which means something like 'battle-play' in Old English (*guþ* is 'war, battle'; *lac* could mean either 'play' or 'sacrifice, gift'). Warfare is the metaphor his hagiographers consistently use to explore the life of this soldier-turned-hermit.

The natural world plays an important role in this spiritual combat. *Guthlac A* explores how the saint's temptations in his solitude come from within as much as from without; demons tempt him to despair or to gloat in his own holiness, and his fight against them is really a battle to maintain control over his own mind. It plays out as a struggle for mastery of his dwelling-place, the barrow-mound: Guthlac fights to keep hold of his hermitage, an island of firm green land amid the lonely Fens, as the devils try to drag or drive him away from it. The land and Guthlac's mind have a close connection, and controlling his own spirit and holding on to his island go hand in hand.

Guthlac endures, and in the end wins the battle. The poem's conclusion offers a beautiful description of the peaceful life the saint attains once he has successfully survived all these trials, and can enjoy his dwelling-place in harmony with the natural world. It's imagined in seasonal terms, as if Guthlac's triumph is mirrored by the victory of spring over winter:

> Triumphant in his victory, the builder
> came back to the barrow. Many species and kinds
> of tree-dwelling birds blessed him
> with unceasing voices, and by these signs proclaimed
> the holy man's return. Often he held out food for them,
> and they would hungrily fly around his hands,
> eager and greedy, glad of his help.
> So the gentle-hearted one separated himself
> from the pleasures of mankind, served the Lord.
> He took his joy in wild creatures, after he had rejected
>   the world.
> Serene was the field of victory and the dwelling renewed;
> fair was the song of the birds, the land blossomed,
> cuckoos heralded the spring. Guthlac, blessed and resolute,
> was able to enjoy his home.
> The green field stood in God's keeping.
> The shepherd, he who had come from heaven,
> had frightened off the fiends. What more beautiful desire
> has been brought to pass in the life of men,
> of those our elders remembered
> or we ourselves have known?

Once Guthlac has secured possession of the barrow-mound, the land comes to life all around him: the birds sing, the trees blossom, and the hermit can live in peace. As in *The Seafarer* and *The Husband's Message*, spring is heralded by the cuckoo, but here there's no mourning in its welcome voice. Such a way of celebrating Guthlac's victory must have seemed particularly appropriate because his feast falls on 11 April, so spring is the time of year when people would be most likely to read about this saint.

Other Anglo-Saxon hermits are also known for their close relationship with the natural world: especially famous is St Cuthbert (*c.* 635–687), who similarly befriended wild creatures in his island hermitage off the coast of Northumbria. Bede tells how Cuthbert had a devotional practice of going out alone at night and standing up to his neck in the sea, praying and praising God; when he had finished, otters would come and dry him with their fur and warm breath.[10] Guthlac has cuckoos instead, but he has an equally friendly and reciprocal relationship with his bird companions. They bless him with their voices, and he feeds them as they cluster around his hands, glad of his help: they're called *hungrige* and *grædum gifre*, 'hungry' and 'eagerly greedy', so we might imagine them swooping and squabbling for food from the hermit's hand. (These are the same words used of the bird-like soul in *The Seafarer*.) As the saint helps the birds, so God and St Bartholomew protect him – Bartholomew is here referred to as a *heorde*, which means 'guardian, protector', and is also the same as the second element in 'shepherd'. It's almost as if Guthlac himself is an animal in Bartholomew's protective keeping.

Altogether there's a beautiful sense that the natural world is *responding* to Guthlac, giving back to him, and he's tending to it now his demons have left him free to do so. The loveliest line here is perhaps *genom him to wildeorum wynne, siþþan he þas woruld forhogde* – 'he took his joy in wild creatures, after he had rejected the world'. Having left behind the pleasures of human society, Guthlac finds new joys in his solitude. After his time of trouble and hardship, the spring has come at last.

5

CHEESE AND ASHES

'A PURE AND HOLY TIME DRAWS NEAR'

In Anglo-Saxon England, the usual word for spring was *lencten*, but this was a word with two co-existing meanings. It referred not only to the season, but to the weeks of fasting before Easter, now 'Lent'. In many European languages, what English calls 'Lent' has a name deriving either from the practice of fasting or from the fast's duration of forty days, such as the French *le carême*, from the Latin *Quadragesima*. When the Anglo-Saxons adopted the custom of Lenten fasting, they did not invent a new word for it; they absorbed it into their idea of spring, and the two meanings of *lencten*, Lent-as-spring and Lent-as-fast, are often difficult to distinguish in medieval English well into the fourteenth century.[1] That suggests something interesting about how inseparable the church season of Lent and Easter was from its springtime setting, and Anglo-Saxon writing about this time of year is very much shaped by the double meaning of *lencten*. Both the natural and liturgical seasons are a time of growth and renewal, when light and life are increasing as the days lengthen.

In the medieval period, there were practical reasons why spring was a good time for a collective fast: with food stocks running low at the end of the long winter months, spring was a time of unavoidable scarcity. With the introduction of Lent, that necessary self-denial was given spiritual meaning. Across the early medieval church, there was some variation in the length of the pre-Easter fast, and therefore in its dating: at the time of the Anglo-Saxon conversion, the

Roman custom was for 36 days of fasting, beginning on the Sunday six weeks before Easter. Around this time, however, the previous four days from Wednesday to Saturday began to be added in order to make forty days, in imitation of Christ's fast in the wilderness.[2] Nonetheless, the idea that the First Sunday of Lent was the real beginning of the season seems to have lingered, and can be traced in Anglo-Saxon sources as late as the tenth century. The First Sunday of Lent has a recorded Old English name, *Halgan Dæg*, 'Holy Day', presumably reflecting its original importance as the beginning of the fast.[3]

For the medieval church, the weeks leading up to Lent formed an important season in their own right, a time of preparation for the coming fast. It was an opportunity to say farewell to various aspects of life which would be restricted during Lent, in order to mark a personal and communal commitment to the fast. This pre-Lent season began nine weeks before Easter with Septuagesima, which takes its name from the Latin word for 'seventieth', because it falls roughly seventy days before Easter. This was followed by the Sundays of Sexagesima ('sixtieth'), Quinquagesima ('fiftieth') and finally Quadragesima ('fortieth'), the First Sunday in Lent. One of the most distinctive features of Septuagesima was the custom of ceasing to sing 'Alleluia' at mass, as a mark of the deepening solemnity of the season. In later medieval England this was popularly called 'locking the Alleluia', a phrase which seems already to have been in use in the Anglo-Saxon period: a number of Old English sources refer to Septuagesima as the Sunday 'when Alleluia is locked' (*þe man belycð Alleluia*).[4] In the late Middle Ages, this was sometimes accompanied with elaborate ceremonies in which a representation of the word might actually be buried in a mock funeral.[5] The word was symbolically locked away, to be unlocked again amid the celebration of Easter; then it was set free from its imprisonment, a moment of liberation paralleling Christ's bursting out of the tomb to free mankind from the captivity of sin.

In his sermon for Septuagesima, Ælfric – following the Carolingian writer Amalarius of Metz – explains the symbolism of this custom:

> We wish to speak to you about this present season, why the holy congregation in God's church omits 'Alleluia' and 'Gloria in excelsis Deo', from this present day until the holy season of Easter. There was a wise teacher named Amalarius, who wrote a book about the church's customs and what the ceremonies of God's servants symbolize through the course of the year; and he said about this present season, which is called Septuagesima, that it acts as a token of the seventy years for which the people of Israel served the king of Babylon in captivity . . . Now God's church keeps this period of seventy, by choice, for their sins, just as Israel of old was forced to keep it in captivity, until merciful God rescued them after their tribulations and led them to their homeland. The prophet Jeremiah prophesied about the people of Israel that during that period of seventy years they should cease from the voice of joy and gladness, the voice of the bridegroom and the bride. Now in emulation of that, God's servants leave the heavenly songs of praise, 'Alleluia' and 'Gloria in excelsis Deo', in this period of Septuagesima, because it is fitting for us that from this present day we pre-pare ourselves voluntarily with a degree of strictness for the spiritual battle, as the liturgy of the church exhorts us to sorrow and repent of our sins.[6]

As Ælfric explains, the church sought to be united with the Israelites in their time of captivity, when they mourned the loss of their songs of joy – the loss famously lamented in Psalm 137, 'By the waters of Babylon we sat down and wept when we remembered Zion. We hung our harps upon the willows . . . How shall we sing the Lord's song in a strange land?' The custom of 'locking the Alleluia' is a liturgical re-imagining of this despairing question, which the medieval church interpreted as the cry of a universal experience of estrangement: all human beings are in exile and captivity on earth, longing for their home in heaven, and every year through Lent and Easter the church re-enacts this progression from exile to homecoming, from grief to joy.

Like other medieval homilists, Ælfric gave his congregation plenty of warning about how to prepare for this solemn season of repentance. Preaching at Quinquagesima, he tells them what they should be doing in the last days before Lent:

> Now a pure and holy time draws near, in which we should atone for our neglect. Every Christian, therefore, should come to his confession and confess his hidden sins, and make amends according to the guidance of his teacher; and let everyone encourage each other to do good by good example.[7]

This custom of preparing for Lent by going to confession later led to the three days before Ash Wednesday being known as 'Shrovetide' – a time for being 'shriven', absolved of sins through confession. On the one hand, Shrovetide was a time for the devout preparations Ælfric describes here, in order to start off Lent in a good spiritual state. On the other hand, by the later Middle Ages, it was also a period of last-chance merrymaking and revelry before the soberness of Lent: a carnival of Shrovetide games, riotous plays, and eating up the rich food which would be off the menu until Easter.[8] This is the etymology of the word 'carnival' itself (from medieval Latin, to do with 'putting away of meat'), and even today many people who don't observe Lent still eat pancakes on Shrove Tuesday, a custom which has its origins in the need to eat up the last of the eggs and dairy products before Lent came in.

We don't have any evidence to show whether this was a custom in Anglo-Saxon England, but there is some indication that the week of Ash Wednesday was known in Old English as 'Cheese Week' (*cyswuce*).[9] This would make perfect sense as a name for the last week when cheese could be eaten before the fast began. Though there's only slight evidence for this name in Anglo-Saxon sources, it parallels many names for this pre-Lent period in other cultures: the famous example is 'Mardi Gras', 'Fat Tuesday', but there are numerous others, including 'Butter Week' and 'Cheesefare Sunday'. The English name 'Shrovetide' is an odd one out in that context, since it's not named for the food that's given up, but there are some traditional English equivalents too: in northern England, the day before Shrove Tuesday used to be 'Collop Monday', when collops of bacon would be eaten up.[10] Now, too, we often speak of 'Pancake Day', a name which is increasingly taking over from 'Shrove Tuesday' in Britain. English is coming into line with other languages in emphasizing the importance of food at this season, instead of the penitential practice of being shriven – but perhaps this is only returning to the way the Anglo-Saxons did it, in 'Cheese Week'.

GOLD IN THE DUST

Unlike the First Sunday of Lent, 'Holy Day', Ash Wednesday seems to have had no vernacular name in Anglo-Saxon England. But it did have a memorable ritual to mark the beginning of Lent, which Ælfric describes as follows:

> On that Wednesday throughout the world, as it is appointed, priests bless clean ashes in church, and then lay them on people's heads, so that they may remember they came from earth and will return again to dust, just as Almighty God said to Adam after he had sinned against God's command: 'In labour you shall live and in sweat you shall eat your bread

upon the earth, until you return again to the same earth from which you came, for you are dust, and to dust you shall return.' This is not said about the souls of mankind but about their bodies, which moulder to dust, and shall again on Judgement Day, through the power of our Lord, rise from the earth, all who ever lived, just as all trees quicken again in the season of spring which were deadened by the winter's chill.[11]

Ælfric here uses the phrase *on lenctenes timan*, 'in the season of spring', exploiting the word's double meaning to connect the revival of the trees in spring with Lent and the spiritual rebirth of human souls. Lent is a reminder of mortality, a solemn admonition to remember that our bodies, like everything in the world, are fragile and decaying things of earth: *þu eart dust and to duste gewendst*, as Ælfric translates the message of the ashes. But as the natural world revives again in spring, it's also a reminder that God's power is stronger than death and can restore life even to the creatures of dust. Ælfric's sermon recalls *The Seafarer* and the effects of spring in that poem: there, too, the coming of spring awakens thoughts both of death and of new life. As the trees show signs of life, they remind the seafarer that our time on earth is short, and he's inspired to seek eternal life through a renewed commitment to God. The voluntary hardship the seafarer accepts on his journey echoes the self-denial of the Lenten fast; invigorated by the energy of spring, he can forgo bodily comfort for a better purpose, just as Christians were taught to do in Lent through penance and abstinence.

This is not the only place where Old English poetry touches on Lenten themes. To read Anglo-Saxon homilies alongside poems like *Beowulf* can be surprisingly enlightening, a reminder that all these texts belong to the same cultural world. Take for instance a homily by Ælfric for the First Sunday in Lent, in which he discusses the duty of helping the poor. He quotes and explains various biblical exhortations to almsgiving, such as Matthew 6:19–21 (given in Old English so you can see his translation):

Be ðisum cwæð Drihten on his godspelle, 'Ne behyde ge eowerne goldhord on eorðan þær ðær omm and moððan hit awestað, and ðeofas adelfað and forstelað; ac hordiað eowerne goldhord on heofenum, þær ne cymð to ne om ne moððe, ne þeofas ne delfað ne ne ætbredað. Soðlice ðær ðær þin goldhord is, þær bið þin heorte.' Hu mage we urne goldhord on heofonum behydan buton ðurh ælmessan? Swa hwæt swa we be anfealdan Godes þearfum for his lufan syllað, he hit us forgylt be hundfealdum on ðam toweardan life.[12]

Of this the Lord said in his Gospel, 'Do not hide your gold-hoard on earth, where rust and moths destroy it, and thieves dig it up and steal it; but hoard up your gold-hoard in heaven, where no rust or moths can touch it, and no thieves can dig it up or take it away. Truly where your gold-hoard is, there is your heart.' How may we hide our gold-hoard in heaven except through alms? Whatever one thing we give to God's needy for the sake of his love, he will repay us for it a hundredfold in the life to come.

With his use of the word *goldhord* in this sermon, Ælfric conjures up resonant associations from Anglo-Saxon poetry. Treasure plays an important role in many Old English poems, as a display of a lord's power and the means by which he rewards his followers for their loyalty: *sincgifa*, 'treasure-giver', is a common term for a ruler, used of earthly kings and of God.[13] But the transient nature of earthly treasure is a recurring theme too – just as the Gospel draws a contrast between the treasures of earth, vulnerable to time and decay, and the treasures which can be stored up in heaven through good deeds. *Beowulf*, a poem which contains many descriptions of precious treasure, ends with just such a transient and vulnerable treasure-hoard. Beowulf's last battle is with a dragon who guards a fabulous gold-hoard, and the poem tells us that this hoard has a long and troubled history.[14] It was originally buried by a mourning man, the last survivor of the people who had owned it. Because his people are all dead, carried away by war, there's nothing for this last mourner to do with their treasures but commit them to the earth; they have no value for him now, once their owners are gone. In time a dragon takes possession of the hoard, and jealously guards it for hundreds of years. Then a thief, by stealing a goblet, drives the dragon into a murderous rage, so that it begins to threaten Beowulf's people. Beowulf – now an aged king – chooses to go into the dragon's lair and fight the beast himself.

Like the Gospel's gold-hoard, eaten by rust (*om*, in Ælfric's translation), the treasure in *Beowulf* is found to be *omige*, 'rusty', from long centuries hidden in the earth:

> Him big stodan bunan ond orcas,
> discas lagon ond dyre swyrd,
> omige, þurhetone, swa hie wið eorðan fæðm
> þusend wintra þær eardodon.

> Beside [the dragon] stood cups and drinking-vessels,
> dishes lay and precious swords,
> rusty, eaten through, as if they had rested
> a thousand winters there in the earth's embrace.

Beowulf slays the dragon and wins the treasure, but is killed himself in the fight. He has saved his people, but left them grieving, leaderless and vulnerable, and without him they have little use for the treasures he has won. In the last lines of the poem, his people build a monument to their beloved king, burying within it the hoard for which he has given his life:

In the barrow they placed rings and jewels,
all the ornaments hostile men
had previously taken from the hoard.
They let the earth keep the warriors' treasure,
gold in the dust, where it still lies now,
as useless to men as it was before.

Though beautiful and precious, the poem suggests, these treasures are only valuable when in use by human beings. Now the treasure-hoard, like Beowulf himself, must return to the earth from which it came – dust to dust.

This is a poem which ends (as it begins) with a king's funeral, as Beowulf is burned to ashes on his pyre; no one who had read *Beowulf* would need to be reminded that *þu eart dust and to duste gewendst*. Ælfric might consciously or unconsciously have drawn on such poetic associations of treasure in his Lenten sermon, and the *Beowulf*-poet might well have been thinking of the same Gospel passage in linking this treasure-hoard with mortality and the brevity of life. In the Old English translation, Christ's statement that 'where your gold-hoard is, there is your heart' is particularly apt, because in Anglo-Saxon poetry the heart itself is often called a 'hoard', the place where the treasures of the spirit are kept. It's the *breosthord*, *feorhhord* or *sawelhord*, the storehouse of thoughts, life or the soul. The Gospel's imagery must have resonated for poets and writers familiar with such metaphors.

In this poetic language, other intangible things can be hoarded too. Several Anglo-Saxon poems, including *Beowulf*, speak of the *wordhord*, 'word-hoard', the store of words treasured up within the memory.[15] When someone makes a wise speech or composes a poem, they are said to 'open the word-hoard' and bring forth the treasures of their mind. The verb usually associated with this process is 'unlocked' (*onleac*) – which might remind us of that other hoarded word, 'Alleluia', locked away every year at Septuagesima and set free at Easter. The association between precious words and a locked treasure-hoard may explain how the same figurative language came to be used for that custom, a symbol of the seasonal movement from captivity to liberation. In the word-hoard metaphor, words are imagined as treasures; they are currency to be passed back and forth, carrying value with them. Poets, preachers like Ælfric, and the many anonymous speakers of Old English who gave names to the seasons and customs of the church year were all drawing on the same hoard of words, and when we read the poetry alongside the sermons, we can begin to understand what kinds of value these words might have had for their audiences.

THE BIRTHDAY OF TIME

For medieval experts in the calendar, spring was the most important time of year. This was the season when they had to work out the timing of Easter and all the dates in the church calendar which depended on it, as well as thinking about leap years and when to add an extra day to February. On top of that, they had to reckon with a sequence of days in late March which marked a set of significant anniversaries – the most momentous anniversaries in the history of the world.

This sequence hinges on 21 March, the date of the spring equinox, and 25 March, which in late antique and early medieval tradition was widely considered to be the historical date of the Crucifixion.[16] That date was worked out from the information given about Christ's death in the Gospels, most importantly its link to Passover and the Jewish calendar: since Christ died at Passover, it was possible to try to establish the date of his death and work out what its equivalent might be in the Julian calendar. The date on which Christ's death and resurrection should be commemorated by the church was a separate issue (more on that later); nonetheless, it was felt important to identify the Crucifixion as a historical event which took place on a particular date. Christ's conception, commemorated by the feast of the Annunciation to the Virgin Mary, was then also fixed to 25 March, because it was thought appropriate that he should have entered the world on the same date that he left it.[17] His life formed a perfect circle, with 25 March both the first and last day of his earthly existence. Add nine months, and you get 25 December as the date for his birth.

For the medieval church, Christ's death was the most significant event in history, so it was thought fitting to link to this crucial date other key events connected to or prefiguring his death and resurrection. One of these was the beginning of time itself. That special date, 25 March, was pinpointed as the last of the days of creation, the eighth day on which God rested after completing his work – the end of another significant circle, the world's first week. If the eighth day was 25 March, it was possible to count back and identify the date on which each day of creation fell, starting with 18 March. Medieval calendars for March sometimes mark this date with a note, 'first day of the world' – just another day among the list of saints' feasts and commemorations.[18] So 18 March was the first day of creation, when God separated light from darkness; on 19 March, he created the sky; on 21 March, the date of the equinox, the sun and moon were created, and that was the beginning of time.

The various arguments which lay behind these systems of dating are too complex to get into here, and it's important to say that this tradition was far from universal in the early medieval church; alternative views were also put forward. In Anglo-Saxon England, however, this schema was the most influential, because it was espoused by Bede. In *De temporum ratione*, Bede explains why the spring equinox was properly dated to 21 March, and why time had to be created on the day when God made the heavenly bodies. (Because how could you have time before there was a sun and moon to measure it by?) He goes on to describe how all this is connected to Christ's resurrection, because the sun and moon themselves prefigure the redemption of mankind:

It is fitting that just as the Sun at that point in time first assumed power over the day, and then the Moon and stars power over the night, so now, to connote the joy of our redemption, day should first equal night in length, and then the full Moon should suffuse [the night] with light. This is for the sake of a certain symbolism, because the created Sun which lights up all the stars signifies the *true* and eternal *light which lighteth every man that cometh into the world*, while the Moon and stars, which shine, not with their own light (as they say), but with an adventitious light borrowed from the Sun, suggest the body of the Church as a whole ... And in the celebration of the supreme solemnity, it was necessary that Christ precede the Church, which cannot shine save through Him.[19]

What underlies this argument is a belief that the created world, in all its aspects, must reveal truths about God's purpose: God, the creator of light, time, measurement and number, would not do anything without meaning, or anything imperfect, so the date on which he chose to create time and redeem the world must be the most perfect time possible. For Bede, that means it's all about trying to identify the most *fitting* date on which these events could take place. He argues that it's fitting that Christ's act of redemption should be linked to the spring equinox, when the days begin to grow longer than the nights and light triumphs over the darkness; that it should be at a point in the solar and lunar cycles when the sun and moon express something about the relationship between Christ and his church; and that it should be in the spring, when life returns to the earth. It is, in every sense, the perfect time.

Bede's arguments and similar ways of thinking about the dates around the equinox shaped learned understanding of this time in the year, though few people could have followed all the intricacies of his analysis. Aspects of this topic are, however, explained in a number of Anglo-Saxon sources, not only by Latin writers like Bede but in vernacular texts too: both Ælfric and Byrhtferth incorporate summaries of this dating system into their English writings on the calendar, making these ideas accessible to a wider audience.[20] It contributes to Ælfric's arguments about the date of New Year, as we saw earlier, and also appears in *The Menologium*, which in its section for March points out the link between the equinox and the creation of time:

> Swylce eac rimcræftige
> on þa ylcan tiid emniht healdað,
> forðan wealdend God worhte æt frymðe
> on þy sylfan dæge sunnan and monan.

> And too the number-skilled
> keep the equinox at that same time,
> because the Lord God created in the beginning
> the sun and moon on that same day.

The Old English word for the equinox here is *emniht*, from *efen* 'even' and *niht* 'night', a literal translation of the Latin word. The poem suggests that only the *rimcræftige*, 'number-skilled', really understand how all this works, and that's probably true. However, *The Menologium* is insistent that though it's the *rimcræftige* who develop the calendar, it's nonetheless experienced by everyone in the world; the experts might calculate it, but we all live through it, and so this poem, like Ælfric and Byrhtferth, makes an effort to explain it in terms everyone could understand.

Since not everyone could calculate the day of the equinox, it was perhaps the connection of these dates with spring which would have been most obvious. The ninth-century *Old English Martyrology* gives a beautiful summary of the link between spring and March's significant dates:

On the twenty-fifth day of the month Gabriel first came
to St Mary with God's message, and on that day St Mary
became pregnant in the city of Nazareth through the angel's
word and through the hearing of her ears, like these trees
when they blossom through the blowing of the wind . . .
And then after thirty-two years and three months Christ
was crucified on the cross on the same day. And as soon as
he was on the cross, the creation demonstrated that he was
the true God. The sun grew black, and day was turned into
dark night from midday to the ninth hour.[21]

This text makes clear the connection between these events in salvation history and the revival of the natural world in spring. At the
Annunciation, Mary becomes like the blossoming trees and like
the tree which became Christ's cross: she brings new life into the
world. Just as the sun's eclipse at the Crucifixion revealed that the
whole world recognized its creator, so every aspect of the seasonal,
solar and lunar cycles could reveal something about God's purpose.

All this way of thinking about the natural world – especially
pinning creation to a specific day of the month – can seem very
foreign to a modern mindset, but it's fundamental to the medieval
understanding of nature and time. It's born of a conviction that, since
God is the designer of the universe, the created world must have
been planned with care and can be understood through the exer-
cise of human reason. In medieval art depicting the creation, God
is often shown with scientific instruments, tools and scales which
are images of balance and precision.[22] When the first divine act of
creation was imagined as careful, scientific workmanship, it would
have seemed only right to be as exact as possible in understanding
the world's origins. That act of creation is also the subject of perhaps the oldest surviving Anglo-Saxon poem, the song attributed to
Cædmon, a cowherd who lived in the seventh century at St Hilda's
monastery in Whitby.[23] As Bede tells the story, Cædmon – who had

never been educated or taught to sing – had a vision one night in his cowshed of an angel, who instructed him to 'sing about creation'. The result was a short poem in praise of 'the might of the Measurer and the thoughts of his mind', telling how God created the world with 'heaven as a roof for the children of men'. The Old English word for 'Creator' is *Scyppend*, meaning 'the one who shapes'; it shares a root with the word for 'poet', *scop*. Cædmon's own act of creation, as he miraculously became a *scop*, mirrored the work of the *Scyppend* whom his poem praises.

Not everyone could be one of the 'number-skilled', like Bede, Ælfric or Byrhtferth, able to follow the intricacies of calendar calculation or work out the dates of leap years and equinoxes. But the point of this way of thinking was that its evidence was visible to everyone – as clear to a cowherd as to an expert in *computus*. It was written all over the world, inscribed in the cycles of the seasons and the sun and moon, which had been imbued with meaning by their divine creator.

6

EASTER

EOSTRE AND EASTER

One reason Bede pays such careful attention to the spring equinox and its link to Christ's resurrection is that this is key to the dating of Easter, a subject on which he wrote extensively. In the first centuries of the church, the date of Easter was a controversial issue, because of problems arising from the difficulties of reconciling the lunar cycle which governs the date of Passover with the solar cycle of the Julian calendar. Early on the principle was established that, to follow a Christianized version of the dating of Passover, Easter should be celebrated on the Sunday following the first full moon after the spring equinox. However, since ways of dating the equinox varied, as did methods for calculating cycles of the moon, different systems of calculation resulted in varying date-ranges within which Easter could be celebrated. At the time the Anglo-Saxons converted to Christianity, this matter had already been under discussion for centuries.[1]

In the years after the conversion, alternative methods for calculating the date of Easter co-existed in the two main cultural spheres of influence that shaped early Anglo-Saxon Christianity, the Roman missionaries and the British and Irish churches.[2] These different ways of calculating Easter could result in problems, since some people would be feasting while their neighbours were keeping the Lenten fast; Bede records that at the court of Oswiu, king of Northumbria (642–70), the king celebrated Easter on a different date from his own wife.[3] In 664 a synod was held at Whitby to discuss the issue, and from that point on the question was essentially settled within the English church. All this was of great interest to Bede, who writes about it at length in his *Historia ecclesiastica*.[4]

Within a century of the conversion, the Christian festival of Easter was well established in Anglo-Saxon England. When people today talk about the Anglo-Saxon history of Easter, however, they're often referring not to the controversy about its dating, the question which so exercised Bede and his contemporaries, but to a theory about Easter's history based on much more scanty evidence – a topic to which Bede devotes just one sentence, and in which other Anglo-Saxon writers seem to have had no interest at all. This concerns the origins of the English name for the festival. In most European languages, the name for the feast of Christ's resurrection derives from the Latin word *Pascha*, ultimately from Hebrew *Pesach*, 'Passover'. Central to the Christian festival of Easter is the belief that Christ became the new Paschal sacrifice, so the Latin name, like the date of Easter, originates in a medieval Christian interpretation of biblical references to Passover.[5]

The English name, 'Easter', is an outlier here. Where did it come from? Bede is the only Anglo-Saxon writer to attempt to answer that question. He does so in his short chapter about the English months, discussing the Anglo-Saxon name for April, *Eastermonað*. He says that this month

> has a name which is now translated 'Paschal month', and which was once called after a goddess of theirs named Eostre, in whose honour feasts were celebrated in that month. Now they designate that Paschal season by her name, calling the joys of the new rite by the time-honoured name of the old observance.[6]

This is all he, or any other Anglo-Saxon source, tells us about a goddess called Eostre, but this brief passage has caused much debate. In the nineteenth century, scholars of comparative mythology, most influentially Jacob Grimm, used Bede's evidence and some German analogues (including a hypothetical goddess Ostara, who is not attested in medieval sources) to argue that Eostre may have been a pan-Germanic goddess – perhaps of spring or the dawn, based on the timing of *Eastermonað* and its etymological link with words relating to 'east'.[7] Aspects of this theory have long been challenged, since it relies heavily on speculation and assumes a cultural homogeneity across the 'Germanic' world which doesn't reflect the complexities of the early medieval period. Some have gone so far as to suggest that Bede invented Eostre as a scholarly hypothesis to explain a name he didn't understand – as Grimm did with Ostara.[8]

However, Bede's claims about Eostre need not be entirely dismissed. Philip A. Shaw has suggested that Eostre may have been neither an invention of Bede's, nor a pan-Germanic deity, but a goddess with a highly localized cult, perhaps centred in Kent in the region around Eastry, a few miles east of Canterbury.[9] He draws a parallel with a group of Romano-Germanic deities called the *matronae Austriahenae*, attested in votive inscriptions dating to AD 150–250, found near Cologne; these inscriptions probably reflect a localized cult, goddesses named in some way from the 'eastern people' who worshipped them. Shaw proposes a similarly named Kentish goddess Eostre, whose name, attached to the spring month closest to April, was borrowed for the Christian festival which most often fell in that month. The influence of Kent and Canterbury in the early days of the Anglo-Saxon church might have enabled this name, though local in origin, to spread to other regions (including parts of Germany, where Christian missionaries from England were active and may have introduced the term). It's plausible that in his explanation of the month-names Bede was using a written source from Canterbury, as we know he did elsewhere in his work. Rather than being a widely known goddess, then, Eostre may have belonged solely to a small – but influential – region of Anglo-Saxon Kent.

The mystery of the goddess Eostre may never be solved. For the purposes of understanding what Easter meant in Anglo-Saxon England, though, it's important to recognize that even if Easter does take its name from a goddess, that only tells us about the origins of the *name* – not the origins of the festival. The Christian festival of Easter long pre-dated the Anglo-Saxon conversion, and its essential features, including the principle behind its dating, had been established for centuries. What's more, we have no evidence of any symbols, customs or rituals that may have been associated with Eostre in Anglo-Saxon England, or anything to suggest how her festival might have been celebrated. Bede mentions 'feasts', in the vaguest terms, but he probably had no idea what those might have involved. Today, it's become a popular myth that symbols linked in modern Britain with Easter, especially eggs, hares or rabbits, derive from the worship of Eostre, but there's no Anglo-Saxon evidence to support that. None of these symbols were linked to Easter in the Anglo-Saxon period; eggs weren't associated with Easter in Britain until the later Middle Ages, hares and rabbits not until much later still.[10] There's nothing to suggest any continuity of customs between the pre-conversion festival and the Anglo-Saxon Christian Easter, and the modern observance of Easter owes nothing to Anglo-Saxon paganism, with the sole exception of its English name.

It's also clear from Anglo-Saxon written sources that though the name survived, it didn't have any pagan connotations for speakers of Old English during the period of our recorded sources. Unlike some of the other festivals discussed in this book, the name *Easter* is plentifully attested in Anglo-Saxon sources, and it's a very stable name, with no recorded vernacular alternatives (unlike Christmas). This suggests that the name took hold early and caught on widely across the English church, quickly losing any pagan associations. Of the many recorded instances of the word *Easter* in Old English sources, all – with the exception of Bede, in the passage quoted earlier – either refer to the Christian festival or use the word in biblical contexts to translate *Pascha*. This means there are in fact more instances in Anglo-Saxon sources where the word *Easter* means 'Passover', in the specific context of Jewish practice, than there are of it referring to a pagan goddess.[11] Anglo-Saxon writers knew very well that the origins of Easter lay in Passover, and would have been bemused by modern attempts to downplay that link or explain its history in any other way. Throughout the recorded history of Anglo-Saxon England, the word *Easter* predominantly meant what it has subsequently meant in English: the chief Christian festival of the year, the equivalent of Latin *Pascha* and the descendant of Passover.

THE SILENT DAYS

So how was Easter celebrated in Anglo-Saxon England? In 877, a law-code of Alfred the Great ruled that labourers should be freed from work for the whole week before and the week after Easter – the longest holiday in the year.[12] This was probably intended not only to give people time for festivity but to allow as many as possible to participate in the sequence of church services that marked the lead-up to Easter. The services of Holy Week formed the high point of the liturgical year: they brought the Easter story to life through the use of sound, light, space and dramatic re-enactment, and they must have been a profound experience to witness and participate in. For the later Anglo-Saxon period, detailed evidence for the observances of Holy Week is provided by *Regularis Concordia*, a tenth-century document which lays out recommended practices and customs for the monasteries of the English church.[13] In combination with sermons and artistic evidence, this gives us a vivid picture of how Anglo-Saxon monastic communities and the wider congregation were encouraged to enter imaginatively into the story of Christ's death and resurrection.

Although some of the rituals in *Regularis Concordia* were performed only by monks, laypeople also attended many of these services. The text specifically mentions lay involvement in some of the rituals, which were for everyone to participate in, not simply to watch. On Palm Sunday, for instance, the whole congregation took part in the re-enactment of Christ's entry into Jerusalem before his Passion. They carried tree-branches in procession, playing the role of the crowd who welcomed Christ into the city with palms. As Ælfric explains in his sermon for Palm Sunday:

> It is the custom in God's church, established by its teachers, that everywhere in God's congregation the priest should bless palm-branches on this day, and distribute them, thus blessed, to the people; and God's servants should then sing the hymn which the Jewish people sang before Christ when he was coming to his Passion. We imitate the faithful ones of that people with this deed, for they carried palm-branches with hymns before the Saviour.[14]

This custom gave its name to the day, which in Anglo-Saxon sources is already called *Palmsunnandæg*. Though Ælfric refers to these branches as *palmtwigu*, real palms are of course not easy to obtain in England, so they probably carried branches of pussy-willow or yew – the traditional substitutes for Palm Sunday 'palms' in Britain until the twentieth century.[15] The use of these 'blossoming palm-branches', as one Anglo-Saxon text calls them, must have engendered a close link between Palm Sunday and the springtime growth of trees and flowers, making the vitality and beauty of the natural world at this season an integral part of the experience of the day. The blossoming branches of Palm Sunday, sprouting their fresh green leaves and cat-kins, also look forward to Good Friday and the cross – imagined in medieval sources, as we'll see later, as a springing tree of life.

At the end of his sermon, Ælfric notes that preaching was not permitted on the last three days of Holy Week, and he calls these 'the silent days' (*swigdagas*). The rituals of these days were left to speak for themselves, impressed on the imagination of participants without the mediation of a preacher. They were meant to take the congregation in mind and heart directly to the time of Christ's Passion, to live again through the last days of his life and experience first the desolation of his death, then the joy of his resurrection. It was a yearly journey from mourning to celebration, experienced communally and through shared ritual, yet often in outward silence.

On the Thursday of Holy Week, the liturgy involved washing the feet of the poor and distributing money and clothes to those in need, acts of service in imitation of Christ at the Last Supper (the *mandatum*, which gave the day its later medieval English name, Maundy Thursday). In a monastic community, as *Regularis Concordia* describes, the abbot would also wash the feet of his monks and drink to the health of each in turn.[16] An image in an eleventh-century psalter from Canterbury shows monks performing the foot-washing ritual next to a king distributing alms to the poor, as later medieval monarchs were to do at the 'royal Maundy' service.[17]

The evening of the last days of Holy Week also saw the intensely dramatic night-time service of *Tenebrae* (named from the Latin for 'darkness'), after the Night Office, in which all lights in the church were extinguished until the place was totally dark.[18] Kneeling in this absolute darkness, the monks would hear the young voices of the children of the choir singing 'Lord have mercy,' and all would sing together, 'Christ the Lord became obedient, even unto death.' This was designed to represent, *Regularis Concordia* explains, the terror of the darkness that covered the whole world at the moment of Christ's death, and it must have been an overpowering experience. Later in the Triduum, the lights would be lit again from the 'New Fire', a blessed flame struck from flint, borne on a candle held in the mouth of a serpent-shaped staff; from this fire, the Paschal candle would be lit on Easter Eve, representing the return of the light of Christ.[19]

Good Friday seems to have been known in Anglo-Saxon England as 'Long Friday' (*Langa Frigadæg*), perhaps because of its sombre mood.[20] Central to this day was the Adoration of the Cross, with the reading of the long Gospel narrative of Christ's death and times of prayer and prostration before the cross as it was held aloft for the congregation to venerate. This ritual provides a useful context in which to explore perhaps the most powerful Anglo-Saxon poem about the Crucifixion, *The Dream of the Rood*. A narrative of Christ's death seen through the eyes of the cross, this poem could be read at any time of year, but it resonates in many ways with the liturgy of Good Friday. It opens with a dreamer receiving a vision of the cross adorned with jewels and banners, as all creation bows in honour – suggesting, perhaps, how an Anglo-Saxon poet might have seen the cross as it was lifted up for veneration on Good Friday.

> It seemed to me that I saw a wondrous tree
> lifted up into the air, wrapped in light,
> brightest of beams. All that beacon was
> covered with gold; gems stood
> beautiful at the surface of the earth, and there were five
> upon the shoulders of the cross. All those fair through
>   eternity there beheld
> the angel of the Lord. That was indeed no criminal's
>   gallows,
> but there the holy spirits beheld him,
> men throughout the world and all this glorious creation.
> Wondrous was that victory-beam and I stained with sins,
> wounded with wickedness. I saw the tree of glory
> adorned with drapery, shining with joys,
> decked with gold; gems had
> worthily wrapped the Ruler's tree.

The jewels and bright drapery here recall images of the cross in early medieval art, including the practice, well attested from Anglo-Saxon England, of decorating crosses with gold and gems.[21] They also echo liturgical texts used in the weeks before Easter, such as the hymn *Vexilla regis*, which describes the cross 'adorned in royal purple'.[22] But this poem's cross, though lavishly adorned, is also bleeding on its right side. It's a paradoxical image of shame and glory, beauty and horror, suffering and joy. These are the paradoxes of the Crucifixion itself, given visual form through the shifting appearance of the cross. The sight produces a strong emotional response in the dreamer:

I was entirely afflicted with sorrow;
I was afraid at the fair vision. I saw that eager beacon
change its clothing and colour; at times it was drenched
   with moisture,
soaked with the flow of sweat, at times adorned with
   treasure.

The language in these opening lines enhances the sense of a shifting, paradoxical vision by exploiting verbal ambiguity, in ways very like the Old English riddles. The poem deliberately avoids the usual word for cross, *rod*, delaying that until later; instead, the object is called a *treow*, 'tree', and a *beacen*, 'beacon', a fire lit as a signal to those far away. It's also called *beama beorhtost*, 'brightest of beams', and *beam* bears a double meaning (as in Modern English): both a shaft of light and a pillar of wood or piece of timber. The cross is all these things at the same time. There's a strange dreamlike quality to the scene: as the cross changes its appearance, everything else remains still. Time stops. The whole universe 'beholds' the cross, gazing upon it together, and that meditative, absorbing gaze of adoration well describes the kind of experience the Good Friday liturgy might provide for worshippers.

While this opening vision imagines a shared experience of adoration, however, the poem also approaches the Passion as an intensely personal encounter. The dreamer receives this vision as he lies alone at night, while the people around him ('all speech-bearers') are sleeping. Into that silence and darkness bursts this vision of light, and he hears – while human voices are silent – an extraordinarily non-human voice: the cross itself speaks to him, narrating its memories of the Crucifixion. Through its eyes, this familiar story is seen from a new perspective. The cross tells how it was cruelly uprooted from its forest home to be made a tool of execution, and how in anguish it witnessed, without being able to prevent, the suffering of the 'young hero, God almighty', who willingly climbed upon it. Christ is imagined as a warrior, the cross as his loyal follower – a relationship reminiscent of other Anglo-Saxon poems, such as *The Wanderer*, where the lord–follower relationship is invested with the most intense emotions of love and grief.

The cross is forced to become the slayer of its Lord, drenched in his blood, pierced with the nails which pierce his hands – but destined to share his glory when he rises from the dead. At a key moment, the tree proclaims its new name:

> Rod wæs ic aræred; ahof ic ricne cyning,
> heofona hlaford.

> As a rood was I raised up; I lifted the mighty King,
> the heavens' Lord.

These lines, with others from the poem, appear in runes on the eighth-century Ruthwell Cross, suggesting that some form of this poem may be among the earliest surviving Old English texts; the fuller version is preserved in the Vercelli Book, from the late tenth century.[23] It offers a version of the Crucifixion story that must have spoken powerfully to Anglo-Saxon warrior culture, though it is also firmly rooted in the liturgy and art of the medieval church.

'THE YOUNG WARRIOR AWOKE'

In medieval tradition, the hours between Good Friday and Easter Day were the time of the Harrowing of Hell, when Christ descended into the underworld to free those kept prisoner there until his resurrection. The apocryphal story of the Harrowing of Hell was hugely popular in the Middle Ages, and formed perhaps the most potent legend of liberation in medieval literature and art: a story telling how the king of justice stormed the prison of evil and set its captives free.[24] It was often imagined as a triumphant military expedition, and that explains its English name: 'harrowing' comes from Old English *hergian*, 'to harry, pillage', a word commonly used of Viking armies and other military threats, but adapted by Anglo-Saxon preachers and poets to refer to Christ's victory over the forces of darkness.

A beautiful poem in the Exeter Book, *The Descent into Hell*, deals with this space of time between Christ's death and resurrection. It movingly describes the pain of the women who mourned him and the sudden, heart-wrenching joy of his rising from the tomb, but it also follows Christ down into hell, to witness the harrowing and his meeting with those he had come to liberate. Here, as in *The Dream of the Rood*, Christ is a warrior, but he wins his battle over hell not with an army but through the sheer power of his presence:

The guardian of the heavens wanted to destroy and
  demolish
the walls of hell, to carry off the people of the city,
most righteous of all kings.
In that battle he gave no thought to helmeted warriors,
nor would he bring mail-clad soldiers
to the gates of that fortress; but the locks fell apart,
the barriers from the city. The king rode in.

As he arrives, he meets the people imprisoned in hell, the faithful men and women of the Old Testament who could not go to heaven before Christ had paid the price of sin with his own death. All these are seen rejoicing as their Lord comes to save them, including John the Baptist, who is made the spokesman for their joy:

> Boldly then the leader of the city-dwellers called out,
> courageous before the crowd, and spoke to his kinsman,
> greeted with words the welcome guest:
> 'Thanks be to you, our Lord,
> because you chose to seek us out, sorrowful ones,
> forced now to languish in these bonds.
> Though many brotherless exiles are ensnared
> by the enemy – he is everywhere hostile –
> there is no one so closely kept in cruel fetters
> or bitterly bound in painful chains
> that he may not easily find courage
> if he trusts in his lord's loyalty,
> that he will release him from his bonds.'

This emphasis on exile and loyalty to his lord casts John in a role familiar from other Anglo-Saxon poems: like other exiles in the Exeter Book, he has suffered painful separation from his lord, chained by psychological as well as physical fetters and bonds. John's role in this poem is also comparable to the cross in *The Dream of the Rood*, since like the cross he describes his personal memories of Christ; he recalls how when he baptized his cousin in the Jordan 'we two bathed in that stream together,' and through his eyes we see this as a moment of intimacy between two kinsmen. As in *The Dream of the Rood*, the reader is encouraged to enter into the Gospel story by imagining the experience of an eyewitness, someone who feels for Christ the love of a devoted follower. John's is the human perspective through which the reader can approach the mystery of this cosmic story, this descent into the underworld.

Among Christ's disciples still on earth, the poem also gives space to the feelings of the grieving women at the tomb, as they set out early in the morning to anoint the body of their Lord.

> Before dawn those noble women began
> to prepare themselves for the journey. The assembled
>   people knew
> the Prince's body was enclosed in an earthen tomb.
> The sorrowful women wanted for a while
> to mourn with weeping the Prince's death,
> to grieve with lamentation. The place of rest had grown
>   cold,
> bitter was the journey of death; but brave were the heroes
> whom they would meet rejoicing at the tomb.
> Mary came, mourning, at daybreak,
> summoned with her another nobleman's daughter.
> The two of them sought, sorrowful, the victorious Son
>   of God,
> alone in the earthen tomb where they knew
> the Jewish men had enclosed him.
> They thought he would have to lie in the grave
> alone on that Easter night. But something very different
> would those women know, when they returned on
>   their way.

Particularly poignant here is the women's distress about their Lord left 'alone' in the tomb – a very human desire to be close to the body of the one they are mourning, because even in death they don't want him to be alone. They go out *on uhtan*, in the hour before the dawn, conventionally in Old English poetry a time for anxiety and lament. But what they find at the tomb is not grief but joy – 'something very different' from their expectations, as the poet says with characteristic Anglo-Saxon understatement.

The Gospel narrative tells how these women met an angel, who announced that the tomb was empty and Christ had risen. In the early medieval liturgy for Easter Eve, this meeting between the women and the angel was re-enacted, with such attention to the dramatic qualities of the scene that it's often been considered one of the earliest examples of medieval drama – perhaps even the origin of the mystery play tradition. *Regularis Concordia* gives full details of this ritual, performed by a group of four monks within the Easter Eve service.[25] The monks took on the roles of the three women and the angel: they wore costumes (cloaks for the women, a white robe for the angel) and carried props (a palm and containers for the spices the women carried to anoint Christ's body). There are even stage directions: in *Regularis Concordia*, the monks playing the women are told how to act as they approach the tomb, 'step by step like someone who is seeking for something', and the angel is instructed to address them 'softly and sweetly'. When they meet, they chant the words of the dialogue from the Gospels:

'Whom are you seeking?'
'Jesus of Nazareth.'
'He is not here. He has risen, as he proclaimed.'

The monks playing the women turn to announce this news, but the angel, 'as if calling them back', invites them to look into the tomb. It contains linens, representing those in which Christ's body was wrapped, and the women display these to the congregation to show that the tomb is empty and the body gone.

All this is unmistakably a form of liturgical play, bringing the story to life through the techniques of drama and the voices of the monks. Although presumably the primary audience was the monastic community, laypeople witnessed this too: a story from the eleventh century tells how a man seeking healing was miraculously cured one Easter Eve as this ritual was being performed in Canterbury Cathedral.[26] This holy night had mighty power, an earth-shaking force of joy, as *The Descent into Hell* describes with marvellous energy:

> Before dawn there came a throng of angels,
> the joy of the host surrounded the Saviour's tomb.
> Open was the earthen vault. The Prince's body
> received the breath of life, the ground shook,
> hell-dwellers laughed; the young warrior awoke,
> dauntless from the dust, majesty arose,
> victorious and wise.

As hell's prisoners are set free from captivity and Christ bursts from the tomb, we may recall the theme of liberation running through the spring poetry we looked at earlier – earth released from its winter chains as the ice melts in a thawing, freeing flood. When Beowulf is imagined delivering the Danes from Grendel's mother with a gush of mingled water and blood, that's probably a deliberate echo of the blood and water that flowed from Christ's side on the cross. Beowulf's passage through deep waters to cleanse the monsters' mere also recalls Old Testament narratives used in the liturgy of Easter Eve, Noah's flood and the crossing of the Red Sea, widely interpreted in medieval tradition as prefiguring Christ's victory over death and the cleansing waters of baptism.[27] In *The Dream of the Rood*, both Christ and his cross bleed blood and water, as if the sap of the tree flows when its Lord's side is pierced, and the poem tells how at the moment of Christ's death 'all creation wept' a healing flood of tears, a kind of universal spring thaw. For these poets, earth's release each year from the bonds of winter replayed the story, written into the signs of nature, of the deliverance brought about by Christ's resurrection.

SUMMER

7

BLOSSOMING SUMMER

TREES OF LIFE

After Easter, the summer months brought a sequence of festivals which allowed people to take advantage of better weather to gather outdoors and celebrate in the sunshine. In the next two chapters we'll look at Rogationtide, Ascension Day, Whitsun and Midsummer, festivals of the height of summer in May and June. But first, let's explore some poetic descriptions of this season, which extol the beauties of the natural world in its summer fullness and give us an insight into how people in Anglo-Saxon England liked to enjoy themselves at this time of year.

Summer in Anglo-Saxon calendars runs from 9 May until 6 August. This is how *The Menologium* describes its arrival, sketching the coming of May and then, close behind it, summer itself:

> [On 1 May] comes to the city
> sweeping swiftly, splendid in its adornments
> of woods and plants, beautiful *Þrymilce*
> to the dwellings; May brings many benefits
> everywhere among the multitudes.
> On the same day those noble companions,
> Philip and James, brave thegns,
> gave up their lives for love of the Lord.
> And two nights afterwards God revealed
> to blessed Helena the noblest of trees,

on which the Lord of the angels suffered
for love of mankind, the Measurer on the gallows
by his Father's will. And after a week,
minus one night, summer brings sun-bright days
to the dwellings for mankind,
with warm weathers. Then the meadows
quickly bloom with blossoms, and joy mounts up
throughout the earth among many kinds
of living creatures; in manifold ways
they speak the praise of the King, extol the glorious one,
the Almighty.

Of all the months, May gets the longest description in *The Menologium*; this passage is like a blossoming hedgerow in May, overflowing with beauties. Its abundance echoes the Old English name for May, *Þrymilce*: Bede claims that this name arose because 'in that month the cattle were milked three times a day', a token of the season's bounteous fertility.[1] The visual beauty of May's greening meadows and blooming flowers is conjured up by the poet's picture of the month as *smicere on gearwum wudum and wyrtum*, 'splendid in its adornments of woods and plants'. In Old English these words have connotations of elegant clothing, as if the world is sporting its best attire when it's dressed in summer foliage.

Then a few days later summer comes, with its 'sun-bright days' (*sigelbeorhte dagas*) and 'warm weathers' (*wearme gewyderu*), its blossom and birdsong – a sound the poem imagines as a chorus of diverse voices singing in praise. These lines evoke all the different sensual pleasures of summer, in sight, touch and sound, and the delight they bring to human beings. The verb used to describe how joy mounts up (*astihð*) in this season, all through the world, will be used later in the poem to describe the sun as it appears to climb higher in the sky in summer. There's an implied link – a note repeatedly struck in this poem – between the seasonal patterns of growth and fertility in the natural world and the joy felt by humans as we live through the cycle of the year, with all its changing, manifold forms of loveliness.

Falling in this part of May are two feasts, St Philip and James on 1 May and the Invention (Finding) of the Holy Cross on 3 May. In this poem, as in Anglo-Saxon sources generally, there seems to be no special significance attached to what would later be called 'May Day'; in the later Middle Ages this became a popular festival celebrating the beginning of summer, but it doesn't seem to have been so in the Anglo-Saxon period.[2] Instead we have these two liturgical feasts, which are carefully described in ways that connect them to their seasonal setting. The phrase used of the cross, *æþelust beama*, 'noblest of trees', seems especially apt amid this forest of flourishing trees in their summer beauty; it echoes language often used of the cross in Old English poetry, including in *The Dream of the Rood*.

With that phrase in mind, we can turn to another Anglo-Saxon poem that marks the feast celebrated on 3 May. This feast commemorates the supposed discovery of the Holy Cross by Helena, mother of the Roman emperor Constantine, in Jerusalem circa 326.[3] The story is the subject of an Old English poem known as *Elene*, which probably dates to the eighth or ninth century and survives in the Vercelli Book. It's by a poet called Cynewulf, one of the few Anglo-Saxon poets whom we know by name; unusually, he 'signed' his works by incorporating his name in runes into the closing sections of his four poems. *Elene* is interesting partly because it puts a commanding female protagonist front and centre. Its heroine Elene (that is, St Helena) is imagined as a powerful queen, much more the focus of attention than her son the emperor. The poem tells how she journeys to Jerusalem to find the cross, on an expedition that is – somewhat incongruously, but very much in keeping with the style of Anglo-Saxon poetry – presented as a military campaign. She's called a 'warrior queen' (*guðcwen*), leading a group of well-armed soldiers on a daring quest. In Jerusalem, Elene convinces the Jewish leaders to search for the cross at her command, and when they dig it up, she has it lavishly adorned with gold and jewels. At the end of the poem, as Elene returns home, Cynewulf brings us forward in time from the world of the story to the present day:

> Elene urged all those
> who praised God in that nation, men and women,
> to honour with mind and might in the thoughts of
>   their hearts
> that famous day on which the holy cross
> was found, most glorious of trees
> which have grown up from the earth,
> flourishing with leaves. Then spring was past,
> all but six nights before the coming of summer,
> in the month of May. For all people
> may hell's doors be shut and heaven's thrown wide,
> the eternal realm of angels opened,
> the joy beyond time, and may their portion
> be appointed with Mary, for those who keep in mind
> the honoured day of the dearest cross
> beneath the skies, which the mightiest
> High King of all embraced with his arms.

Much as in *The Menologium*, the cross is described as *mærost beama*, 'most glorious of trees', and Cynewulf presents it to us, like other trees, as *geloden under leafum*, 'flourishing with leaves'. The cross is imagined as a living tree, just like many others that have 'grown up from the earth', and yet greater than them all, the superlative tree.

This way of envisioning the cross as a real tree, with leaves and branches, and often blossom and fruit, is widespread in medieval literature and art. In early medieval depictions of the Crucifixion the cross is often shown sprouting tendrils of growth, or coloured green to make it an emblem of life and vitality.[4] The emphasis on the cross as a living tree, not a dead wooden object, helps to underline the parallel between the cross and that other tree in the Garden of Eden: 'through a tree came to us death, when Adam ate the forbidden fruit, and through a tree came to us again life and redemption, when Christ hung on the cross to redeem us,' as Ælfric says in one of his sermons.[5] The pairing of the trees connects the sin and the redemption, the sickness and the remedy – the tree of death and the tree of life.

For Anglo-Saxon poets, this imagery would have been inspired by medieval Latin hymns such as the sixth-century *Crux fidelis*, which sets the cross in comparison with other trees of the forest:

> Steadfast cross, among all others
> the one most noble tree;
> no wood can bear such surpassing
> foliage, blossom, or fruit.
> Sweet wood, sweet nails,
> upholding so sweet a weight![6]

Sung in the spring, on Good Friday and the cross's feast in May, this hymn's imagery reflects the blossoming that worshippers would see in the natural world around them. It is Christ himself who is the blossom and fruit of this tree, its 'sweet weight'.

This view of the cross as a living being also underlies the central poetic idea of *The Dream of the Rood*, in which the tree is so fully alive, with its own memory and voice. As it's transformed into the *wuldres beam*, 'tree of glory', it is – like the tree of the *Crux fidelis* – presented as faithful and steadfast: 'I trembled when that man embraced me,' says the cross, 'yet I dared not bow to the ground, fall to the surface of the earth; I had to stand fast.' In its opening image of the cross towering as tall as the heavens, worshipped by all beings in the world, *The Dream of the Rood* shows us this great tree as the steady axis around which the universe revolves, the world-tree. As such images found their way into Old English poetry, they must have resonated with older beliefs, since there's evidence for the veneration of sacred trees in pre-Christian Anglo-Saxon culture as well as in the Christian tradition.[7]

In *Elene*, as in *The Menologium*, the tree imagery seems especially appropriate because the feast of the Invention of the Cross falls on the cusp of spring and summer. When Cynewulf says 'spring was past, all but six nights before the coming of summer,' he's referring with careful precision to the date of 3 May, six days before 9 May, the first day of summer. This seasonal allusion chimes very well with the image of a tree springing with fresh growth of leaves. By turning to the liturgical celebration of the feast in the closing lines of the poem, Cynewulf brings his story forward from its fourth-century historical setting into the time of his Anglo-Saxon audience, who can commemorate these long-ago events in their own lives every May. Living this out each year in the recurring cycles of seasonal and liturgical time, they can find their way to heaven, a 'joy beyond time'.

SUMMER PLEASURES

Cynewulf's description of the cross as *geloden under leafum*, 'flourishing with leaves', is echoed by another Anglo-Saxon poem which celebrates a tree in its summer prime. This is *The Old English Rune Poem*, which contains several verses dedicated to trees, among them a tree identified as *beorc*.

> Beorc byþ bleda leas, bereþ efne swa ðeah
> tanas butan tudder. Biþ on telgum wlitig,
> heah on helme hrysted fægere,
> geloden leafum, lyfte getenge.

> The *beorc* has no fruit, but still bears
> shoots without seed. It is beautiful in its branches,

its high canopy gloriously adorned,
flourishing with leaves, pressing up into the air.

Beorc is the root of the Modern English word 'birch', but it's usually
thought that the tree described here is actually a poplar.[8] What's
notable about this verse is its emphasis on the tree's beauty, which
distinguishes it from the other trees included in the *Rune Poem*. In
their respective verses, the oak, ash and yew are all characterized by
their important functions in human society: the ash provides wood
for weapons, the oak timber for ships and the yew firewood, a 'joy
in the home'. But this verse offers instead a vision of the living tree,
its branches stretching high into the air. It's described with two of
the most popular Old English poetic words for 'beautiful', *wlitig*
and *fægere* (Modern English 'fair'), and the last word, *getenge*, is
very tactile, suggesting the boughs thrusting or pressing close to the
sky itself. The tree is said to have a *helm*, which evokes a canopy or
covering, but also perhaps a crown. You can't read this verse without imagining yourself under the tree, beneath the shade of its high
branches, looking up at the leaves against the sky.

Slight as this verse is, there's something about it which feels very
summery. What it implies about the pleasure of sitting under a tree
on a summer's day, gazing up into the branches, recalls a story from
eleventh-century England – one of the little stories we find in saints'
lives which give a memorable glimpse into everyday Anglo-Saxon
life. It's a tale told of St Wulfstan, Bishop of Worcester from 1062 to
1095, one of the few high-ranking English churchmen to retain his
position after the Norman Conquest. On one occasion, Wulfstan
was invited to Longney, a village on the River Severn, to dedicate
a church. When he arrived, he was annoyed to find the church was
overshadowed by a large nut-tree, 'which provided shade with its
spreading leaves, but whose luxuriant branches denied light to the
church'. The bishop summoned his host, a man named Ælfsige,
and ordered that the tree should be cut down. But Ælfsige refused,

because 'he had a habit of spending his leisure time under the tree, especially on a summer's day, playing at dice or feasting, or amusing himself in some other way.' He was so fond of the tree that he felt he would rather leave the church undedicated than have it felled. Wulfstan, angered by his obstinacy, laid a curse on the tree, and it shrivelled up so badly that it had to be cut down after all.[9]

This miracle is, of course, supposed to show Wulfstan's saintly power, and perhaps to echo the Gospel story of Christ cursing the fig-tree in Matthew 21:18–21. Wulfstan doesn't come across very sympathetically; many of the stories told about this bishop suggest he had a formidable character, but then you did have to be strong-minded if you wanted to survive in Norman-ruled England. (To be fair, Wulfstan was no stranger to outdoor fun himself. As an old man, he used to tell a story from his teenage years about a day when he was out in the fields running races against a group of other boys, and was forced to jump into a thorn-bush to avoid a girl trying to seduce him.[10]) Despite the poor nut-tree's untimely fate, this story gives us a nice insight into what someone in Anglo-Saxon England might like to do on a summer's day: sit under a spreading tree in the sunshine, playing a game and having a feast. It sounds very pleasant, and you can't really blame Ælfsige for preferring it even to the honour of St Wulfstan's company.

Another glimpse into Anglo-Saxon summer pleasures is provided by an unusual text in the Exeter Book known as *The Rhyming Poem*. In this poem a first-person speaker, who appears to be a king or high-ranking lord, describes the course of his life from beginning to end. He tells his story not through narrative but through a succession of swiftly changing pictures, each vivid in its turn but quickly passing into the next without a clear connecting thread. The poem falls almost precisely into two halves. In the first half, the man describes a time of increasing prosperity and happiness, when he successfully wields a high social position, surrounded by friends, wealth and pleasure. In the second half, this has been replaced by trouble:

without giving specifics, he speaks now of a life filled with betrayal, war, hatred and at last the grave. He concludes by saying that since death is inevitable, we should fix our thoughts on heaven, where true happiness is to be found. In those respects, this poem has much in common with others we've already looked at, such as *The Wanderer*. Once again we have a speaker who is grieving, remembering lost happiness and reflecting on the transience of worldly prosperity. In other ways, though, this poem is very unusual: it makes extensive use of rhyme, as few Anglo-Saxon poems do, and uses words in ways untypical of Old English poetry, with senses and forms which don't appear elsewhere. The author was clearly someone with an idiosyncratic approach to language, a poet excavating his word-hoard to the very depths and displaying his treasures in his own unique way.

The two-part structure of the poem reflects not just the comparison of two states – past happiness and present sorrow – but an arc, moving from a time of growth to a time of decay, waxing to waning, gain to loss. Behind this, there's an underlying seasonal framework: it's a movement from summer to winter, or more specifically from the season of growth and flourishing (spring/summer/harvest) to the season of decay and death (autumn/winter). Leaving the sadder seasons aside, let's look at the opening of the poem, which describes the man's happy early days – the spring and summer of his life.

He gave me life, who brought forth this light
and drew out that brightness, graciously revealed it.
I was glad with songs, decked with colours,
in pleasure's hues, blossom's tints.
Men beheld me, feasts never ceased,
they rejoiced in the gift of life. Ornamented horses
bore me across the meadows on paths of joy,
beautifully hung about with long branches.
Then growth was awakened, the world came alive,
stretched up under the skies, covered with strength.

Guests came, mingled with noisy chatter,
pleasantly lingered, adorned with delights.
The appointed ship sailed, glided skilfully into the open;
a path was on the ocean where no vessel failed me.
I had high rank; nothing was lacking to me in the hall,
there where the proud troop rode.

The general sense here is an outward movement of growth and expansion, a young man coming into his prime. We're presented with a kaleidoscope of pictures, all typical of the life of an Anglo-Saxon nobleman: a feast, a horse-ride, a ship, a hall, a proud troop of warriors. There's swift travel, music and the sound of chattering voices; everything's bright, colourful and full of life.

The seasonal framework mostly lies not on the surface level but in the connotations of the words. Those which connote spring occur largely in the first four lines, especially in the line *blissa bleoum, blostma hiwum*, 'pleasure's hues, blossom's tints'. In medieval English poetry the alliterating words 'blossom' and 'bliss', especially in conjunction, conventionally evoke spring. The opening references to light – presumably a description of the speaker's birth – might also suggest spring, *lencten*, the time of lengthening days.

But the next lines strongly evoke summer, as if the man is reaching the May and June of his life. He describes his horse carrying him through green meadows, past trees which touch him with their long branches. The word used for 'meadows', *wongas*, connotes open green spaces, far-spreading plains and downs – the kind of landscape where a spirited horse with a fearless young rider could really let itself go. All this time the world is waking up, coming into fullness of growth: its *wæstm* is increasing, a word which means 'produce' or 'growth' when speaking of plants and 'strength' or 'stature' when used of human beings. As the plants are sprouting, so is the man himself, shooting up under the skies like a tall tree. We see him surrounded by companions and friends in the sociable environment of the hall, and he mentions a successful journey by sea – a typical summer activity, as we'll see later. There's a clear parallel between the growth of this young man and the earth as it moves from the first signs of spring to the height of its summer flourishing.

With its delight in feasting, sailing and horse-riding, this poem seems to show us a glimpse of the summer pleasures of young Anglo-Saxon aristocrats. The descriptions of these activities work both literally and metaphorically: the riding and the sea-journey are pastimes we could well imagine a young man enjoying in the summer, but the speaker is also thinking of his life, at this period, as being like a pleasant ride across green fields or a smooth journey on the sea. As the year moves on, things will take a turn for the worse; but for the moment this young man is like the year itself, strong and happy in the summer of life.

ETERNAL SUMMER

Let's close this chapter by looking at the most sun-drenched poem in the corpus of Anglo-Saxon literature: *The Phoenix*, another poem from the Exeter Book. This tells the myth of the regenerating phoenix, interpreting the bird's story, as was common in medieval Christian thinking, as an allegory of Christ's resurrection and the rebirth of the redeemed human soul. Based on learned Latin sources, principally the fourth-century *Carmen de ave phoenice*, the poem first describes the idyllic landscape in which the phoenix lives, and then tells how the bird, when he grows old, builds himself a nest in a sun-dappled tree.[11] As the sun's rays become hotter at the height of summer, the nest is kindled into flame. The bird is consumed by fire and reborn, young again.

This poem contains some of the loveliest nature writing in Old English. The phoenix lives in a paradise of eternal summer, a beautiful land untouched by rain or snow, hail or frost – a place where the leaves never wither and the fruit never falls. Considering that much Old English poetry is decidedly wintry in character, this makes *The Phoenix* something of a rare treat. As we've seen, Anglo-Saxon poets were adept at describing winter landscapes and could probably compose word-sketches of stormy seas and snow-battered cliffs in their sleep; this poet, for a change, dwells with delight on scenes of blazing sunshine, leafy glades and cooling rivers.

> That is a joyous plain, a green weald,
> spacious under the skies. There neither rain nor snow,
> nor the blast of frost, nor the blaze of fire,
> nor the fall of hail, nor the descent of rime,
> nor the sun's heat, nor the bitter cold,
> nor turbulent warm weather, nor winter showers
> can cause any harm; the field remains
> blessed and unimpaired . . .
> Serene is that plain of victory; the sunny grove glitters,
> the joyous wooded holt. The fruits never fall,
> bright branches, but the trees stand
> ever green, as God commanded them.
> Winter and summer the wood is alike
> laden with foliage; no leaf ever withers
> beneath the sky, nor does fire harm them eternally.

The serene beauty of the phoenix's home is conveyed by some skilful choices of language: the word *lixeð*, for instance, which means 'glitters', seems to evoke the flickering play of light in a tree-shaded grove, a dappled sunlight that shifts with the rustling of the leaves. The phoenix worships the sun, paying homage to it each day as it rises, so the poem offers many descriptions of radiant light, heat and sunshine. Despite the poem's Latin sources, its imagery and metaphors are drawn from the traditional stock of Anglo-Saxon poetic vocabulary. Look, for instance, at how the sun is described in this passage:

[The phoenix] beholds the journey of the sun
and comes to meet God's candle,
eagerly watches the jewel of gladness
when that noblest of stars rises up
above the waves, gleaming from the east;
the Father's ancient work glimmers with ornaments,
bright token of God.

God's candle, jewel of gladness, noblest of stars: the sun is described
with a dazzling array of images, five different metaphors in just seven
lines. In the next chapter, we'll see how the image of the sun as a
jewel, rising to its highest at the summer solstice, could suggest for
an Anglo-Saxon poet the divine Son, the ascended Christ, and since
the phoenix's resurrection is meant to parallel Christ's, perhaps that
should be in the back of the reader's mind here too. Both Christ and
the sun might be called 'bright token of God'.

As the phoenix grows old, it leaves its paradisal homeland to
live on earth and makes a nest nearer the human world, at the top
of a lofty tree, its 'roots fast fixed under the roof of the heavens':

To that tree the King, mighty in glory,
Measurer of mankind, has granted – I have heard –
that alone of all trees
which lift up their branches upon the earth
it blooms the brightest. No wicked thing
can do it any harm; it is shielded for ever,
abiding untouched, as long as the world stands.

Again, there are delicate echoes here of Old English Christian poetry,
especially the poetry of the cross we looked at earlier. The tree is
called *heanne beam*, 'lofty tree', a phrase used in other poems (including *Elene*) to describe the cross, and its unique beauty, 'alone of all
trees', recalls the *Crux fidelis*, which emphasizes the uniqueness of

the cross among the trees of the forest. The phoenix's tree too is steadfast, standing 'as long as the world stands', like the faithful cross of *The Dream of the Rood*.

High in this tree the phoenix builds a nest, preparing for the cleansing fire that will be kindled by the sun's heat at the height of summer.

> When the wind dies down, the weather is fair,
> the holy gem of the heavens shines brightly,
> clouds are dispersed, the tumult of the waters
> grows still, every storm beneath the skies
> is calmed, the burning candle of the air
> shines from the south, giving light to men,
> then he begins to build in the branches . . .
> He collects and gathers the sweetest spices
> to that dwelling-place, every kind of noble fragrance,
> pleasant herbs and fruits of the woods,
> which the King of Glory,
> Father of every beginning, created
> across the world for the glory of mankind,
> sweet under the skies. There he carries
> bright ornaments into that tree;
> there the wild bird builds his house
> in the wilderness, on the tall tree,
> fair and joyous, and there he dwells
> alone in that sunny chamber, and on the outside
> surrounds himself, body and feathers,
> in the shade of the leaves, on every side
> with blessed scents and the noblest
> fruits of the earth.

The phoenix's nest is described as a *solere*, a striking choice of word: borrowed from the Latin *solarium*, it means in Old English an upper chamber in a house, a room that gets lots of sun. Not many Anglo-Saxon houses had upper rooms, so the phoenix is special in having this sunny chamber all to himself, up in his tree amid the *leafsceade*, 'shade of the leaves'.

> When in the summer
> the jewel of the sky, the sun at its hottest,
> shines above the shadows and fulfils its destiny,
> gazing far across the world, then his house
> is heated by the brilliant radiance.
> The herbs are warmed, the beloved hall smokes
> with sweet fragrances; then, seized by fire,
> the bird burns in the flames within its nest.

Consumed by fire, the phoenix regenerates and takes again his youthful form; then the cycle is repeated. As the poem describes it, this process of self-immolation mirrors the seasonal cycle of growth, death and rebirth: the bird building his nest suggests the spring, it's the height of summer when the fire is kindled, then comes the harvest and the cycle begins again. In our world, unlike the paradisal landscape of this poem, summer does fade and pass into autumn, and the earth experiences a kind of death – but every year it's reborn like the phoenix, with the return of the spring.

8

FESTIVALS OF THE LAND AND SKY

HOLY AND HEALTHY DAYS

May and June are marked by three festivals linked to the end of the Easter season: Rogationtide, Ascension Day and Whitsun, which all fall in the fortnight between five and seven weeks after Easter. The feast of the Ascension is celebrated on the Thursday forty days after Easter Sunday, and the preceding Monday, Tuesday and Wednesday of that week form Rogationtide. Because of the moveable date of Easter, the timing of Rogationtide varies, but it nearly always falls in May. In the medieval church Rogationtide was a time for prayer, fasting and processions around the countryside, asking for God's blessing on the land and the crops of the future harvest. As one Anglo-Saxon homilist put it, the aim was to 'bless our earthly abundance, the acres and woods and our cattle and all the things that God has given us to enjoy'.[1] The customs of Rogationtide are widely attested in Anglo-Saxon sources, and they illustrate well how the liturgical calendar could intersect with the cycle of the seasons. These days provided an opportunity to reflect on the bounty of nature and its role in sustaining human life; they were a time to give thanks for the natural world as a visible expression of God's creative power and loving care.

The origins of Rogationtide lie in fifth-century Gaul, around 470, when Mamertus, Bishop of Vienne, instituted three days of penance before Ascension Day in response to troubles afflicting his city.[2] Soon adopted by the wider church, the custom is first recorded in Anglo-Saxon sources in the eighth century.[3] On the Rogation Days, clerics and laypeople would process out from church, carrying relics of saints and other holy items such as Gospel books and crosses. They would proceed through the surrounding area, stopping at appointed stations – other churches or shrines – for prayers and blessings. The idea was that by carrying these sacred objects out into the world, beyond the walls of the church into the fields and woods, the processions were carrying God's blessing with them. This belief is reflected in one of the earliest Anglo-Saxon allusions to Rogationtide, in Bede's narrative of the arrival of St Augustine's mission in Kent in 597. He says that the missionaries processed towards Canterbury carrying a cross and an image of Christ and singing a text from the Rogationtide liturgy, asking God for his mercy and blessing.[4] This story may be a tradition of Bede's time rather than Augustine's, but it illustrates the combined purpose of Rogationtide processions: they were a form of collective penance, asking God for forgiveness for sins, but they also sought to consecrate and hallow physical space. Just as Augustine, in the minds of Anglo-Saxon writers, claimed Canterbury and England for Christ, so Rogation processions diffused God's presence out from the church building through the surrounding countryside.

Preaching was also a regular part of these days, and as a result there are numerous surviving Old English sermons for Rogationtide. Anglo-Saxon preachers offered their congregations various different explanations for the history of the custom they were engaged in: some related its institution by Mamertus, but others claimed it was a Christianized version of a pagan Roman processional ritual, the Amburbium, adapted by St Peter in his time as Pope.[5] Ælfric wrote several homilies for Rogationtide, a season he calls the *Gebeddagas*, 'Prayer Days' ('Rogation' comes from the Latin *rogare*, 'to ask' or 'to pray', and *gebed* is related to Modern English 'bid'). During these three days, Ælfric explains, 'we should pray for abundance of our earthly fruits, and for health and peace for ourselves, and, what is still greater, for the forgiveness of our sins.'[6] In his Rogationtide homilies he takes the opportunity to teach his congregation about some key ideas and practices of the Christian faith, including fasting, the Lord's Prayer and the relationship between the body and soul. In one, he explores the doctrine of the Trinity by discussing the nature of the sun:

> The sun that shines above us is a physical creation, but nevertheless has three properties: one is its physical substance, that is the orb of the sun; the second is the light or brightness always shining from the sun, which enlightens the whole world; the third is the heat, which comes to us with its beams. The light is always coming from the sun, and is always with it; and the Son of Almighty God is always begotten of the Father, and always dwelling with him . . . We speak about God – the mortal about the immortal, the weak about the all-powerful, wretches about the merciful. But who may worthily speak about that which is beyond speech? He is without measure, because he is everywhere. He is without number, because he is eternal. He is without weight, because he upholds all creation without labour; and he ordained it all with three things, that is, measure, number and weight. But know that no man can speak fully about God, since we cannot even search out or reckon up the creation which he made. Who may speak in words of the ornaments of the heavens, or the fruitfulness of the earth? Or who may sufficiently praise the course of all the seasons, or all other things, when we cannot even fully comprehend with our sight the physical things which we can see?[7]

This is a beautiful bit of writing – so many words, carefully arranged, to describe what is beyond words. Ælfric encourages his congregation to 'consider the sun, how high it climbs, and how it sends its light throughout the whole earth':

Now think how much greater is God's presence, and his power, and his visitation everywhere. Nothing withstands him, neither stone walls nor broad barriers, even though they withstand the sun. To him nothing is hidden or unknown.

In this image of the sun, there's an implicit relevance to the Rogation-tide context: Ælfric talks about how the fruitfulness of the earth, the course of the year and the seasons reveal the gap between divine knowledge and human perception, and that's the gap Rogationtide seeks to bridge by asking for God's blessing on the earth. The sun is a good topic for a summer sermon, since if you're praying for a successful harvest, the sun's light and heat, which make the crops grow, may seem tangible manifestations of divine favour. Ælfric's emphasis on the omnipresence of God, permeating even further than the light of the sun, reminds his congregation that their processions are helping to spread that divine presence, consecrating the whole world as sacred space. Perhaps it was a sunny May day when Ælfric wrote this homily, and he imagined the congregation looking up at 'the sun that shines above us'.

The processions of Rogationtide gave the season one of its Anglo-Saxon names, *Gangdagas*, 'Walking Days', from *gangan*, 'to walk, to go'. This name, 'Gang Days', survived as a common English name for the season well into the nineteenth century. A description from the *Old English Martyrology* gives a more detailed explanation of how these processions worked and who took part in them:

On those three days should come to God's church both men and women, both old people and the young, both male and female servants, to ask favour from God, because Christ's blood was shed equally for all. On those three days

Christians ought to leave their worldly occupations at the third hour of the day (that is, at *undern*) and process with the relics of the saints until the ninth hour (that is, at *non*). These days are rightly appointed for fasting and for the use of those foods which are used during the forty-day fast before Easter. It is not permitted during these days to let blood or drink purgative drinks, or to travel very far on worldly business from the place where one ought to serve God. These three days are medicine for the human soul and a spiritual tonic; so they are to be kept with compunction of heart, that is, with weeping prayers and generous alms and full good will towards all human enemies, because God will forgive us his anger, if we forgive our fellow men.[8]

This emphasizes that everyone was supposed to join in these processions; they were an event for the whole community, and that communality was important in shaping the character of the Gang Days. Rogationtide falls in early summer, when springing crops bring promise of the harvest to come, so it was a natural time of year to pray for good weather and a bountiful harvest. But not coincidentally, early summer is also the loveliest time of year to go walking in the countryside. Though their penitential function was serious, these days don't seem to have been particularly solemn occasions; with crowds of people going for a walk through the summer woods and fields, the atmosphere must have been pretty sociable. In an early Anglo-Saxon reference to the Rogation Days, in the decrees of the Council of Clofesho in 747, people are warned not to mix the religious customs of the days with sports, horse-racing and feasting – and if that prohibition was necessary, it suggests that this had already become a time for more general summer festivity.[9]

There's a story from Ramsey Abbey in the late tenth century, told by Byrhtferth, which conveys this atmosphere nicely. He describes how on one occasion a Rogationtide crowd made their way 'with heartfelt joy' through the landscape surrounding their Fenland monastery, which in this watery region meant travelling by boat as well as on foot. In their excitement, too many people piled into one of the boats, so that it almost sank – but fortunately Ramsey's founder St Oswald was at hand to pray for them and bring them safely back to land.[10] The festive atmosphere of the event is clear, despite its near-fatal consequences. Another reference to Rogationtide, from a few decades later, reinforces this picture of a merry, bustling crowd. In the mid-eleventh century, Leofric, Earl of Mercia, had a vision of heaven in which he was led to a beautiful and sweet-smelling field. It was full of a huge crowd, all dressed in white, listening to St Paul giving a blessing – as Leofric described it, 'such a great crowd as on the Gang Days'.[11] Reaching for words to convey what he had seen in his heavenly vision, a joyous crowd in a beautiful and blessed field, it was of Rogationtide that he thought.

This element of holiday festivity continued into the later medieval observance of the Rogation Days. By the late Middle Ages, the processions would follow parish boundaries, combining the function of blessing the surrounding area with an opportunity to reinforce territorial rights.[12] Parishes treated these as expressions of local pride, and would sometimes even get into fights with processions from neighbouring parishes. The stopping-places on the procession would be the boundary-markers of the parish – trees, walls, large stones – and these might be fixed in the memory of onlookers by 'beating the bounds' with sticks or marking them with crosses.[13] Descriptions of these events are full of noise and colour, with music, bells, banners and feasts provided for the participants. After the Reformation, Rogationtide processions survived in a secularized form as inspections of parish boundaries, with the feasting and merriment but minus the carrying of relics and crosses. In this form the custom remained widespread for hundreds of years, only beginning to die out in the eighteenth century; it has been increasingly revived in recent decades.

Rogationtide's stated function may have changed over time, but its expression and key themes remained remarkably similar over the course of more than a thousand years. Anglo-Saxon preachers talk of penitence and blessing; later medieval writers speak of the processions driving away evil spirits, purifying the air and protecting crops from harm; post-Reformation descriptions instead extol the perambulations for promoting good neighbourliness and gratitude to God. All would, perhaps, have agreed with the idea commonly found in Anglo-Saxon sermons that these are 'days holy and healthful and medicinal for our souls' – a 'spiritual tonic', as the *Martyrology* puts it.[14] As penance purifies the soul, the processions cleanse and make holy the physical world. They are healing and hallowing and they promote community wholeness – three ideas which all go back to the same Old English root, *hal*, meaning 'healthy, sound, whole'. Etymologically speaking, 'to heal' and 'to hallow' are both 'to make whole'. The Rogation Days seek physical and spiritual health for the individual, the community and the natural world; all are connected, one harmonious whole.

THE SON RISING: ASCENSION DAY

Ælfric's decision to preach on the sun during Rogationtide reflects not only the summer timing of the season and its focus on the natural world, but also the well-established association between Christ and the sun – as we saw earlier at Midwinter – which made this theme especially appropriate for the days leading up to the Ascension. In discussing the Ascension, early medieval writers play with the idea that this is a feast of 'the Son rising', interpreting a phrase from the prophet Habbakuk, *elevatus est Sol*, as prefiguring Christ's ascent into heaven.[15] Since the feast of the Ascension falls in May or early June, with the summer solstice just weeks away and the sun perceived as 'climbing' higher in the sky, this was timely.

This image, along with other metaphorical ways of approaching the mystery of Christ's Ascension, is explored in an Old English poem by Cynewulf, known as *Christ II*. Scholars have given it this (rather uninspiring) title because it follows the *Advent Lyrics*, often called *Christ I*, in the Exeter Book, although the two poems were probably composed by different people. One thing *Christ II* does have in common with the *Advent Lyrics* is that it's a sophisticated theological meditation on its biblical theme, using the traditional language of Anglo-Saxon poetry but also drawing on a range of patristic and medieval interpretations of the story. Cynewulf's principal source is a sermon by Gregory the Great, which supplies him with some rich material to turn into verse.[16] After telling the story of the Ascension, contrasting the angels' delight at Christ's return to heaven with the disciples' grief at parting from their Lord, the poem turns from narrative to reflection, and takes some dizzying leaps into metaphor. As Christ ascends into the sky, he is imagined as a bird, moving with ease between heaven and earth:

> So the beautiful bird took to flight.
> Now he sought the home of the angels,
> that glorious country, bold and strong in might;
> now he swung back to earth again,
> sought the ground by grace of the Spirit,
> returned to the world.

This is a wonderful image of power and liberty: a bird soaring through the air, completely in command of its flight, free and weightless as earthbound humans can only dream of being. Cynewulf's Christ is a dynamic figure, always in movement, the embodiment of unfettered energy. The poem develops this by exploring Gregory's discussion of the 'leaps of Christ', which identifies Christ with the lover of the Song of Solomon (2:8–13), springing across the mountains to seek his beloved. This extraordinary passage begins with a paraphrase of Solomon's prophecy:

'The King of angels, the Lord mighty in strength,
will come springing upon the mountain,
leaping the high uplands; hills and downs
he will garland with his glory, and redeem the world,
all earth's inhabitants, by that glorious leap.'
The first leap was when he descended into a woman,
an unblemished virgin, and there took human form
without sin; that became a comfort
to all earth's dwellers. The second bound
was the birth of the boy, when he was in the manger,
wrapped in cloth in the form of a child,
the glory of all glories. The third leap
was the heavenly King's rush when he climbed upon
    the cross,
Father, Comforting Spirit. The fourth bound
was into the tomb, when he relinquished the tree,
safe in the sepulchre. The fifth leap
was when he humbled the host of hell's inhabitants
in living torment; the King bound within
the advocate of the fiends in fetters of fire,
the malignant one, where he still lies
fastened with chains in prison,
shackled by sins. The sixth leap,
the Holy One's hope-play, was when he ascended
    to heaven
into his former home. Then the throng of angels
in that holy tide was made merry with laughter,
rapt with joy. They saw the glory of majesty,
first of princes, seek out his homeland,
the bright mansions. After that the blessed
    city-dwellers
endlessly delighted in the Prince's play.

This sums up Christ's whole life in less than thirty lines, and every-thing that happens is propelled by his triumphant vigour, even his 'rush' towards the cross and his leap into the tomb when he chooses to be buried. His Ascension is not a passive lifting-up into heaven but an active bound towards his homeland, and in this the poem echoes depictions of the scene in early medieval art, such as the Benedictional of St Æthelwold, where Christ is shown leap-ing into heaven.[17] In this passage, the 'leaps' through the universe are imagined as the acts of a shape-shifting life force, which moves at will and at speed through earth, hell and heaven, one moment taking the form of a baby, then an adult warrior, never still or stable but constantly in motion. It's an almost unsettling vision of restless, limitless power – something deeply unhuman and alien. But it's a force of joy: his leaps are called *plega*, 'play', movement as swift and natural as the play of fire or light, but with the implications of skill and strategy we would associate with athletic play. The Ascension is described as a *hyhtplega*, a beautiful compound: *hyht* means both 'hope' and 'joy', so this is a 'play of hope', 'an action which brings joy' to all those in heaven, who spend eternity delighting in the 'Prince's play'.

WHITSUN

In *Christ II*, Cynewulf also explores the sequel to the Ascension, Pentecost, the descent of the Holy Spirit to the disciples. Pentecost falls fifty days after Easter, because the biblical event it commem-orates took place when the disciples were gathered in Jerusalem to celebrate the Jewish Feast of Weeks, Shavuot, seven weeks after Passover. Descending with wind and fire, the Holy Spirit gave the disciples the gift of tongues (Acts 2); Pentecost is also associated with other biblical lists of 'gifts of the Spirit', such as 1 Corinthians 12:4–13. Cynewulf's poem incorporates this theme of spiritual gifts, but in a distinctively Anglo-Saxon way:

He honoured us then, he who created the world,
God's Spirit-Son, and gave us gifts:
eternal dwelling on high with the angels,
and also the manifold wisdoms of the mind
he sowed and established in the hearts of men.
To one he sends wise speech
into his mind's thoughts through the breath of his
    mouth,
fine perception. One whose spirit is given
the power of wisdom can sing and speak
of many things. One can play the harp well
with his hands loudly among men,
strike the instrument of joy. One can tell
of the true divine law. One can speak of the course of
    the stars,
the vast creation. One can skilfully
write with words. To one is granted success in battle,
when archers send quivering arrows flying
over the shield-walls. One can boldly
drive the ship over the salt sea,
stir the thrashing ocean. One can climb
the tall upright tree. One can wield a weapon,
the hardened sword. One knows the expanse of earth's
    plains,
far-flung ways. Thus the Ruler,
God's Son on earth, gives to us his gifts.

The gifts of the Holy Spirit typically associated with Pentecost include faith, healing and prophecy – no mention of harp-playing, tree-climbing, seafaring and the rest. But these are all forms of skill and knowledge, part of the 'manifold wisdoms of the mind'. This celebratory approach, honouring practical as well as intellectual and spiritual gifts, accommodates the biblical theme to a topos found in Anglo-Saxon wisdom poetry: there's a whole Old English poem on this subject known as *The Gifts of Mortals*, which adds to the list such varied skills as architecture, swimming, metalworking, looking after horses, tasting wine, hunting and hawking. Anglo-Saxon poets loved to praise craft and skill, extolling the technical ability and power of thought which goes into making beautiful and useful things, and these poetic lists of 'gifts' paint an appealing picture of a society in which everyone's contribution is valuable, however mundane it might seem. In the king's hall, in a smith's forge, in a monk's cloister, 'there are many gifts, but the same Spirit'.

From the late Middle Ages until the mid-twentieth century, Pentecost – usually known as Whitsun – was the principal summer holiday of the year in Britain. Whit Sunday and the days that followed were a popular time for communal festivity, including fairs, plays, games and processions. Many records from the later medieval period testify to the holiday spirit of Whitsun, especially after the development of 'Whitsun ales' – feasts that combined shared festivity with the useful function of fundraising for the parish church.[18] The festival continued to flourish after the Reformation, and by the end of the nineteenth century Whit Monday was a statutory bank holiday. In some ways, Whitsuntide took the place of the Rogationtide processions after their decline: in the early twentieth century it was marked in northern England by 'Whit Walks', when mills and factories would be closed and churches and Sunday schools would come together in huge crowds to walk in procession with banners and music.[19] All this changed in 1971, when the Spring Bank Holiday was fixed to the last Monday in May rather than the moveable Whitsun. The holiday lost its centuries-long link to Whitsun, and consequently even the name is now widely forgotten.

Most of the festivities historically associated with Whitsun bear little relation to the feast of Pentecost; more significant was the timing of the festival in May or June, an auspicious season for outdoor events. There's not much evidence for this kind of festivity at

Whitsun in Anglo-Saxon England, but we do know it was a popular date for baptisms and other public ceremonies, and that must have helped make it an occasion for more general celebration. The English name 'Whitsun' is first recorded in the eleventh century: it probably comes from 'White Sunday', referring to the garments worn by the newly baptized. This link with baptism was already established early in the Anglo-Saxon church: Bede records that the baby girl he calls 'the first of the Northumbrian race to be baptized', Eanflæd, daughter of King Edwin of Northumbria and his wife Æthelburh, was baptized at Pentecost in 626.[20]

Among the forms of ceremony thought appropriate for Whitsun in Anglo-Saxon England were coronations. The first attested use of the word 'Whitsun' is in the *Anglo-Saxon Chronicle*'s record of the coronation of William the Conqueror's queen, Matilda, at Westminster on *Hwitan Sunnandæg* in 1068, and in this respect the new Norman rulers were following in the footsteps of previous English kings.[21] The most significant precedent had been set by King Edgar, who was crowned in Bath at Whitsun 973. This was a grand ceremony staged in front of a large crowd, its details carefully planned to evoke important political and spiritual resonances. Edgar was not only crowned but anointed, and his monastic supporters, including St Dunstan, saw the king's divine authority as essential to furthering their programme of church reform.[22] This Whitsun marked an important day for Edgar and his supporters, and it's commemorated in the *Anglo-Saxon Chronicle* with an intricate poem:

> Here Edgar, ruler of the English,
> was consecrated as king, among a great crowd,
> in the ancient city, *Acemannesceastre*,
> the same which island-dwellers also call
> by another name, Bath. There was great bliss
> for everyone on that blessed day,

which the sons of men name and call
Pentecost Day. There was a crowd of priests,
a great throng of monks, I have heard,
a gathering of the wise. At that time had passed
ten hundred winters in the tally of reckoning
from the birth-time of the glorious King,
the Guardian of Lights, except there were left
a number of winters, as the writings say,
seven and twenty, so that nearly a thousand
had run for the Lord of Victories when this occurred.
And he, Edmund's heir, had
nine and twenty winters in the world,
doughty in war-work, when this was done,
and in the thirtieth was consecrated as lord.[23]

What makes this poem interesting for our purposes here is the attention it pays to the reckoning of time, which is much more prominent
than the subjects you might expect instead, such as praise of the king
or details of the ceremony. The poet locates the event precisely in
space and time, giving all these lines to what might, in other *Chronicle*
entries, have been noted in very few words: 'in Bath at Pentecost
973'. We get two names for Bath, *Baþan* and *Acemannesceastre*, the
latter probably recalling the city's Roman name, Aquae Sulis (with
the suffix *ceastre* in Anglo-Saxon place-names which designates a
Roman city, as in Winchester, Dorchester and so on). The choice
of Bath for Edgar's consecration must have been deliberate: Bath
had some of the most impressive Roman ruins in the country –
perhaps described, as we've seen, in *The Ruin* – and the aim was
probably to confer some Roman imperial glamour on Edgar and
his 'island-dwellers', the English.

In the second half of the poem, the focus turns to placing the
event in history, and we see how even the tallying of years could be
turned into poetry. This is a special day – a 'blessed day', the poet

calls it, playing with the king's own name (*eadgan dæge* echoes the name *Eadgar*). So its date matters, and here time itself, like the king, is consecrated and hallowed. This poem uses the same 'one step forwards, two steps back' approach to counting as *The Menologium*: the poet tells us this event took place in the year 1000, minus seven and twenty, that is, 973. Those thousand years are measured against the much shorter span of the king's own lifetime, his nine-and-twenty *wintra on wurulde*, 'winters in the world'. The two timescales align the earthly and the heavenly king: Christ and Edgar are linked not only by the use of phrases that could apply to both rulers – 'the glorious king' – but also by the emphasis on the fact that Edgar was in his thirtieth year, since thirty was the age at which Christ was baptized. The poet tells us that Edgar's 29 winters had been marked by conflict, and in fact the young king had only two more years to live in 973. But with that still in the future, this Whitsun day must have seemed to promise a glorious summer ahead.

9

MIDSUMMER

THE SUNSTEAD

In medieval England, the high point of summer was the solstice: the longest day of the year, the time of maximum light before the turn towards the waning days of autumn. References to this day feature in many different contexts in Anglo-Saxon sources, suggesting it had wide and deep cultural importance. Since the winter solstice seems to have been significant in the pagan Anglo-Saxon calendar, it's very likely there was also some kind of festival linked to the summer solstice before the conversion – but if so, we know nothing about it, and there's no recorded evidence of a summer equivalent to *Modraniht*.

Instead, Anglo-Saxon writers participated in the observances of the date which were shared across Europe, in which scientific and spiritual interpretations of the solstice were united in the June festival of Midsummer, the feast of the Nativity of John the Baptist. The date of the solstice now falls between 20 and 22 June, and this was also the case in the Anglo-Saxon period; Bede, along with other contemporary writers, argued that it should fall on 20 June.[1] As with the dating of Christmas, however, there was already a slight disparity between the solstice date preferred by these writers and the day to which the liturgical calendar had assigned a significant festival. The feast of the Nativity of John the Baptist is one of the oldest in the church's history, and had been fixed very early on to 24 June, exactly six months before Christmas Eve, in accordance with what was at that time the accepted date of the solstice in the Roman calendar.[2] Bede and other Anglo-Saxon writers seem fairly relaxed about this disparity, and it doesn't prevent them from linking John's feast to the solstice, as we'll see.

The result is that in most Anglo-Saxon sources St John's Day and the solstice are treated as synonymous, their celebration merged in one festival, Midsummer. This continued to be the case throughout the medieval period, and for long afterwards; the names 'Midsummer Eve' and 'St John's Eve' were interchangeable well into the twentieth century. Since Midsummer was a very popular festival, its cultural significance marked by its use as a quarter-day, it stuck firmly to its date, despite the ever-growing disparity produced by calendar drift over the centuries; by the early modern period 24 June was more than a week out of sync with the actual date of the solstice, but it was still called 'Midsummer'. This endured through the calendar reform that brought the dates closer together again, and it's only recently that observance of the solstice has become detached from the feast of St John and fixed to the slightly earlier, more accurate date.

Like many medieval scholars, Anglo-Saxon writers could interpret the solstice from a scientific point of view. A concise vernacular description of the solstice as they understood it is given by Ælfric in *De temporibus anni*:

> When the day grows longer, the sun goes northwards until it comes to the sign which is called Cancer. The summer solstice is there, because there it turns back again southwards, and then the day grows shorter until the sun comes again south to the winter solstice, and there stands still. When it is moving northwards, it causes the spring equinox in the middle of its course, and when it is moving south, it causes the autumnal equinox. The further south it goes, the closer winter draws near, and the winter chill follows after it. But when it turns again, it drives away the winter chill with its hot rays.[3]

Later he explains how the length of the solstice day varies in different parts of the world, observing that it's seventeen hours long in England, and adding, 'in the northern part of that land, the nights in summer are as light as if it were day all night long, as we ourselves have very often seen.'[4]

The name Ælfric uses for the solstice is *sunstede*, a direct English translation of the Latin *solstitium*. The Latin name derives from the belief that at the solstice the sun briefly stands still in the sky; its second element is from *sistere*, 'to stand still'. In using *sunstede*, Ælfric follows the common Anglo-Saxon practice of finding vernacular translations for technical Latin terms, so the second part of *sunstede* is from Old English *stede*, meaning 'fixed place, point of standing still'. This survives in a number of familiar Modern English words – 'homestead', 'bedstead', 'instead' – and in place-names such as Hampstead. If it had caught on, we'd call the solstice the *sunstead*. However, this name doesn't seem to have been widely used in Anglo-Saxon England; it was invented by, and probably only used by, scholars like Ælfric and Byrhtferth who understood its relationship to the Latin term.

Instead, the standard English name for the solstice was 'Midsummer' (*midsumor*, and variants thereof), a term very widely attested in Anglo-Saxon sources. This features as a common time-marker in the *Anglo-Saxon Chronicle*, where events are often said to have taken place 'before Midsummer' or 'between Midsummer and Lammas', and so on. In such uses the name can refer generally to the days around the solstice, but in many cases it clearly means the day itself, in a phrase such as 'nine nights before Midsummer'. 'Midsummer' of course parallels 'Midwinter', the popular name for Christmas Day, and like Christmas, the summer solstice had its eve: an eleventh-century *Chronicle* entry speaks of *midsumeres mæsseæfene*, 'Midsummer's mass-eve', the eve of the Midsummer festival.[5] Both terms are probably remnants of the ancient two-season division of the year, pre-dating the conversion to Christianity, and they proved extraordinarily durable, continuing in popular use for many centuries after these two pivotal points of the year had taken on new Christian significance.

The liturgical importance of Midsummer could not rival Christmas, but the days were linked in the Christian calendar too. As we've already seen, the solstices and equinoxes were a fundamental structuring principle in the medieval church year: while the spring equinox was crucial for the dating of Easter, the solstices were tied to the celebration of the birth of Christ and his herald, John the Baptist. St John's feast has a special status because he is the only saint in Christian tradition other than the Virgin Mary to have a feast commemorating his birth as well as his death (the feast of his beheading is in late August). His birth is significant because of his importance as Christ's forerunner, but also because of the interrelated timing of the Gospel narratives of his birth and that of Christ, his near relation. Their mothers were pregnant at the same time, and the meeting between the two expectant women is tenderly told in the Gospel of Luke (1:39–56), where John leaps in his mother's womb at the approach of the unborn Saviour.

Since John was born six months before Christ, their births are celebrated at the four key points of the solar year: just as Christ was said to have been conceived at the spring equinox and born at the winter solstice, so John was conceived at the autumn equinox and born at the summer solstice. We saw Bede explain this earlier, and Ælfric elaborates on the idea in his sermon for the Nativity of St John:

> It is not without meaning that the herald's birth at this season came to pass when the earthly day is waning, and the Lord's birth when it is waxing. This meaning John himself revealed with these words: 'It is fitting for Christ that he should wax greater, and for me that I should wane.' John became known to people through his famous actions earlier than Christ was, because Christ did not reveal his divine

power before he had lived thirty years in human nature. So it seemed to the people that he was a prophet, and John was Christ. But then Christ made himself known through great signs and his fame waxed throughout all the world that he was truly God, who had previously seemed a prophet. John's fame was indeed waning, because he was recognized as a prophet, and herald of the heavenly Prince, who a little while before was believed to be Christ by uncertain guesses. This waning is betokened by the waning day at the season of his birth, and the increasing day at the Saviour's birth signifies his increasing power according to his human nature.[6]

Christ and John were, as Ælfric puts it, *anes geares cild*, 'the children of one year', not just because they were born so close together but because the pattern of their coming into the world maps onto the structure of the year itself. If Christ is the light of the rising sun, born at Midwinter when light begins to increase, John is the light that will wane with the shortening days.

For medieval Christians, the concurrence of the solstice with these key feasts made the cycle of the sun a revelation of the plan of their creator – and this could also be discerned in other aspects of the natural world, for those who had eyes to observe its cycles of growth and decay. Such knowledge could be put to very practical use. One of the contexts in which we find references to Midsummer in Anglo-Saxon sources is in medical recipes and rituals, which seek to harness the power of this special time of year for the purposes of healing. In these texts, Midsummer is sometimes recommended as the best day on which to gather specified plants and herbs for use in medicines and remedies.[7] As we saw at New Year, certain days in the year were perceived as having great potency, and Midsummer was clearly one of them. A fascinating example occurs in a short fragment of a ritual to cure lung disease in cattle. The Old English text is damaged, but can be reconstructed as follows:

. . . hill, and burn it to ashes on Midsummer [Eve, and add]
holy water to it, and pour it in their mouths on Mid[summer]
morning; and sing these three psalms over them: [Miserere]
nostri, Exurgat deus, and Quicumque vult.[8]

Since the text is fragmentary – the manuscript, coincidentally, has
been scarred by fire – we unfortunately don't know *what* you're
supposed to burn to produce this cure. Comparison with other
Anglo-Saxon rituals provides some possible suggestions: a particular
plant or combination of plants is most likely, though some prescribe
burning animal teeth, bones or other body parts and using the ashes
to create a drink or medicinal paste. Damage to the manuscript has
also made the word following *middan sumeres mæsse* illegible, so we
can't be sure whether the first part of the ritual is supposed to take
place on Midsummer Eve or Midsummer Day. Most editors of the
text have assumed Midsummer Day, but comparison with other
rituals can again be helpful: this would suggest the preparation is
meant to take place on the eve, and the application of the remedy on
the following morning.[9] Either way, this healing ritual is evidently
designed to channel the power of this important time of year.

This remedy survives among a group of miscellaneous texts in
an eleventh-century manuscript from a monastery in Winchester.
It's a psalter, to which has been added a collection of prayers, rituals,
calendar information (such as how to calculate the date of Easter)
and medical lore (good and bad days for bloodletting, lucky days
to be born and so on).[10] If you wanted to perform this ritual, you
could find the Latin texts recommended for use – two psalms and
the Athanasian Creed – elsewhere in the psalter. What all these texts
have in common is a belief that understanding the calendar offers
knowledge that can be beneficial in all kinds of ways, spiritual and
practical. Knowing when to celebrate Easter, when to let blood and
when to perform this ritual to cure sick cattle are all related forms
of knowledge, depending on similar kinds of calendrical data. They

share an attitude to the natural world in which the bodies of humans and animals, the growth of plants and the cycles of the sun and moon correspond with each other in meaningful ways, all part of the essentially ordered nature of the created world. Understanding the calendar was a way of accessing this knowledge.

It's particularly interesting that this text links Midsummer with a ritual of burning, because in later tradition there was a strong association between Midsummer and bonfires. In the late Middle Ages and afterwards, bonfires on St John's Eve were a widespread custom found across northern Europe. By this time Midsummer had become a hugely popular celebration, when houses were decorated with lights and greenery and feasts and parades would take place with pageantry and music.[11] Bonfires were the most consistent element of these celebrations, and it was believed that these fires had protective powers, able to purify the air and drive away evil spirits. At the time, Midsummer was still closely identified with the feast of John the Baptist: medieval writers like the fourteenth-century preacher John Mirk saw bonfires as appropriate for St John because the saint himself was a 'lantern burning', a herald seen from afar like a beacon of fire.[12]

Although the custom of Midsummer bonfires isn't attested before the thirteenth century in England, it's often been suggested it may reflect a pre-Christian practice of celebrating the solstice with fire.[13] That some kind of popular festivities did take place in Anglo-Saxon England on this date is suggested by a brief reference in an eleventh-century story from Wilton Abbey, which concerns the healing of a teenage boy named Sigeric by St Edith, the young Anglo-Saxon princess who was Wilton's patron saint. The story says that Sigeric, who had been born without a tongue, was promised that he would be healed if he kept vigil all night at St Edith's shrine on St John's Eve. Though he intended to do so, he was distracted on the eve by taking part in 'the boys' games at night which are customarily celebrated on that festival in accordance with ancient tradition'.[14]

(Alas, no more details are given.) Sigeric remembered his promise before it was too late, ran to the abbey, and awoke in the morning miraculously healed and able to speak. Perhaps bonfires were part of the Midsummer games Sigeric and his friends were enjoying; though we can't know for sure, the obvious association between fire and the sun may well mean the solstice bonfire tradition is older than surviving records can prove. If so, there might be a trace of it in the fragmentary ritual from Winchester – perhaps a belief that a fire which burned on this special night had particular power. It's ironic that the text itself has been damaged by fire; if the flames which attacked this manuscript, leaving it curled and charred, had eaten just a few more inches, any trace of Anglo-Saxon Midsummer fires would have been entirely lost.

After the Reformation Midsummer bonfires were suppressed in England, though the tradition long endured in other parts of Europe, especially Ireland and Scandinavia. Despite the attempts to put down Midsummer 'superstition', however, many customs recorded by later folklore-collectors preserve the sense of Midsummer Eve as an especially magical time, a night for ghosts and love-divination.[15] Also lastingly popular was the idea found in the Anglo-Saxon medical remedies that plants gathered at Midsummer had special potency: St John's wort, which gets its name because it flowers at this time of year, was used to decorate houses at Midsummer, and shared the healing and protective powers attributed to St John's bonfires.[16]

Over the course of the twentieth century, the cultural importance of Midsummer waned in Britain, as a result of the increased attention paid to the astronomical date of the solstice, as well as a growing belief that the solstice marks the beginning of summer, rather than its midpoint. In modern Britain, most people's immediate association with the solstice is now probably the crowds who gather on that day at Stonehenge, rather than any customs of St John's Eve or Midsummer Day.[17] The disparate uses to which Midsummer is put in Anglo-Saxon texts can seem strange to modern eyes, accustomed as we are to drawing firm dividing lines between the scientific and the religious, the Christian and the pagan. Midsummer, perhaps more than any other date in the year, illustrates how artificial it is to read these divisions back into the Anglo-Saxon period. For the Anglo-Saxons, an interest in the solstice, the healing properties of plants and the story of John the Baptist were all interrelated, and they all converged to make Midsummer an immensely powerful time of year.

THE SUMMER-LONG DAY

The distinctive feeling of the Midsummer season, the days of longest light around the summer solstice, is sensitively evoked in a number of Old English poems. *The Menologium* has a beautiful description of the solstice in its section for June:

> Then after six nights the next month,
> *ærra Liða*, brings long days to town for us,
> June into the dwellings, in which the jewel climbs up
> highest in the year into the heavens,
> brightest of stars, and descends from its place,
> sinks to its setting. It likes then
> to gaze longer upon the earth and to move more slowly
> across the fields of the world, the fairest of lights
> and of all created things. Then after thirteen and ten
>   nights
> the thegn of glory, the Prince's darling,
> John, was born in days of old;
> we keep that feast at Midsummer, with great honour.

Here the sun is personified as it 'climbs' to its highest point in the year: it's as if the days are longer at the solstice because the sun is lingering above the earth, unwilling to depart, lovingly beholding the world and wanting to travel more slowly across the summer fields. As often in Anglo-Saxon poetry, the sun is called a 'jewel', *gim*, a gem of precious brightness and warmth.

Since the solstice offers the greatest quantity of light of any day in the year, it can serve as a powerful image of spiritual enlightenment. One such metaphorical use occurs in an anonymous poem from the late ninth or early tenth century, in the Old English translation of Boethius' *Consolation of Philosophy*.[18] This sixth-century work, much read and beloved in the Middle Ages, was first translated into English as part of Alfred the Great's project to make important works of Latin learning available in the common tongue. Written in prison, Boethius' deeply personal book is concerned with philosophical questions of fate, free will and the nature of true happiness, but also with psychological trouble – how philosophy can be a consolation when things go badly wrong. This may have been a theme that appealed to Alfred and his translators, perhaps because of what the Old English preface to the translation calls the king's own 'various and manifold worldly cares which often troubled him both in mind and body', including physical illness and warfare against Viking invaders. After being translated into English prose, the verse sections of Boethius' work were also translated into poetry. In one of these poems, the translator, seeking an image that could encapsulate the highest form of spiritual illumination, turns to the metaphor of the sun at the solstice. Anyone who wants to find truth, he says, should look not outside but inside their own mind:

> He must seek then within his mind,
> and utterly forsake, as often as he can,
> every anxiety which is useless to him,
> and gather, as much as he can,
> all into one his inner thought;
> say to his mind that it can discover
> all within itself which it is now so often

always seeking outside itself:
every good. He will then perceive
all the harmful and useless things
which he had long kept within his inner chamber,
just as clearly as he may look upon the sun
with his present eyes;
and he will also perceive his inner thought,
lighter and brighter than the radiance
of the sun in summer, when the jewel of the sky,
serene star of the heavens, shines most brightly.

This is a wonderful passage of consolation, as the sorrowing mind is urged to remember that however difficult its outward circumstances, even in times of greatest darkness, gleams of light always remain within the soul. Seek inwards, burrow deep into your own mind, and within that enclosure – which the translator calls a *runcofa*, a 'secret chamber' – truth and goodness can still be found. The comparison with the sun is mentioned by Boethius, but the Anglo-Saxon poet expands it with familiar metaphors and the seasonal reference: we're encouraged to picture the sun in summer, *sunnan on sumera*, the time of the year when it's at its superlative brightest, gleaming gem and radiant star. Glorious as that sun is, there's something even 'lighter and brighter', *leohtre and berhtre*: your own mind, if you let go of useless anxieties and learn how to be illuminated by the light within you.

A very different poetic use of the height of summer is offered by a poem in the Exeter Book, *The Wife's Lament*. Like some of the poems we've already looked at, it's a moving reflection on enforced solitude, exile and grief; but unlike *The Wanderer* or *The Seafarer*, where sorrow is associated with the desolation of winter, this poem situates its isolated speaker in the opposite seasonal setting, the long days of summer. It's a haunting poem, difficult to translate and interpret, and in many ways mysterious. It opens like other Old English laments, with a first-person speaker – in this case a woman – who promises to tell of her sorrows:

> I utter this song, very sorrowful, about myself,
> my own journey. I can tell
> what I have known of hardships, since I grew up,
> recently and long ago, never more than now.

As she goes on to describe her situation, the account she gives is puzzling, perhaps deliberately enigmatic, alluding to troubles she never fully explains. She says that her 'lord' (possibly, but not necessarily, her husband) left his people to travel across the sea, and she, after a time of uncertainty, set out on her own journey, perhaps to seek him. She has experienced feud, violence and murder; it may be that, like Hildeburh in the Finnsburh episode in *Beowulf*, she has found herself caught up in conflict between her husband's family and her family of origin. Possibly her husband's kinsmen have persuaded him to reject her. Whatever happened, she's now living alone, in a very strange dwelling-place:

> I was commanded to dwell in this forest grove,
> under an oak-tree, in this earthy barrow.
> Ancient is this earth-cave; I am entirely seized with
>   longing.
> The valleys are dark, the hills lofty,
> the fortifications bitter, overgrown with briars,
> a dwelling-place without joys. Very often here my lord's
>   absence
> cruelly comes over me. There are living in the world
> dear lovers, who lie in their beds,
> while I before dawn must walk alone
> under the oak-tree, through this earthy cave.
> There I must sit all the summer-long day,

there I may weep for my exile,
my many hardships, for I never can
set at rest my sorrowful heart,
nor all the longing which has seized me in this life.

This is a threatening landscape of ancient and ominous associations. She seems to be living in a burial mound or some kind of prehistoric earthwork; it may be that her cave is in fact a tomb. There are challenges of translation which complicate the question: for instance, she describes her dwelling as a *herheard*, a compound that might suggest a temple or grove for pagan worship, but interpretations vary.[19]

Why is she here? Has her husband betrayed and imprisoned her, or sent her into sanctuary in a sacred place for her own protection? Or is she dead, speaking from the grave? We don't know. In Anglo-Saxon England, landscapes such as the one she describes – the barrows, ditches and earthworks of the prehistoric past – were viewed with a mixture of awe and horror.[20] While poets could situate ruined Roman cities within their knowledge of history, they knew nothing of the peoples who had built these older monuments, and perhaps thought they were not built by human hands at all. The numinous antiquity of these places is often encoded in their Anglo-Saxon names, which link them with mysterious beings who were thought to have built them or to dwell in them: monsters, dragons, the legendary smith Weland, or the god Grim (a name for Odin).[21] If such beings are lurking, this woman's earth-cave is a frightening place.

Along with its unforgettable description of the eerie space this woman inhabits, the poem also locates her very precisely in time, offering two almost unique words which transport the reader into the exact moment of her sorrow. First is *uhtcearu*, a compound which means 'sorrow before dawn' or 'grief at early morning'. In Old English *uht* is the name for the last part of the night, the empty chilly hours just before the dawn, an especially painful time for grief and loneliness (as well as other kinds of threat: the dragon in *Beowulf* is called an *uhtfloga*, a creature who flies before dawn). The word suggests the sting of waking to the memory of sorrow, or the anxiety of lying awake in the early morning, worrying over what the day will bring.

And after dawn there's a whole day of sorrow to be lived through, which the woman describes in equally memorable language: 'there I must sit all the summer-long day.' The implication, of course, is that the length of a midsummer day is a very long time – seventeen hours, as Ælfric tells us – and so a weary stretch for a woman who has nothing to do but think of her troubles. It almost sounds as if it might have been proverbial: 'as long as a summer's day'. Unlike *uhtcearu*, which appears nowhere else, the word *sumorlang* is not quite unique, but also appears in Cynewulf's poem *Juliana*. There, the dauntless saintly heroine captures a demon who has been tormenting her and holds him prisoner until she's forced him to confess all his wickedness. He says he could not relate all the suffering he has caused in the world 'even if [he] were to sit the length of a whole summer's day', in very similar language to the woman in the earthy barrow.

The Wife's Lament is unusual in linking its speaker's sorrow to summer. We've seen that in Anglo-Saxon poetry grief is often imagined as a winter-like experience, and if 'summer-long day' is being used as a semi-proverbial measurement of 'a very long time', you might think a 'winter-long night' would do as well. But the seasonal marker gives this poem an unforgettably different character from other Old English laments. While their exiled men battle against winter, journeying through icy seas, here a woman dwells solitary and stationary in her summer grief. Perhaps part of her pain is that, while winter is a bad time for a journey, summer is supposed to be a good season for travelling – but she can't escape, however much the long days seem to offer her an opportunity. Unlike the woman in *The Husband's Message*, waiting for summer so she can go to join her lover, for this woman the summer days bring no release.

There's something vivid and nightmarish about the idea of her sorrow accompanying her all through the glaring light of a long midsummer day, from early dawn to late dusk, as she's hemmed in by the oak-tree and briars around her barrow in the full choking force of their summer growth.

The 'summer-long day' might also suggest her state of mind, an indication of how time is dragging. The *length* of the day echoes the word she most frequently uses to characterize her sorrow: *longing*. She uses variants of this word no fewer than four times, and the echo between 'summer-long' and 'longing' connects her yearning desire with the day that seems so endless. As the poem closes, she imagines her lover sitting 'beneath a stormy cliff, covered with frost', grieving and lonely. She pictures him in the hostile winter landscape familiar from other Old English poems, but perhaps this winter, too, is less a literal reality than a state of mind. The two of them are probably not simultaneously living through different seasons, but they might as well be, they are so far apart. The last line of the poem brings us back again to their separation, taken now out of time and lengthened into eternity: 'Grief must be for the one who, longing, waits for the beloved.'

MONTHS OF GENTLENESS

Before we move into autumn, the last thing to consider is the Anglo-Saxon name for the months of June and July, *Liða*. As with the period around the winter solstice (*Geola*, 'Yule'), the Old English name *Liða* corresponds to two months in our calendar: June is called *se ærra liða*, 'the earlier *Liða*', and July *se æftera liða*, 'the later *Liða*'. Bede explains that in the old Anglo-Saxon calendar, in years when there were thirteen lunar months rather than twelve, an extra month would be assigned to summer to help keep the lunar calendar roughly in line with the solar year; such years were called *Þriliði*, that is, 'three-*liða*'. He interprets the meaning of the name by saying that

'*Liða* means "gentle" or "navigable" because in both these months the calm breezes are gentle, and they were wont to sail upon the smooth sea.'[22] Bede here proposes an etymological link between the month-name and two Old English words: the adjective *liðe*, which means 'smooth, calm, serene', and the verb *liðan*, 'to sail'. He speculates that both words may have influenced the month-name: in June and July the weather is calm, so people go sailing, so they call it *Liða*. This is a reasonable hypothesis; the only problem is that the verb isn't etymologically connected to the adjective, since they go back to different Proto-Germanic roots. To a speaker of Old English, however, such a link must have seemed obvious, especially in light of the conventional association between spring/summer and sea-journeys which we saw in *The Seafarer*, *The Husband's Message* and *The Rhyming Poem*.

The idea that summer weather is characteristically *liðe* must also have seemed very plausible. This adjective is common in Old English, with universally positive connotations in all its different applications. It's often used of serene, pleasant weather, particularly balmy summer days. In *De temporibus anni*, Ælfric uses this word in explaining the difference in weather between the two halves of the year, either side of the solstice – what he calls 'the lengthening day' and 'the shortening day'. While 'the lengthening day is cold because the earth is permeated with the winter chill, and it takes a long time before it is warmed again', it's the opposite during the days after the summer solstice, when 'the shortening day has balmier [*liðran*] weather than the lengthening day, because the earth is all bathed in the summer heat, and does not so swiftly cool down again.'[23]

Not only weather is *liðe*, however; many things can be. The word also means 'mild, pleasant, sweet, gentle' when used of food and drink, medicine, words and gestures. It can apply to people, too, where it implies 'merciful' and 'kindly', so it's sometimes used of God, as in an Old English translation of Christ's words in Matthew 11:29: 'Learn from me, for I am merciful (*liðe*) and humble, and you shall find rest for your souls.'[24] At the end of *Beowulf*, the hero is mourned as the 'gentlest of men and most courteous, most gracious to his people', *leodum liðost*. Many of these meanings – though not the month-name – survived into Middle English, where the word continued to be used of serene weather, sweet food and gentle people. Then it began to die out, and by the eighteenth century only one usage of the word was still prevalent, the only sense in which it survives today: 'lithe', meaning 'supple, flexible'. That sense isn't attested in Old English, but the underlying link must be the idea of smooth, easy movement, like the calm sailing that Anglo-Saxon writers associated with the summer seas of June and July. The history of the word seems to connect such freedom with kindness, generosity and the summer weather of the bright months around the solstice – a season of balmy and peaceful days, a climate which helps plants and people thrive.

AUTUMN

10

HARVEST

THE FEAST OF BREAD

Of the four seasons of the year, none has undergone a greater change between its medieval and modern conceptions than autumn. Say 'autumn' and what springs to mind are probably the sights and sensations of October: carpets of tawny fallen leaves, misty mornings with a chill in the air, darker and ever-shortening days. What was in Anglo-Saxon calendars the first month of autumn, August, is now in Britain considered the height of summer, when schools are out and many people go on holiday. Our seasonal shift from summer to autumn starts in September, when the schools go back, and modern autumnal celebrations tend to cluster in October and November – think of church harvest festivals, Halloween or Thanksgiving in Canada and the USA.[1]

It was very different in the Middle Ages. Though we'll get to the poetry of fallen leaves in the next chapter, there's really no word in Old English corresponding to what English-speakers today would call 'autumn' or 'fall'. To the Anglo-Saxons the fourth season of the year was *hærfest*, 'harvest', and that continued to be its usual name throughout the medieval period. In the four--season pattern of the year, *hærfest* was used as the equivalent of Latin *autumnus*, and theoretically ran from 7 August until 6 November. However, in general use *hærfest* referred more loosely to the period when harvesting was actually being done, from late July to September. In that sense it's the latter part of summer, as it would have been in the older two-season cycle – and once it's over, winter begins.

It's difficult to overstate the importance of the harvest in Anglo-Saxon England, as in any agricultural society. A good harvest was essential for sustaining life through the winter months, and bringing in the harvest required a huge amount of hard work, communal labour necessary for everyone's survival. The significance of harvest in an agricultural society is often difficult for modern Western audiences to imagine; most of us rarely have to think about food in terms of scarcity or season, or plan ahead to gather in enough stores to get us through the winter. This is a relatively recent privilege. Well into the nineteenth century, harvest retained something of the importance it had in medieval society; August wasn't holiday time, but the season when many people were doing their hardest work of the year.

The pragmatic side of harvest – the labour it required and the basic need for food – is not the whole story, however. In cultures where survival depends on a bountiful harvest, there's often a pro-foundly spiritual aspect to this season of the year: it may be felt important to pray for divine help with the harvest, to give thanks for it when it comes and to share its produce in festivals and cele-brations. In looking at the *Æcerbot* field-blessing we saw how one Anglo-Saxon ritual sought sacred assistance to protect crops and ensure a good harvest, invoking God's aid and the fertility of Mother Earth to counteract damaging spiritual influences. References to harvest in Old English literature suggest this was a time, more than any other, when divine power was thought to be displayed on the earth. Praying for and celebrating the fruits of the harvest seem to have been part of Anglo-Saxon culture both before and after the conversion to Christianity. There are traces of pagan Anglo-Saxon harvest festivals in August and September, while the medieval church, following biblical precedent, also laid emphasis on giving thanks to God for the fruits of the harvest. In Old English poetry the abundance of harvest is lyrically, joyfully praised; harvest is a season for celebrating the earth's life-sustaining plenty.

The first harvest festival of the Anglo-Saxon year was Lammas, celebrated on 1 August. Lammas is something of a mystery. The meaning of its name, *hlafmæsse* in Old English, is straightforward enough: it comes from *hlaf*, 'loaf, bread', and *mæsse*, 'mass, festival'. That suggests it was a celebration of the wheat harvest – a feast of bread. The evolution from *hlaf-* to *la-* in the modern form is comparable to two words with the same root, 'lord' and 'lady': these words ultimately derive from the Old English compounds *hlafweard* and *hlæfdige*, which originally meant something like 'bread-guardian' and 'bread-kneader', suggesting those who protect and provide for a household. That bread should be associated with such important social roles is an indication of how central it was to medieval life, and it's not surprising that it should have been honoured with a harvest festival.

Lammas is mentioned numerous times in Anglo-Saxon sources, but it's difficult to pin down what actually happened at this festival. As it falls in August, it was probably a festival of first-fruits, perhaps when loaves of bread made from the first corn of the harvest were blessed ('corn' in this context means wheat or barley, the main cereal crops in Anglo-Saxon England).[2] This is a plausible supposition, but it's never explicitly stated in any Anglo-Saxon text.[3] As there are no clear parallels in the wider medieval church for a harvest festival on this date, scholars have often proposed that Lammas may be related to the Irish festival of Lughnasadh, which also fell at the beginning of August. This festival, named for the god Lugh, was celebrated with large gatherings at open-air assembly sites, involving games, feasts and sacrifices.[4] With this comparison in mind, it's been hypothesized that Lammas may be the survival of an older harvest festival celebrated in Britain and Ireland before the conversion to Christianity. This certainly seems possible, but there's no definitive evidence for any continuation of pre-Christian practices at Lammas into the post-conversion period. Nothing among the surviving Anglo-Saxon references to Lammas indicates that it was perceived to be a festival with pagan elements, and there are in fact no obvious links between the customs practised at Lughnasadh in Ireland and parts of Britain and anything Anglo-Saxon sources connect to Lammas – including the key element, bread. Furthermore, whatever the origins of the festival, the name *hlafmæsse* can only have been coined in a Christian context, since the second element *mæsse* was borrowed from Latin and has its roots in Christian liturgical language. It belongs with the other English names given by the Anglo-Saxon church to Christian festivals introduced into England – Christmas, Candlemas and the rest. It is, therefore, a name which can only have been formed after the adoption of Christianity; if the origins of Lammas lie in a pagan festival celebrated by the Anglo-Saxons before the conversion, that festival must have had another name.

The majority of references to Lammas in Old English sources simply treat it as another name for 1 August, without describing any customs associated with the day. Clearly the date was well known, but there's little to tell us how it was celebrated. Bede doesn't mention it. It first begins to be attested in the ninth century, the earliest reference probably appearing in the *Old English Martyrology*: this doesn't use the name Lammas, but refers to 1 August as the day of *hlafsenunga*, 'bread-blessing'.[5] In this word *senung*, from *segnian*, 'to make the sign of the cross', is another borrowing from Latin (*signare*), so like *hlafmæsse* this must be a name coined in a Christian context. The first recorded use of the word *hlafmæsse* itself is in a text from the late ninth or early tenth century, which refers to 1 August in passing (while telling the story of Antony and Cleopatra) as 'the day we call Lammas'.[6] It crops up regularly in the *Anglo-Saxon Chronicle* from the tenth century onwards, though again only as another name for 1 August. Events are dated 'after Lammas', or 'between Lammas and Midsummer': one example occurs in an entry for 917, when 'before Lammas' the renowned female ruler of Mercia, Æthelflæd – known by the title 'Lady of the Mercians', *Myrcna hlæfdige* – won a battle to recapture the Viking-held town of Derby.[7]

Even Ælfric, usually such a helpful guide to the cycle of the church year, only mentions Lammas as a date reference.[8] But it could be a very useful date to know. A brief comment in a compilation of medical texts informs the reader, 'Fifteen nights before Lammas and thirty-five nights afterwards bloodletting is to be avoided, because at that time all venomous things fly and greatly injure human beings ... Physicians also say that growing herbs are best to prepare at this time, whether for potions, salves or powder.'[9] The reason is that these are the 'dog days' of summer, when the Dog Star, Sirius, the brightest star in the night sky, is visible above the horizon. Anglo-Saxon scholars knew that in Greek and Roman astronomy these sultry late-summer days were associated with disease, fever, thunderstorms and lethargy.[10] This knowledge formed part of learned calendar lore, and Old English medical texts adapt this belief to an Anglo-Saxon context by adding references to Lammas.

All this suggests widespread knowledge of Lammas as a date, but tells us nothing about either its popular or liturgical celebration. In liturgical sources, Lammas doesn't appear in the places we might look to find it, such as calendars or service books. In particular, if bread was blessed on this day, we might expect to find blessings for Lammas loaves included in Anglo-Saxon manuscripts. There are quite a few items blessed on particular days through the course of the church year: candles, ashes and palms are blessed on their respective days in the spring, and the medieval church also assigned days for blessing other crops of the harvest, such as grapes on 6 August. Texts for all these blessings regularly feature in Anglo-Saxon manuscripts, but there's nothing specific to Lammas, though there are general blessings for bread and other crops which could be used. It's possible we should interpret this to mean that by the late Anglo-Saxon period Lammas had become for many people simply a name for the beginning of harvest, rather than a festival with any specific rituals or customs. This was the case in the later medieval and early modern period, when Lammas continued to be widely known, but mostly served as a fixed date for various secular customs rather than a festival in its own right. It was a popular day for fairs and local feasts, and one of the regular dates on which rents would be paid, debts settled, contracts made and labourers hired.[11]

However, a special connection between Lammas and blessed bread is suggested by the most interesting reference to Lammas in an Anglo-Saxon source. This is a ritual, comparable to *Æcerbot* but much shorter, which tells you how to protect harvested sheaves from mice and other pests. The text is damaged, but can be translated as follows (the italicized text is in Latin in the original):

> [Take two] long pieces of four-edged wood, and on each piece write a Pater Noster, on each side down to the end. Lay [one] on the floor of the barn, and lay the other [across] it, so they form the sign of the cross. And take four pieces of the consecrated bread which is consecrated on Lammas Day, and crumble them at the four corners of the barn. This is the blessing for that. *So that mice do not harm these sheaves, say prayers over the sheaves and [then] hang them up without speaking. City of Jerusalem, where mice do not live and cannot have power, and cannot gather the grain nor rejoice with the wheat.* This is the second blessing. *Lord God Almighty, who made heaven and earth, bless these fruits in the name of the Father and the Son and the Holy Spirit. Amen. And Pater Noster.*[12]

This text comes from the same eleventh-century manuscript as the Midsummer ritual for curing sick cattle, the psalter with its added calendar information and medical lore. This ritual similarly uses a variety of Christian symbols and practices – the cross, Pater Noster and consecrated bread – to seek divine help and blessing. In this case, the idea is to surround the harvested sheaves with a sacred space of protection, a square divided by a cross, marked in the middle of the barn and at its four corners. This demarcation of space parallels the ritual protection invoked by *Æcerbot* and other medieval liturgical practices of blessing, such as Rogationtide processions.[13]

This ritual is our best evidence that there was something special about the bread blessed at Lammas. It's possible, however, that the bread referred to is in fact the Eucharistic host consecrated at mass on Lammas Day. Bread is, of course, blessed at every mass; it may be that the reason we don't find Lammas blessings in the service-books is that the special bread of Lammas Day was the Eucharist, for which, perhaps, the first harvested wheat was used. Such a practice would again find close parallels in other Anglo-Saxon Christian rituals of healing and protection, which prescribe using sacred and liturgical items – including consecrated wine, patens, church bells and holy water from the baptismal font – to make or administer medicine.[14] For an eleventh-century Anglo-Saxon audience, any 'feast of bread' would potentially have had Eucharistic overtones, given the centrality of bread to both the celebration of the mass and the fundamental prayer of Christian worship, the Pater Noster; it's no wonder that the Pater Noster, with its prayer for 'our daily bread', plays a key role in this ritual for protecting the sheaves. It's an indication of how seriously this was being taken. Guarding your crops, once you had harvested them, was hugely important; that's your food for the winter, and you don't want to let the mice have it. This ritual is a reminder that harvest-time might be an anxious season as well as a joyous one.

HARVEST KINGS

Growing crops involves a great amount of human labour – long, hard, steady work throughout the year, from seed-time to reaping-time. But there's still much about the process that is beyond human control: farmers can plant, tend and gather crops, but can't master all the forces that will affect the harvest (especially the weather). As a result, there remains something mysterious about harvest, and poets writing about this season often reflect on what might be the ultimate source of nature's bounty, the invisible power that makes the crops grow.

That mysterious power is reflected in the story of one of the most important legendary hero-kings in Anglo-Saxon culture, who seems to have been closely linked to the harvest. This was Scyld Scefing, whose name and legend associate him with sheaves of corn and the fertility of the land. Scyld features in medieval sources from England and Scandinavia, which all give slightly different versions of his legend, but his most famous appearance is in the opening lines of *Beowulf*.[15] His story starts the poem: Scyld is the ancestor of the Danish king whom Beowulf will save from the attacks of Grendel and his mother. The legend says that Scyld was found by the Danes as a boy drifting in an open boat, alone and destitute. No one knew where he had come from, but the Danes took him ashore, and he grew and flourished and became a famous king. He was a mighty ruler, successful in war and founder of a great royal dynasty, and in his time there was much prosperity. When at last he died his people returned him to the waves, sent out to sea again in a ship laden with treasure. He came from mystery and returned to it again; as *Beowulf* says, 'No one can tell for certain, neither counsellors in the hall nor heroes under the heavens, who received that cargo.'[16]

Scyld's link to the harvest is in the name 'Scefing', which means 'son of Sceaf'. In Old English *sceaf* is 'sheaf', as in 'wheatsheaf', while *scyld* means 'shield'. The sheaf and the shield together represent two of the most important aspects of early medieval kingship: the king's duty to provide for and defend his people. It's the same connection that explains the development of the word 'lord' from *hlafweard*, 'bread-guardian', suggesting the lord's responsibility to maintain a secure food supply, metonymically indicated by bread. As a mythic king of the sheaf and shield, Scyld is the ideal provider and protector: *Beowulf* says of him emphatically, 'that was a good king'. In some versions of Scyld's story, he's found drifting in the boat with a sheaf of corn lying beside him. Though this isn't mentioned in *Beowulf*, the poem speaks of a 'golden banner' set up to wave high above Scyld's head on his funeral ship – surely a sheaf, or an image of one. Scyld leaves behind him a son called Beow, a name which means 'barley'. *Beowulf* says of this son that *blæd wide sprang*, his 'glory spread far and wide'. This language implies he's flourishing like a young shoot of barley, since *blæd* also means 'growing thing' or 'fruit of the harvest', while *sprang* is (as in Modern English) a word very appropriate for the growth of a plant.

From Beow are descended the Danish kings who feature in the early part of *Beowulf*, the Scyldings, 'descendants of Scyld'. Outside the poem, Scyld was indeed claimed as an ancestor by the kings of Wessex and of Denmark, including the Danish kings who ruled in England in the Anglo-Saxon period. The names Scyld and Sceaf feature in the genealogy of the West Saxon royal house, among the ancestors of Alfred the Great, but Cnut's poets also hailed him as 'strong Scylding' as they praised his conquest of the English.[17] Scyld was clearly a mighty ancestor and a name to conjure with, and the mystery of his origins and his fate suggests that he was perceived as something more than human – a semi-divine royal progenitor. He's almost an embodiment of the harvest itself: he comes out of nowhere, driven or summoned by some unknown force, and brings great prosperity, but when his days reach their end he vanishes, no one knows where. It may be that in this story we can catch a glimpse of a pre-Christian fertility myth, an Anglo-Saxon hero of the harvest.

Another harvest king can be traced, more distantly, in the story of the man in *The Rhyming Poem*, whose life-course, as we saw earlier, is mapped onto the cycle of the year. After his time of youthful

growth and flourishing, this ruler's mature life is imagined in terms
of harvest – a season of settled wealth and success, as he reaps the
rewards of worldly prosperity.

> Thus hope's gift held me, a household enfolded me;
> I possessed properties, ruled the goings of men,
> as the earth gave nourishment. I held the high seat,
> chanted charms. The joy of peace did not fail;
> the year was constant in gifts, the harp-string resonant ...
> Courage burgeoned, prosperity shone like a beacon,
> gave wisdom to the nobles, success to the strong.
> The mind expanded, love rejoiced,
> truth branched forth, glory abounded,
> fame prospered,
> gold was ready, jewels passed around,
> treasure was artfully wrought, kindred grew close.
> Strong was I in armour, noble in adornments,
> lordly was my joy, my life full of pleasure.
> I protected the land, was gentle to my people;
> my life was long among my countrymen,
> touched by glory, surrounded by good things.

This is a picture of a ruler at the height of his power, succeeding in
all the ways expected of an Anglo-Saxon king. He defends his land
and governs his people well; riches abound in his hall as he rewards
his followers with gold and treasure. He prospers not only in material
wealth, but in abstract goods too – in strength of mind and the
ability to foster wisdom and loyalty among his people. Earlier in the
poem, the man's youth is characterized by movement, as he travels
by horse and ship, but here he's settled, established in his hall. This
period of his life is a season of *ead*, which means 'prosperity, happiness, blessing'; we're told it *beacnade*, 'shone like a beacon'. *Ead* is a
common element in Anglo-Saxon personal names, including some

still in use, such as Edward and Edmund (*Eadweard* and *Eadmund*), meaning happy/blessed 'guardian' and 'protector', respectively. These names – and others beginning with *Ead* – were used by many Anglo-Saxon kings, and they suggest aspirations for ideal kingship: if rulers prosper, so will their people.

In these lines there's much to echo *Beowulf*'s portrait of Scyld Scefing, and here too the poetic language evokes harvest, linking a ruler's success to the bounteous produce of the earth. This man also has *blæd*, with its double meaning of 'glory' and 'growth'. We're told that in his time *treow telgade*, and this has a significant dual meaning: *treow* can mean 'truth, integrity', and that must be the primary sense here, but *treow* also means 'tree', and the verb, *telgian*, is one that strongly connotes the growth of a tree, meaning 'to branch forth, put out shoots'. There's a suggestion that truth and fidelity flourish in this king's hall like a tree at the height of its growth, stable and strong. In this season of prosperity, the man implies, the harvests were always good to him: *wæs gefest gear*, 'the year was constant in gifts.' While the year is generous in bringing forth its produce, the lord can fulfil his duty to feed and sustain his people.

THE SEASON OF GIFT AND GLORY

In *The Rhyming Poem*, as often in Old English poetry, the word *gear* means not exactly 'year' in the sense we would use it, but 'the season of growth and harvest', the opposite half of the year from winter. *Gear* is also a letter in the runic alphabet, so there's a verse dedicated to it in *The Old English Rune Poem*:

> Gear byþ gumena hiht, ðon God læteþ,
> halig heofones cyning, hrusan syllan
> beorhte bleda beornum and ðearfum.

> *Gear* is a joy to men, when God,
> holy King of heaven, causes the earth
> to give bright fruits for nobles and the needy.

There again is the word *blæd*, in the alliterating phrase *beorhte bleda*, 'bright fruits'. It would make sense to translate *gear* here as 'harvest', but there are other contexts (such as *Beowulf*'s story of Hengest) where it has to be translated as 'spring'. It might seem odd to have a word that could equally denote what are, to us, clearly distinct seasons of the year, but *gear* really covers both those seasons – the growing and the gathering. Spring and harvest are not so distinct if what matters most is the whole process of producing crops; in fact, they're so fundamentally linked that it may seem impossible to separate them. Here the source of joy is all the earth's plenty as the year runs through its course, from the first shoots of green to the ripe crops of the harvest.

There's emphasis on the idea that the harvest is for everyone, rich and poor; it's God's gift to all humanity. This verse has close parallels to the description of harvest in *Maxims II*:

> Hærfest hreðeadegost; hæleðum bringeð
> geres wæstmas, þa þe him God sendeð.

> Harvest is most glory-blessed; it brings to men
> the *gear*'s fruits, which God sends them.

Harvest is the season most blessed with *ead*, and here that's seen as a revelation of God's generosity in sending the fruits of nature to provide for human needs. In a Christian context, too, harvest is praised in *The Menologium*:

> And after seven nights
> *Weodmonað*, brightened by summer, slips

into the dwellings; everywhere August
brings to peoples of the earth
Lammas Day. So harvest comes,
after that number of nights but one,
bright, laden with fruits. Plenty is revealed,
beautiful upon the earth.

The Old English name for August, *Weodmonað*, is explained by Bede
as 'the month of weeds', because 'they are very plentiful then'.[18] An
alternative name for August, recorded only in one early Kentish
source, is *Rugern*, probably referring to the harvest of rye – another
cereal crop to add to the wheat and barley of the Scyld legend.[19]

These lines in *The Menologium* provide the sole reference in
Anglo-Saxon poetry to Lammas, as part of the transition from
summer to *hærfest* (here suggesting both harvest and autumn).
After a final week of summer's brightness, the new season arrives
on 7 August, and the emphasis is on harvest's plenty and beauty.
Harvest arrives *wæstmum hladen*, 'laden with fruits', a phrase that
evokes trees and vines bowed down by the weight of fruit, or
the heavy heads of ripened wheat – the fullness of earth at the
pinnacle of its productive growth. The rest of *The Menologium*'s
section for August describes the feast-days of four major saints:
Lawrence, Bartholomew, the Dormition of the Virgin Mary and
the Beheading of John the Baptist. The theme of harvest also colours the language in which the poet records all these feasts, making
this harvest month a reflection on growth, fruitfulness and the
rewards of labour. Here, for instance, is the section about the
Virgin Mary:

And five nights after this the fairest of maidens,
glory of women, sought the Lord of Hosts
because of kinship with her son, a victorious home
in the fields of Paradise. The Saviour repaid the virgin

with a beautiful reward for her nurturing,
for all eternity.

By the late Anglo-Saxon period, the harvest season contained two feasts of the Virgin Mary, less than a month apart, celebrating both the end of her life and its beginning: 15 August commemorated her departure from earthly life, 8 September her birth. Like the word *gear*, these two harvest feasts unite the beginning and end of a life-cycle, the first shoot of growth and the mature plant bearing fruit. In later medieval England, both feasts became known as 'Lady Day in Harvest', to distinguish them from 'Lady Day in Lent' (the Annunciation, 25 March) and 'Lady Day in December' (the Feast of the Conception, 8 December).[20] In *The Menologium*, the feast is implicitly linked to harvest by the emphasis on 'reward' – appropriate for an August feast in the season when those who have worked hard all the year can at last enjoy the fruits of their labours.

11

FALLOW AND FALL

THE HOLY HARVEST MONTH

Seprember marks a transitional point in the year: it's the month of the autumnal equinox, the end of harvest and the first sight of winter coming over the horizon. According to Bede, the Old English name for September was *Haligmonað*, which means 'holy month'. Unusually, Bede doesn't offer any explanation for why this month should be thought holy, but only gives a Latin translation, *mensis sacrorum*, 'month of sacred rites'.[1] Possibly he didn't know what those rites consisted of, and chose not to guess. However, it's reasonable to assume that the name has some connection to harvest, the main agricultural event of this time of year. If the first-fruits of the Anglo-Saxon harvest season were celebrated in early August, around the time of Lammas, *Haligmonað* might have seen rituals marking the end of harvest, such as the bringing-in of the last sheaves. Celebrations for the end of harvest are widely recorded in later British sources from the sixteenth century onwards: examples include ceremonies of cheering as the last sheaf was cut and traditions of decorating the last cart to come in from the fields, with the labourers following it on their way to a 'harvest-home' feast.[2] Though the first records for such customs date from centuries after the Anglo-Saxon period, the importance of harvest makes it likely that something similar existed in early medieval England too. One Old English source suggests that reapers were entitled to a feast at harvest-time as a reward for their labour, and implies that farmers were also expected to provide feasts for their workers during the seasons of ploughing and haymaking.[3]

As we've seen, some of the old names of the Anglo-Saxon months, such as *Eastermonað*, continued in use because they were transferred to Christian festivals. Perhaps because there was no obvious replacement in the church calendar for *Haligmonað*, however, the name soon died out. The most important Christian festival at this time of year was Michaelmas, the feast of the Archangel Michael on 29 September, which later became the autumnal quarter-day. Popular throughout the medieval church, St Michael was credited with stupendous power: he was seen as a warrior against the forces of evil, a psychopomp who guided souls to the afterlife and the bearer of the scales of divine justice.[4] Most often depicted battling the Devil in the form of a dragon, he was a hero to suit the Anglo-Saxon imagination. His feast was a high point in the church year, and its English name, Michaelmas, derives from the Anglo-Saxon name for the festival (*Michaeles mæsse*). *The Menologium* calls this feast 'the high-angel's tide in harvest', while an Anglo-Saxon homily speaks of St Michael himself as a harvester: 'the holy archangel St Michael, the prosperous sower of Christ's fields and the reaper bearing the fruit of the bright lands, who fills his Lord's barns with the purest wheat.'[5]

September has two attested names in Old English: while Bede calls it *Haligmonað*, Ælfric refers to September as *Hærfestmonað*, 'harvest month'.[6] Though not elsewhere recorded in Anglo-Saxon sources, the name *Hærfestmonað* is paralleled in other Germanic languages: for instance, a list of Old Norse month-names recorded by the Icelandic writer Snorri Sturluson includes *Haustmánuðr*, cognate with the English 'harvest month'.[7] This is the only name in Snorri's list which finds a parallel in recorded Old English month-names, but it supports the idea that this was a name for September in English too. Snorri observes that this harvest month was considered the last month before winter, and that also appears to have been the case in Anglo-Saxon England. Though *hærfest*, when used as a name for autumn, theoretically extended until 6 November, in practice it seems to have been felt that as soon as the last of the harvest was in, winter began. *Gerefa* reminds the reeve that in harvest, as well as bringing in the crops, he needs to be making sure that the farm buildings are in good repair: he should mend the thatch and attend to the cattle-shed and pigsty 'before harsh winter comes to the estate'.[8]

The swift transition from harvest to winter is evoked in a beautiful passage from *The Phoenix*, the poem we looked at earlier for its paradise of eternal summer and sun-filled glades. Amid its descriptions of that unchanging summer landscape, the poem offers one brief passage which summarizes the whole cycle of the year – a little vignette of the winter, spring and harvest of this earth, which never touch that land. It's a description of what happens when the phoenix is reborn in fire, comparing it to the cycle of death and regeneration the earth undergoes as it passes through the seasons.

> At that time the flesh becomes
> born again, entirely renewed,
> sundered from sins, somewhat like
> how in harvest people carry home
> the fruits of the earth for sustenance,
> pleasant nourishment, before winter comes,
> in the reaping-time, lest the showers of rain
> destroy them beneath the clouds. There they find
>   sustenance,
> joy in feasting, when frost and snow
> with overwhelming force wrap the earth
> in winter garments. From those fruits
> shall grow again the blessed plenty of men,
> according to the nature of the grain which first is sown
> as pure seed, when the sun's light,
> life's sign, in spring
> wakes the world's wealth, so that these fruits

according to their own nature are born again,
ornaments of the earth.

Compared to the phoenix's endless and perfect summer, this is a
more down-to-earth glimpse of the human experience of harvest,
winter and spring. This sketch of the seasonal cycle foregrounds
the essential dependence of human beings on the earth, provider
of the food we need for survival. Though the earth's produce, its
'blessed plenty', is beautiful, it's necessary too: the harvesters are
laying in stores for the winter ahead, when frost and snow will
'wrap the earth in winter garments'. There's perhaps a hint of harvest
celebrations in the alliterative link between 'harvest' and 'home';
'harvest-home' was later to become the familiar English name for
end-of-harvest feasts, and it occurs here in the phrase *on hærfeste
ham gelæded*, 'carry home in harvest'. The fruits of the earth are
described as *woruldgestreon*, 'world's wealth': they're imagined as
the earth's store of treasures, hidden underground in the winter
like a hoard of gold, and coming to light again when the spring
sun begins to shine.

As this poem suggests, winter follows hard on the heels of the
harvest. After the equinox *langað seo niht and wanað se dæg*, 'the
night lengthens and the day wanes', as Byrhtferth puts it.[9] Bede
suggests that the full moon following the autumnal equinox was
considered by the pagan Anglo-Saxons to be the first moon of winter,
and gave its name to the month equivalent to October: 'They called
the month in which the winter season began *Winterfylleð*, a name
made up from 'winter' and 'full moon', because winter began on the
full moon of that month,' he says.[10] Though the name *Winterfylleð*
soon fell out of use, the moon closest to the autumnal equinox kept
its significance long after the end of the Anglo-Saxon period. The
fourteenth-century poem *Sir Gawain and the Green Knight* includes
(rather like *The Phoenix*) a brief, beautiful poetic description of
the cycle of the year as it passes from winter through spring and

harvest and back to winter again.[11] Harvest ends with the coming of what the poet calls the 'Michaelmas moon', which must be the full moon (and perhaps the month) closest to Michaelmas at the end of September. This moon brings with it *wynter wage*, meaning the first 'pledge of winter'. We might think of that as the first chill in the air in an October dusk, or the first time it seems to be getting dark too early, or the first breath of mist in the morning – anything which says that summer is gone and the dark half of the year is coming. In September, amid the bounty of harvest-home, it may feel as if summer's hardly over, but winter's only one full moon away.

THE COMING FALL

While descriptions of harvest are plentiful in Anglo-Saxon poetry, there are fewer poems which concentrate on autumn as we might think of it today. Between the bringing-in of the last sheaves and the arrival of winter, there isn't much space for dwelling in what we might call an October mood, relishing the last lingering warmth or admiring the shades of autumnal leaves. For Anglo-Saxon writers, the established conventions of literary melancholy were almost inextricably linked to bleak winter landscapes, not the tender tints of autumn, and allusions to this season in Old English poetry are coloured by the awareness that autumn's beauties foreshadow winter's coming.

Sometimes we get glimpses of autumn in the middle of poems on other topics. In *Solomon and Saturn*, for example, the wise Solomon uses the fall of the leaves as an ominous metaphor for the fall of doomed men:

> A little while the leaves are green;
> then they fallow again, fall to the earth,
> and die, turn to dust.
> Just so fall those who for a long time

continue in their crimes, live in wickedness,
hide their treasures, hoard them eagerly
in safe places at the pleasure of the Devil.

This passage offers three alliterating verbs to describe what happens
to the leaves in autumn: *fealewiað, feallað, forweorniað*. The last two
mean 'fall' and 'die' respectively, while the first means 'to turn *fealo*' –
and *fealo*, 'fallow', describes a colour. Colour-names are notoriously
difficult to translate from one language to another, but we can get
a sense of what *fealo* means from the way it's used in Old English
sources. In some contexts, its meaning is clear: in poetry it's used of
the colour of fire, gold-hilted swords and light-brown lindenwood
shields, bay horses and autumn leaves. That suggests a yellow-gold
or brown-bronze kind of shade, and perhaps also a certain effect of
light – a burnished glow like that of metal or a horse's coat. *Solomon
and Saturn* contrasts the green leaves of spring and the fallow leaves
of autumn, which feels fitting: the unfurling leaves of early spring
are yellow-green in their beginning, as the falling leaves of autumn
are yellow-brown in their dying.

The colour *fealo* also appears in some more surprising contexts. It
is, for instance, several times used to describe the sea in Old English
poetry: in *Beowulf* the sea is 'the fallow flood', while *The Wanderer*
miserably contemplates 'fallow waves' as he watches the seabirds who
are his only company. Certainly the sea can be pale yellow or brown,
especially in winter – at least northern seas can be, such as those the
Anglo-Saxon poets knew. But who would think of using the same
word for that colour as for the shade of autumn leaves? That's part
of the fascination of colour-words in ancient languages; you have
to try and see with the eyes of the people who named them, and
often they yoke together things we would not connect. As a colour-
name 'fallow' survived into Middle English, but gradually became
restricted to describing the coats of animals. By the fifteenth century
it had given its name to the fallow deer, probably the only context

in which we might encounter it today. (It's not related to the word 'fallow' used of arable land left to lie uncultivated.)

The verb *fealewian*, 'to turn *fealo*', is only used in Old English of trees and plants, and that came to influence the connotations of the word. What it really means is 'to do what leaves do in autumn', and they don't only change their colour from green to gold; they also fade and wither, lose their strength. That gives the word poignant overtones, especially since it often – as in *Solomon and Saturn* – alliterates with the verb *feallan*, 'to fall'. Alliterating words which so closely echo each other had a tendency to draw together in the minds of Anglo-Saxon poets, and so it is with 'fallow' and 'fall'. After leaves fallow, they inevitably fall; as autumn declines into winter, the fallowing leaves must die and decay. And so must all mortal things. What in *Solomon and Saturn* is said only of wicked people becomes commonly extended, in later medieval poetry, to all people living in the world: we fallow, fade and fall like the flowers.

There are some places where leaves don't fallow or fall: in the eternal summer of *The Phoenix*, where the trees are never touched by autumn, *ne feallað þær on foldan fealwe blostman*, 'blossoms never there fall fallow to the ground'. On earth, however, the association with autumn leaves and mortality often lends this word a tinge of melancholy, even when it's being used as a colour description. This is how it appears in *The Battle of Maldon*, a poem that commemorates the defeat of an English army in battle against the Vikings on the coast of Essex in 991.[12] Though the poem opens with an exchange of defiant speeches between the English leader, Byrhtnoth, and the Vikings, it soon becomes clear that Byrhtnoth and his men will lose this battle: they are facing death, and the poem explores how they cope with that prospect as it comes to seem inevitable. This is a poem about courage in the face of disaster – about how we choose to act when we know death is near.

For Byrhtnoth, a noble and experienced warrior, that moment of choice comes midway through the battle. He is pierced by a Viking spear and mortally wounded, but he fights on until the time comes when he can fight no more:

> Then the fallow-hilted sword fell to the ground;
> he could not hold the hard blade,
> wield the weapon. Yet still the grey-haired warrior
> spoke words, encouraged the soldiers,
> commanded them to press onwards as good comrades.
> Then he could no longer stand steady on his feet.

There again are the alliterating words, 'fallow' and 'fall', and the use of the autumnal colour to describe his sword strikes a mournful note: the old soldier has received his death-wound, and his fall is coming. Now all his men are facing death, and they give speeches in which they grimly announce their choice to stay and fight to the end rather than flee the battlefield. They don't speak of fighting for their land or king; their only wish is to live up to the oaths they have sworn Byrhtnoth and each other, and to go to their deaths bravely. The last and most famous speech belongs to one of the oldest warriors, whose words sum up the mood and message of this deeply moving poem:

> Courage must be the firmer, heart the keener,
> mind must be the greater, as our strength diminishes.
> Here lies our leader all cut down,
> a good man in the dust. Anyone who chooses to leave
> this battle-play now will always regret it.
> I am old in years; I will not go,
> but by the side of my lord, the man so dear,
> I mean to lay myself down.

THE TREE'S GRIEF

This association between the fall of the leaves and the inevitable approach of death recurs several times in Anglo-Saxon poetry. One powerful example appears in the wisdom poem *Maxims I*, from the Exeter Book. In this compilation of proverb-like observations about life and the natural world, the poem moves from one concise statement to another without any obvious link; the reader is left to draw their own connections, reflecting on what brings these ideas or images together. In the following lines, we're presented with three seemingly unrelated statements, but it's not difficult to perceive what links them:

> A woman and man must bring into the world
> a child by birth. A tree on the earth
> must lose its leaves, the branches mourn.
> Those who are ready must go; the doomed die
> and every day struggle against their departure
> from the world.

The verb translated here as 'mourn', *gnornian*, is elsewhere used of human mourners, so the attribution of emotion to the tree is very deliberate: it's grieving for the loss of its leaves. The sound of the word contributes to its melancholy mood, echoing the noise of a wailing wind in bare branches as their leaves are stripped away.

The tree's grief, so tenderly described, is set in parallel with human experiences of loss. The poem places it between two statements about birth and death, and – without any overt link – uses the tree's sorrow to connect the two. The tree's mourning gives voice to what is *not* being said: that when parents bring a child into the world, they give birth to someone who will die, grieve and be grieved for. The tree mourning its leaves and the human parents become one, a bond strengthened by the language in which they are described:

the alliteration links *bearn*, 'child, bairn', and *beam*, 'tree', two words that look and sound alike, and the word used for the trees' branches is the human-like *leomu*, 'limbs'.

This mood is echoed in *The Fortunes of Mortals*, a catalogue poem which explores one of the traditional themes of Anglo-Saxon wisdom literature: the different ways people can die. It's a solemn and gloomy subject, yet the poem has a beautiful opening:

> Very often it happens, through the power of God,
> that a man and woman bring into the world
> a child by birth, and clothe it in garments,
> coax it and cheer it, until the time comes
> with the passing of years that the young limbs,
> life-filled members, become fully grown.
> So the father and mother carry and lead,
> provide and prepare. God alone knows
> what the winters will bring the growing child.

This is a remarkable depiction of Anglo-Saxon parenthood. It begins just like the lines from *Maxims I*, but develops the idea beyond the child's birth to describe the years of its growth and the mutual care of mother and father as they lovingly tend to their child. Yet the parents can only do so much: they can bring the child up, but only God knows what will happen next – what the winters will bring.

And from the ensuing catalogue we learn that what the winters bring is always ultimately, in some way, death. The poet begins to list all the different ways in which people can die: devoured by a wolf, destroyed by hunger, killed in battle and many more. It's the strangest of subjects from a modern perspective, and yet it's weirdly mesmerizing. By dwelling on the details of these deaths, the poet conjures up vivid scenes of everyday life. At one point he shows us a tree, and a man falling to his death:

One in the wood must from a high tree
fall, featherless yet in flight,
dancing in the air, until he is no longer
a growth of the tree; then he drops
to the roots, spirit darkening, bereft of his soul,
falls to the ground. His spirit takes a journey.

These lines have a kind of horrible beauty. As the man falls, the poet chooses to pause in this stomach-churning moment, giving six lines for the split-second instant between fall and landing. As the man slips, suddenly he's flying: in that moment he dances in the air, light as a leaf as it drifts to the ground. The next moment he drops to the roots with a thud, no longer weightless but heavy as a ripe apple, and body and soul part ways. It's sudden, vertiginous and very unsettling. Once again, we see an association between human progeny and the produce of a tree, but with grim irony in this scene of death. All this poem's deaths are given more pathos by being framed with that opening description of parenthood: you can't help seeing the man falling from the tree as somebody's child, the recipient of some parent's loving care. The tree doesn't mourn for him, but no doubt his parents do.

A link between trees and grief seems to have been deeply rooted in the Anglo-Saxon poetic tradition, since it's also found in Old Norse poetry. Old Norse sometimes offers close parallels to Old English wisdom poems like *Maxims I*, and when that happens we may be looking at remnants of the ancient oral tradition out of which both Anglo-Saxon and Scandinavian wisdom poetry grew.[13] In Norse mythology, a link between trees and humans goes right back to our beginnings. The Norse gods are said to have made the first pair of humans out of driftwood they found on the shore: endued with life and intelligence, these trees became the father and mother of mankind.[14] It may be that something like this myth lies behind the frequent association between trees and humans in Old Norse poetry, sometimes specifically in the context of parental grief and the severing of the family line through the death of a child.[15] Leafless trees are used as a figure for the desolate mourner, made vulnerable by the loss of children, kinsmen or friends. One example occurs in a poem called *Hávamál*, 'Sayings of the High One'.[16] This poem is a collection of wisdom statements, in many ways comparable to *Maxims I* and with some close echoes of the Anglo-Saxon poem; here, however, the sayings are attributed to Odin, father of the gods. One likens a friendless man to a fir-tree:

> The fir-tree withers
> which stands in a field;
> neither bark nor needles shelter it.
> So it is for a man
> whom no one loves;
> why should he live long?

The implication is that friends and family give shelter to a man, as the branches of a tree protect the trunk; stripped of its foliage, the tree is vulnerable, withering away without the hope of new growth. Odin – who made humans from trees, who hanged himself from a tree to gain wisdom – knew all about trees, but also all about grief.[17] Like the parents of *Maxims I*, Odin too was imagined as a grieving father: Old Norse sources tell how he lost his son Baldr, the bright and beautiful god, and knew as he mourned him that his son's death would mean the coming of Ragnarök, the end of the gods, heralded by the most terrible winter the world will ever know.[18] Perhaps that fear of apocalyptic winter is part of what lurks behind all these images of desolate trees, bare forever and never expecting another spring. But it's not all hopeless. According to Norse myth, human beings, unlike Odin himself, will survive Ragnarök – shielded from its danger in a wood, perhaps beneath Yggdrasil, the great world-tree.[19]

Our final example of Anglo-Saxon autumnal poetry comes from *The Seafarer*, a moment of melancholy which occurs as the poem contemplates earthly transience and death. Reflecting on the fleeting nature of worldly glory, the seafarer laments:

> The days are departed,
> all the glories of the kingdom of the earth;
> there are now no kings nor caesars
> nor gold-givers such as once there were,
> when they performed among themselves so many
>   magnificent deeds,
> and lived in most lordly majesty.
> Fallen is all that troop, joys are departed,
> weaker ones now live and possess the world,
> gain use of it by their labour. Glory is bowed down,
> the nobility of earth ages and grows sere,
> as now does every man across the world.
> Old age comes on him, his face grows pale,
> the grey-haired one grieves, knows his friends of old
>   times,
> the sons of princes, have been given up to the earth.

This is a picture of societal as well as individual decline, the autumn of a whole civilization. Just as every mortal grows old, so the earth itself is ageing and its best days are over. The great kings and emperors of the past (called *caseras*, 'caesars', evoking a long-dead Roman glory) have been replaced by the weaker generations of the present day. As we saw back in Advent, this was a very common idea in early medieval thinking, and it's often expressed in autumnal terms.

The autumn tints in *The Seafarer*'s version of this theme lie in the words *blæd* and *searað*, which both bear senses relating to plants and trees. As we've seen, *blæd* can mean 'glory', but also 'growing thing' – it refers to any produce of a plant, from fruits of the harvest to flowers and leaves. It's this *blæd* which is now 'bowed down' as the earth ages, and as it passes into autumn, it grows 'sere'. If 'fallow' refers to the colour of autumn leaves, 'sere' describes their texture: it means 'dry, withered', like plants when all moisture and power of growth is gone. Like 'fallow', this was a word which could be easily transferred from leaves to human beings. Here it suggests the failing strength of the waning world and the human body withering with age; to grow 'sere' is to grow old, to lose strength, to be brittle and dry in spirit and body.

This word survives in one sense in Modern English: it's the same as 'sear', meaning 'to burn, scorch', and you can see how the idea of dryness and withering up might link the senses of the word. The older, autumnal meaning of 'sere' is now less well known, but it has been kept alive as part of the poetic language of autumn, almost solely as a result of its use in Shakespeare's *Macbeth*. Towards the end of the play, as Macbeth contemplates his coming defeat and death, he says of himself:

> I have lived long enough: my way of life
> Is fall'n into the sere, the yellow leaf;
> And that which should accompany old age,
> As honour, love, obedience, troops of friends,
> I must not look to have.

This soldier, facing the autumn of his life, articulates the same sense of decline and loss as *The Seafarer*, even the same regret at the absence of 'troops of friends', the noble companions mourned by the Anglo-Saxon poem. Unlike the old soldiers of *The Battle of Maldon*, who face death together, he stands alone in the autumn of his days.

As it happens, *Macbeth* is the only one of Shakespeare's plays to take place in the same world as Anglo-Saxon poetry. Its Scotland is contemporary with the reign of Edward the Confessor, who lends his aid to the army that is, at this moment in the play, on its way to defeat Macbeth. At distant remove, the story of the play – though not the witches and ghosts – is based on actual events of the 1050s, as recorded in medieval sources including the *Anglo-Saxon Chronicle*.[20] The ageing Macbeth is to be replaced as king of Scotland by the young Malcolm, who would eventually marry Edward's great-niece, Margaret – thus uniting himself to the last surviving branch of the Anglo-Saxon royal family and helping to ensure its continuation after the Norman Conquest. A famous medieval prophecy imagined the Anglo-Saxon royal line as a green tree, cut down at Edward's death and severed from its trunk, growing withered and sere; after the daughter of Malcolm and Margaret, Edith, married the Norman king Henry I in November 1100, it was said that the dead tree miraculously came back to life again and had another spring.[21]

That was far in the future when *The Seafarer* was written. We don't know exactly when that was, but we do know that the manuscript which preserves the poem was given to Exeter Cathedral in around 1072, just about the time Margaret was settling into her new life in Scotland. As we approach the end of the Anglo-Saxon year, we might imagine what it could have been like to read these lines from *The Seafarer* in that particular historical moment, in the immediate aftermath of the Norman Conquest. The poem's regret for the departed glory of past kings might have seemed especially poignant, and the lament for lost troops might have awakened recent griefs. This autumnal mood is timeless, but at certain times it can strike close to home.

12

THE MONTH OF BLOOD

THE HELPFUL DEAD

The beginning of November is now marked by a chain of three
linked days, a season for remembering the dead: Halloween, All
Saints' Day and All Souls' Day. Of these three, only one was observed
in Anglo-Saxon England. During the first millennium, feasts in
celebration of all the saints developed on different days across the
international church, and a feast of All Saints on 1 November began
to appear in Anglo-Saxon sources in the late eighth century.[1] In
Old English it was called *ealra halgena mæssedæg*, 'the mass-day of
all hallows'; *halga* is the usual Old English word for 'saint', related
to *halig*, 'holy'. By the later Middle Ages, this had become *halwe* or
halow, and so the season of All Saints was known by names such
as 'All Hallowmas', or simply 'Hallowtide'.[2] The other two days of
Hallowtide were later additions to the English festival calendar. All
Souls' Day, for remembering the faithful dead not yet in heaven, ori-
ginated at Cluny and began to be regularly observed in England from
the thirteenth century. The widespread observance of Halloween
in England is more recent still; the eve of All Saints' Day seems
never to have been an important part of the Anglo-Saxon or later
English Hallowtide, at least not in the form we understand it today,
as a time for encountering ghosts or spirits.[3] In the past few decades Halloween has become popular throughout Britain, but even
a hundred years ago it was absent from most of England, while
being widely kept in Ireland, Scotland, Wales and parts of northwest

England.[4] This seems to reflect a clear dividing line between regions of what we might call Anglo-Saxon and Celtic culture in Britain and Ireland, and that's supported by the complete absence of Halloween from Old English sources.

All Saints' Day, however, reflected a profound devotion to the saints which was as deeply felt in Anglo-Saxon England as it was anywhere in the medieval church. For medieval Christians, the saints were the helpful and familiar dead, always only a prayer away, ready to rush to the aid of the living. Unlike the spirits of the modern version of Halloween, they were not to be feared or avoided, unless one had done something to offend them; they possessed a power that could be awe-inspiring, but they only ever worked for the forces of good. Medieval Christians were constantly speaking to the dead, appealing for their help and coming close to them in their relics. To believe in the saints was to be part of a vast community, a fellowship that encompassed the living and the dead in one.

By the end of the Anglo-Saxon period, the English church commemorated a huge number of saints, many of them shared throughout the wider church, many English-born. Ælfric, writing at the end of the tenth century, comments proudly that 'the English are not deprived of the saints of God,' and he means it as an emphatic understatement.[5] From saintly abbesses like Æthelthryth of Ely and Hilda of Whitby to hermits like Guthlac and Cuthbert, bishops like Dunstan or kings like Oswald of Northumbria, from the missionaries of the seventh century to the martyrs of the Viking wars, the English church had hundreds of holy men and women to celebrate.

Ælfric makes this comment at the end of his *Passion of St Edmund*, in which he tells the story of one of Anglo-Saxon England's most popular saints – Edmund, king of East Anglia, who had been killed by a Viking army in November 869. Edmund's story forms part of a collection of saints' lives which Ælfric probably wrote in the 990s. He introduces this collection with some remarks, phrased in appealingly matter-of-fact tones, about the company of the saints:

> We will write about many wonders in this book, because God is wonderful in his saints, as we said before; and the wonders of his saints bring honour to him, because he worked those wonders through them. An earthly king has many thegns and various officers; he cannot be a worthy king unless he has the things that are fitting to him and such attendants to offer him obedience. So it is also with Almighty God who created all things: it is fitting for him that he should have holy thegns, who carry out his will, and of these there are many among mankind, whom he chose from the world, so that no learned person – even if he knows many things – can write down their names, because no one knows them. They are beyond number, as is fitting for God. But we wanted to compile this book about some of them, for people's encouragement and for our protection, so they may intercede for us with Almighty God, just as we make their wonders known in the world.[6]

For all his talk of wonders, Ælfric makes it sound very ordinary: God, like any human king, has 'thegns' – noble followers and soldiers – to do his work, and the living can interact with them as readily as with any earthly attendants. The daily company of the dead is seen as entirely normal and profoundly reassuring.

In the context of Ælfric's *Lives of Saints*, the metaphor of saints as God's 'thegns' is one chosen to suit a specific audience. The book is dedicated to Ælfric's patrons, a father and son named Æthelweard and Æthelmær, who were themselves officers of an earthly king. As we near the end of our journey through the Anglo-Saxon year, the fortunes of this family, over three generations, can tell us something about how England was changing as the Anglo-Saxon period itself drew to an end. These men belonged to one of the most powerful families in tenth-century England, descended from the royal line of the kings of Wessex through one of the brothers of Alfred the Great (which means they claimed Scyld Scefing as an ancestor).[7] Æthelweard served as ealdorman of the western shires, governing a region in southwest England and acting as an influential counsellor to King Æthelred.[8] In the closing years of the tenth century, as Viking raids posed an ever-increasing threat to the stability of Æthelred's kingdom, Æthelweard was prominent in negotiations with the Vikings, hoping to exchange money for peace. Neither these arrangements, nor military resistance such as Byrhtnoth and his men tried to mount at Maldon in 991, kept the Vikings away for long. Under the pressure of these attacks the king's court became riven by internal conflict, and Æthelmær, who succeeded his father as ealdorman, fell out of favour. The ideal relationship between God and his thegns which Ælfric describes in his *Lives of Saints* could be a long way from the human reality, as Æthelweard and Æthelmær must have known.

Amid these worldly cares, both father and son occupied themselves with literary and spiritual interests. Æthelweard wrote a chronicle in Latin – a very unusual achievement for an early medieval layman – and for many years he and Æthelmær gave material support to Ælfric's work as a preacher and teacher.[9] Æthelmær was the founder of Cerne Abbey in Dorset, where Ælfric wrote most of his works, and in 1005 he founded another abbey, in the village of Eynsham near Oxford, and made Ælfric its first abbot. Ælfric spent the last years of his life there in retirement, though the troubles of the day pressed close at hand, with Viking armies raiding just miles from Eynsham.

In the autumn of 1016, these years of warfare came to an end with a final battle. On 18 October 1016 the young Danish king Cnut defeated Æthelred's son, Edmund Ironside, at the Battle of Assandun in Essex and won control of England. As he established his power, Cnut had one of Æthelmær's sons killed, but another son, a monk, was chosen to anoint him as king, and in 1020 became Archbishop of Canterbury. This son, Æthelnoth, adapted himself to the reign of the new king with the same political skill his father and grandfather had shown. With Æthelnoth's guidance, Cnut became an enthusiastic patron of the English church – and especially of English saints. King and archbishop worked together to honour saints including Edith of Wilton and Ælfheah of Canterbury, a recent martyr of the Viking invasions.[10] Cnut also supported the veneration of St Edmund, the king whose story prompted Ælfric's comments on the proliferation of English saints. In the 1030s, Cnut founded a church at Bury St Edmunds and it was consecrated on the anniversary of the Battle of Assandun, as if the Viking king was dedicating his victory to the Anglo-Saxon saint. In part through shared veneration of the saints, Æthelnoth helped to ensure a degree of continuity from the past in Danish-ruled England. He died a day or two before All Saints' Day in October 1038, three years after Cnut, and was remembered by those who had known him as 'Æthelnoth the Good'.[11]

BLOOD AND BLESSING

As we arrive back in November, we've come full circle; winter is once more in sight. The last festival we'll explore takes us back to the beginning of Anglo-Saxon history, very close to the place where we began, but also points us forwards beyond the traditional end of the Anglo-Saxon period in the autumn of 1066. This festival is Martinmas, the feast of St Martin of Tours, celebrated on 11 November. St Martin (d. 397) was a soldier in the Roman army in Gaul who converted to Christianity and became a monk and bishop. The patron saint of soldiers, he's usually shown in medieval art as a soldier mounted on a horse, cutting his cloak in half to share it with a beggar – an act of charity appropriate for a saint with a winter feast.

Ælfric, recounting this story in his homily for Martinmas, tells how Martin met a beggar 'in midwinter's chill' and 'couldn't find it in his heart' (*ne mihte on his mode afindan*) not to help him.[12]

In the Middle Ages Martinmas was a popular festival across Europe, partly because it fell on the cusp of autumn and winter. It was associated with the slaughter of animals – especially pigs and cattle – in preparation for the winter, the laying-in of stocks of meat to be cured and salted to last through the barren months ahead. This meant it was a good time for a feast, with a supply of meat on hand and the prospect of cold dark months to come. When it reached Anglo-Saxon England, Martinmas seems to have directly replaced a similar festival at this time of year in the pre-Christian calendar. Bede tells us that the month equivalent to November for the pagan Anglo-Saxons was called *Blotmonað*, 'month of sacrifices', because at that time 'the cattle which were to be slaughtered were consecrated to their gods'.[13] He adds, 'Thanks be to you, Good Jesu, who has turned us away from such vanities and granted to us to offer you the sacrifice of praise.' These rituals were presumably linked to the winter slaughter of animals: if *Haligmonað* was holy because of customs celebrating the end of harvest, this is the next stage in the agricultural calendar, important enough to mark with sacrifices to the gods.

The first element of the month-name is *blot*, 'sacrifice', though some Anglo-Saxon sources instead give the form *Blodmonað*, 'blood-month'. The words *blot* and *blod* aren't always easy to distinguish in Old English, and there's good reason for their similarity: they're etymologically linked, probably connected by the use of blood in pagan sacrificial rituals and rites of consecration. The nature of *blot* rituals at different times of the year is much more fully attested in Scandinavian sources and archaeological evidence than in anything from Anglo-Saxon England, but there are likely to have been some parallels.[14] Our knowledge of how the pagan Anglo-Saxons might have made these sacrifices is blotted out by such comments as Bede's, drawing a veil over the details of rituals he considered 'vanities', but the month-name records at least that they did take place.

Not all was obliterated, however. Bede draws his readers' attention to the contrast between those pagan rituals of sacrifice and the Christian replacement, 'the sacrifice of praise'. One interesting aspect of that process of replacement was how the language of paganism was preserved and adapted by the Anglo-Saxon church, even as its rituals were discarded. The vocabulary of sacrifice is a striking example. In surviving Old English sources *blotan*, 'to sacrifice', is used of pagan worship, in the context of classical antiquity as well as the Anglo-Saxon past. In that form, the word eventually died out and didn't survive into later English. But the related verb *bletsian*, 'to consecrate with blood', was chosen early in the history of the Anglo-Saxon church as an equivalent to Latin *benedicere*, so it survived and came down to the present-day as a very common word: 'bless'. The root of *benedicere* in Latin relates to 'speaking well', so it's about words of praise and blessing, not rituals of blood-sacrifice; over time *bletsian* gradually took on those senses, losing its bloody connotations. It became part of the standard vocabulary of Anglo-Saxon Christianity, used in a variety of contexts regarding blessing, consecration and hallowing with words or rituals such as the sign of the cross. As *bletsung* became *blessing*, the similarity between the alliterating *bless* and *bliss* meant they often appeared together in medieval poetry and began to influence each other's meaning. It's a remarkable semantic development, hiding in plain sight: 'bless' has come so far from its bloodstained origins, yet the basic sense, 'to make holy', has not actually changed – only the means of doing it. Such Christianization of pagan vocabulary seems to have been a regular part of the conversion process in early Anglo-Saxon England, and there are other, less dramatic examples of pagan words given Christian meanings, as we've seen with festivals like Easter. Where concepts really were unfamiliar, it was necessary to borrow from Latin, and words like 'bishop', 'monk' and 'mass' represent early borrowings from Latin into Old English. But in the case of several fundamental religious concepts, some old words were preserved in surprising ways.

It wasn't only the language of the pagan past that was given new meaning. In November, in what had been *Blotmonað*, the slaughter of animals in preparation for winter didn't cease to be necessary, even once the pagan gods had ceased to oversee it. In the Christian era, it quickly became absorbed into the celebration of Martinmas. St Martin was already a well-established saint long before the Anglo-Saxons converted to Christianity – and here we return to the place we started, with Æthelbert, king of Kent, and his wife Bertha. The oldest Anglo-Saxon building in England still in use is an ancient church, just outside the walls of Canterbury, which is dedicated to St Martin. This was, Bede tells us, Queen Bertha's own church, where she used to pray in the days when her husband and his kingdom were still pagan.[15] It probably has an even older history than this, since it has Roman bricks built into its walls. The dedication to St Martin must reflect Bertha's influence: Bertha was a member of the Frankish royal dynasty, which had close links with Tours and the veneration of St Martin, and he would have been a natural choice as patron of her church.[16] St Augustine, on his way to convert Æthelbert and his kingdom, probably passed through Tours, and it's likely that St Martin's feast was among the first to be celebrated by the new English church.

It might not have been long before the sacrifices of *Blotmonað* became the festivities of Martinmas. Bede speaks of replacing animal sacrifices with the sacrifice of praise, but this replacement must have involved much continuity, if the focus was the same pre-winter slaughter. Gregory the Great, writing to the Augustinian mission to advise them how to deal with the pagan Anglo-Saxons, specifically mentions replacing the sacrifice of cattle to pagan gods with Christian festivals:

Because they are in the habit of slaughtering much cattle as
sacrifices to devils, some solemnity ought to be given them
in exchange for this ... Do not let them sacrifice animals to
the devil, but let them slaughter animals for their own food
to the praise of God, and let them give thanks to the Giver
of all things for His bountiful provision.[17]

Martinmas seems a perfect example of this process of adaptation.
It was still essential to prepare for winter, whatever the source of
blessing they sought to help them through it.

At Queen Bertha's church in Canterbury, St Martin is associated
with one of the earliest dedications in the history of Anglo-Saxon
Christianity – older than the English church or England itself. But
he's linked with one of the latest, too. St Martin was popular in
Normandy, as in England, and as the patron saint of soldiers he
was often associated with military victories. In the eleventh century, when William the Conqueror, new king of England, founded
an abbey in Sussex to commemorate his victory at the Battle of
Hastings – supposedly on the very site of the battle itself, where so
much blood had been shed – he chose to dedicate it to St Martin.[18]

THE AUTUMN OF ANGLO-SAXON ENGLAND

That dedication, even as it marked a seismic moment of political and
cultural change, illustrated an important form of continuity too.
In many ways, the transition from Anglo-Saxon to Anglo-Norman
England made very little difference to the pattern of the year which
we've been following in this book. As the abbeys founded at Battle
and Bury St Edmunds commemorate, England was conquered twice
in the eleventh century, in battles fought fifty years apart – almost
to the very day – on 18 October 1016 and 14 October 1066. It would
be neat, coming round again to the beginning of winter, to end like
this: just as in the quotation from *The Menologium* with which we

began Chapter One, where 'Winter's Day' marches in with armies of frost to capture the summer fields, so on these autumn days first Cnut, then William the Conqueror, seized the kingdom of England.

But that would be too simplistic. In terms of the human relationship to the cycle of the seasons, political upheavals don't necessarily introduce huge changes. Wars and invasions may temporarily disrupt the harvest and interfere with a society's ability to feed itself; Viking raids did that, as did William's terrible Harrying of the North in the years after the Norman Conquest. The rhythm of the agricultural year remained consistent, though, and so did the feasts and festivals that marked its turning. Among the new Norman leaders imported in the years after the conquest to govern English churches and monasteries, there was some initial scepticism about a few of the feasts kept by the Anglo-Saxon church: some saints came under question, and some local festivals fell out of use.[19] But it did not last long. The basic structure of the church year was already shared by the Normans and the English, as were many saints – such as St Martin – and by the twelfth century the Normans were enthusiastically adopting English saints too. St Edmund became one of their favourites, as he had been one of the Danes'.[20]

As the liturgical year and the agricultural cycle kept on turning, the work of many of the Anglo-Saxon writers who had thought about or celebrated these cycles remained relevant and necessary. The granaries of Anglo-Saxon libraries were heaped with harvested stores, and many kinds of learning were not forgotten, but reused and remade. Bede, in particular, was highly honoured by Anglo-Norman historians, who made extensive use of his work, as well as of Byrhtferth's writings and the anonymous annals of the *Anglo-Saxon Chronicle*, to construct their own narratives of English history.[21] Ælfric's works, too, continued to be read and adapted long after the Norman Conquest. While invasion and cultural change in the centuries after his death altered other aspects of Anglo-Saxon literature, the pastoral work of the church for which Ælfric had laboured went steadily on: the festivals he had explained so carefully in his sermons continued to be celebrated, so his work still provided an important resource for later preachers and teachers.[22]

What did not survive, however, was the tradition of Old English poetry which we have been drawing on throughout this book. The new Norman elite had their own forms of poetry, in their own language, and they knew or cared little about stories like *Beowulf* or the poems of the Exeter Book. As the English language changed in the centuries after the conquest, the complex and archaic vocabulary in which most Anglo-Saxon poetry is composed became gradually more and more incomprehensible, and this poetic tradition withered and died. That might have happened even without the conquerors, since the tradition was probably already in retreat some decades before 1066. The four major manuscripts in which most Old English poetry survives all date to the years around 1000, but the poems they contain were likely written many years earlier. Along with some short eleventh-century poems in the *Anglo-Saxon Chronicle* commemorating the deaths of kings (including William the Conqueror), *The Battle of Maldon* is one of the last surviving new poems written in the Old English tradition – almost self-consciously so in its deployment of heroic language and tropes. This poem about facing death looked back to a way of life that was already dying. By the time poetry in English began once more to be composed in quantity, in the thirteenth and fourteenth centuries, poetic culture and especially literary interpretations of the seasons had been heavily influenced by the tastes of the French-speaking elite. In the seasonal poetry of Chaucer and his contemporaries, praising May as a time for lovers, there is essentially no continuity from the Anglo-Saxon tradition.

At the time when the two poems we considered in the Introduction, *The Menologium* and *Maxims II*, were written down in a manuscript of the *Anglo-Saxon Chronicle* in the mid-eleventh century, they too were part of this waning tradition. They were intended to serve as a preface to the particular view of history represented by the *Chronicle*: one that situates human events within the larger context of the natural world and the cycles of sacred time, which go on turning whatever upheavals the course of history may bring. By using these poems to introduce the *Chronicle*, the compiler of the manuscript draws our attention to how the events of history and the cycle of the year may intersect with each other. *The Menologium* begins with the birth of Christ, and so does the *Anglo-Saxon Chronicle*, though it locates the event in reference not to the festival of Christmas but to a historical era: 'Octavian ruled 56 winters, and in the 42nd year of his reign Christ was born.' From that similar starting point the two texts follow their divergent courses, reckoning their different kinds of time. The poem describes a single, unchanging yearly cycle, while the *Anglo-Saxon Chronicle* follows a linear model of history covering more than a thousand years, but the two intersect repeatedly, every time the *Chronicle* dates events by reference to festivals and seasons of the year. The last entry in this version of the *Chronicle* is for 1066, and it contains a memorable cluster of significant events dated to points in the festival year. From Edward the Confessor, spending Christmas in Westminster at 'Midwinter' but dead and buried by 'Twelfth Day', the year runs through moments of political crisis dated to Easter, harvest and the Nativity of the Virgin Mary, as Harold Godwineson first gained, then fought to keep, the English crown. The last events recorded are a battle in Yorkshire between an English army and the forces of the Norwegian invader, Harald Hardrada, on 'the Vigil of St Matthew the Apostle' (20 September), then a few days later Harold Godwineson's triumphant defeat of the Norwegian king at Stamford Bridge. Here the entry breaks off, and the *Chronicle* stops before reaching Hastings. For whatever reason, the chronicler was unable to write about that last autumn day.

When Christmas came that year, England had a new king, and would never be the same again. But Midwinter itself would have looked no different, and the cycle began another round. That last tumultuous year – in one sense, the last year of Anglo-Saxon history – was full of surprises and upheavals, yet the yearly cycle was stable and unchanging. And so it continued for many centuries. All the festivals named in this entry for 1066 would still have been familiar five hundred years later, when the architects of the English Reformation set about adapting or suppressing them. Even after the Reformation, when many saints' days were stripped from the calendar, the high points of the festival year – from Christmas to Lady Day, Midsummer to Michaelmas – remained the same. It was really only over the course of the twentieth century, with its dramatic social and cultural change, that the cycle the Anglo-Saxons knew became increasingly distant and unfamiliar, especially as more and more people lost touch with the rhythms of the agricultural year. Some ancient festivals which were celebrated continuously for a millennium or more pass almost unnoticed today. But in recent years others, such as Candlemas and Lammas, have been experiencing a revival, and in secular modern Britain it's not only those drawn to their religious significance who find meaning in these feasts. Such festivals offer opportunities to mark the passage of time, to gather in community with others and to acknowledge the profound value of our relationship with the natural world. In a time of ecological crisis, Anglo-Saxon poems which recognize how fundamentally we are connected to the rhythms of nature – how dependent we are on the well-being of the earth, how grateful we should be for its gifts and its beauties – speak truths we still need to hear.

The cycle of the seasons, to which poets have so often turned as a reminder that nothing in this world is stable, is in fact one of the great constants in life. In some ways, the thousand years or more that have elapsed since the poems in this book were written have changed our world beyond recognition – but every year, when the blossom springs and the leaves fall, we see what the Anglo-Saxon poets saw. The revolving cycle finds us each year at a different moment in the story of our own lives; the unfolding events of history change us, but the seasons do not change. Every year, the familiar sights, words and stories of the passing seasons will bring forth new fruit for us, because every year we bring different things to them and take different things away. So, year by year, the cycle may give meaning to the passing of our own brief days, and we may become, like the winter-weathered sage of *Maxims II, fyrngearum frod*: 'wise with by-gone years'.

REFERENCES

INTRODUCTION: THE ANGLO-SAXON YEAR

1   For a useful overview of the history of the calendar in England, see Steve Roud, *The English Year* (London, 2008), pp. xxv–xxxiv.
2   For discussion of the influence of climate, agriculture and economic factors on the early medieval calendar, see P. S. Langeslag, *Seasons in the Literatures of the Medieval North* (Cambridge, 2015), pp. 1–26, and on Anglo-Saxon farming, see Debby Banham and Rosamond Faith, *Anglo-Saxon Farms and Farming* (Oxford, 2014). Surviving liturgical calendars from Anglo-Saxon England are collected in Rebecca Rushforth, ed., *Saints in English Kalendars before AD 1100* (London, 2008).
3   Bede, *The Reckoning of Time*, trans. Faith Wallis (Liverpool, 2004).
4   Ibid., p. 53.
5   See R. I. Page, 'Anglo-Saxon Paganism: The Evidence of Bede', in *Pagans and Christians: The Interplay between Christian Latin and Traditional Germanic Cultures in Early Medieval Europe*, ed. T. Hofstra, L.A.J.R. Houwen and A. A. MacDonald (Groningen, 1995), pp. 99–129; Philip A. Shaw, *Pagan Goddesses in the Early Germanic World: Eostre, Hreda and the Cult of Matrons* (London, 2011), pp. 49–50.
6   Bede, *Reckoning of Time*, p. 101.
7   Earl R. Anderson, *Folk Taxonomies in Early English* (Madison, NJ, 2003), pp. 219–66.
8   Langeslag, *Seasons in the Literatures of the Medieval North*; Anderson, *Folk Taxonomies*, pp. 219–66.
9   Thomas J. Talley, *The Origins of the Liturgical Year* (Collegeville, MN, 1991); C. Philipp E. Nothaft, *Dating the Passion: The Life of Jesus and the Emergence of Scientific Chronology (200–1600)* (Leiden, 2012).
10 John Blair, *The Church in Anglo-Saxon Society* (Oxford, 2005), pp. 8–49.
11 Bede, *Ecclesiastical History of the English People*, ed. Bertram Colgrave and R.A.B. Mynors (Oxford, 1969), pp. 108–9.

12 See Mary Clayton, *The Cult of the Virgin Mary in Anglo-Saxon England* (Cambridge, 2002), p. 37.

13 Bede, *Ecclesiastical History*, pp. 334–5; on Hadrian and Theodore, see Bernhard Bischoff and Michael Lapidge, eds, *Biblical Commentaries from the Canterbury School of Theodore and Hadrian* (Cambridge, 1994).

14 For discussion of changes in agricultural practice during the Anglo-Saxon period, see Banham and Faith, *Anglo-Saxon Farms and Farming*, pp. 293–300; on climate change across the period, see pp. 3–4.

15 Bede, *Ecclesiastical History*, pp. 566–7.

16 See Patrick Wormald, *The Times of Bede: Studies in Early English Christian Society and Its Historian*, ed. Stephen Baxter (Oxford, 2006), pp. 106–34; Sarah Foot, 'The Making of *Angelcynn*: English Identity before the Norman Conquest', *Transactions of the Royal Historical Society*, VI (1996), pp. 25–49.

17 Christine Rauer, ed., *The Old English Martyrology: Edition, Translation and Commentary* (Cambridge, 2013).

18 Thom Gobbitt, ed., 'Gerefa', *Early English Laws*, https://earlyenglishlaws.ac.uk, accessed 14 October 2021.

19 On the dates of royal assemblies, see Levi Roach, *Kingship and Consent in Anglo-Saxon England, 871–978: Assemblies and the State in the Early Middle Ages* (Cambridge, 2013), pp. 71–6.

20 On the development of the *Chronicle*, see Pauline Stafford, *After Alfred: Anglo-Saxon Chronicles and Chroniclers, 900–1150* (Oxford, 2020); for a translation of the different versions, see Michael Swanton, trans., *The Anglo-Saxon Chronicles* (London, 2000).

21 Ælfric, *De temporibus anni*, ed. Martin Blake (Cambridge, 2009).

22 Byrhtferth, *Enchiridion*, ed. Peter S. Baker and Michael Lapidge (Oxford, 1995), pp. 66–7.

23 Katherine O'Brien O'Keeffe, ed., *The Anglo-Saxon Chronicle MS. C* (Cambridge, 2001); Stafford, *After Alfred*, pp. 190–206.

24 For an edition and translation of *The Menologium*, and discussion of other metrical calendars of this type, see Kazutomo Karasawa, ed., *The Old English Metrical Calendar (Menologium)* (Cambridge, 2015).

25 For discussion of Anglo-Saxon attitudes to animals and the natural world, see Jennifer Neville, *Representations of the Natural World in Old English Poetry* (Cambridge, 1999).

1 FROM WINTER INTO WINTER

1 Bede, *Ecclesiastical History of the English People*, ed. Bertram Colgrave and R.A.B. Mynors (Oxford, 1969), pp. 162–89.

2 Mohamed Eric Rahman Lacey, 'Birds and Bird-Lore in the Literature of Anglo-Saxon England', PhD thesis, University College London, 2013, pp. 167–95.

3 For discussion of this episode, see R. I. Page, 'Anglo-Saxon Paganism: The Evidence of Bede', in *Pagans and Christians: The Interplay between Christian Latin and Traditional Germanic Cultures in Early Medieval Europe*, ed. T. Hofstra, L.A.J.R. Houwen and A. A. MacDonald (Groningen, 1995), pp. 99–129.

4 Michael Swanton, ed., *Beowulf* (Manchester, 1997), pp. 84–9, lines 1063–160.

5 Bede, *Ecclesiastical History*, pp. 50–51 and 150–51; J. E. Turville-Petre, 'Hengest and Horsa', *Saga-Book of the Viking Society*, XIV (1953–7), pp. 273–90.

6 On the use of runes in Anglo-Saxon England, see R. I. Page, *An Introduction to English Runes* (Woodbridge, 1999).

7 Janet Backhouse, D. H. Turner and Leslie Webster, eds, *The Golden Age of Anglo-Saxon Art, 966–1066* (London, 1984), pp. 136–7.

2 MIDWINTER LIGHT

1 On Roman ruins in Anglo-Saxon literature, see Nicholas Howe, *Writing the Map of Anglo-Saxon England: Essays in Cultural Geography* (New Haven, CT, 2008), pp. 75–100.

2 Ælfric, *Catholic Homilies, The First Series: Text*, ed. Peter Clemoes (Oxford, 1997), p. 528; for the sources of this homily, see Ælfric, *Catholic Homilies: Introduction, Commentary and Glossary*, ed. Malcolm Godden (Oxford, 2000), pp. 334–44.

3 Snorri Sturluson, *Edda*, trans. Anthony Faulkes (London, 1998), pp. 52–3; Carolyne Larrington, trans., *The Poetic Edda* (Oxford, 1999), pp. 8–13.

4 Ælfric, *Catholic Homilies, First Series*, pp. 520–21.

5 On the relationship between these poems and their sources, see Susan Rankin, 'The Liturgical Background of the Old English Advent Lyrics: A Reappraisal', in *Learning and Literature in Anglo-Saxon England*, ed. Michael Lapidge and Helmut Gneuss (Cambridge, 1985), pp. 317–40.

6 Thomas J. Talley, *The Origins of the Liturgical Year* (Collegeville, MN, 1991), pp. 85–99.

7 Bede, *The Reckoning of Time*, trans. Faith Wallis (Liverpool, 2004), p. 87.

8 Ibid., p. 53; I have used my own translation here.

9 Audrey L. Meaney, 'Bede and Anglo-Saxon Paganism', *Parergon*, III (1985), pp. 1–29.

10 See for instance Felix Lieberman, ed., *Die Gesetze der Angelsachsen* (Halle, 1903), vol. I, p. 78.
11 Ælfric, *Catholic Homilies, First Series*, p. 286.
12 G. P. Cubbin, ed., *The Anglo-Saxon Chronicle* MS. D (Cambridge, 1996), p. 81.
13 Tiffany Beechy, '*Eala Earendel*: Extraordinary Poetics in Old English', *Modern Philology*, CVIII (2010), pp. 1–19. This poem and the name 'Earendel' served as significant inspirations for the young J.R.R. Tolkien as he developed his own imagined mythology; see Stuart Lee and Elizabeth Solopova, *The Keys of Middle-Earth: Discovering Medieval Literature through the Fiction of J.R.R. Tolkien* (Basingstoke, 2015), pp. 113–20.
14 On religious observances at Christmas in the early Anglo-Saxon church, see Arthur W. Haddan and William Stubbs, eds, *Councils and Ecclesiastical Documents Relating to Great Britain and Ireland* (Oxford, 1869–78), vol. III, pp. 412–13.
15 Dorothy Whitelock, ed., *English Historical Documents, c. 500–1042* (London, 1996), p. 416.
16 Ælfric, *Catholic Homilies, The Second Series: Text*, ed. Malcolm Godden (Oxford, 1979), p. 11.

3 NEW YEAR TO CANDLEMAS

1 Bede, *The Reckoning of Time*, trans. Faith Wallis (Liverpool, 2004), p. 53.
2 Christine Rauer, ed., *The Old English Martyrology: Edition, Translation and Commentary* (Cambridge, 2013), pp. 34–5, 42–3.
3 Michael Swanton, trans., *The Anglo-Saxon Chronicles* (London, 2000), pp. xv–xvi.
4 Ælfric, *Catholic Homilies, The First Series: Text*, ed. Peter Clemoes (Oxford, 1997), p. 228; Ælfric, *Catholic Homilies: Introduction, Commentary and Glossary*, ed. Malcolm Godden (Oxford, 2000), pp. 45–53.
5 For discussion of the eighteenth-century calendar reform and its background, see Robert Poole, *Time's Alteration: Calendar Reform in Early Modern England* (London, 1998).
6 Steve Roud, *The English Year* (London, 2008), pp. 1–8.
7 On Ælfric's comments, see R. M. Liuzza, ed., *Anglo-Saxon Prognostics: An Edition and Translation of Texts from London, British Library, MS. Cotton Tiberius A III* (Cambridge, 2010), pp. 45–7.
8 M. L. Cameron, *Anglo-Saxon Medicine* (Cambridge, 1993), pp. 161–2.
9 Ibid., pp. 162–3.

10 The texts quoted here can be found in László Sándor Chardonnens, ed., *Anglo-Saxon Prognostics, 900–1100: Study and Texts* (Leiden, 2007), pp. 483–5, 491–500.

11 See ibid., pp. 1–15.

12 Susan Irvine, ed., *The Anglo-Saxon Chronicle MS. E* (Cambridge, 2004), p. 86.

13 Roud, *The English Year*, pp. 10–13.

14 Thom Gobbitt, ed., 'Gerefa', *Early English Laws*, https://earlyenglishlaws.ac.uk, accessed 14 October 2021. On ploughing in Anglo-Saxon England, see Debby Banham and Rosamond Faith, *Anglo-Saxon Farms and Farming* (Oxford, 2014), pp. 41–59.

15 Ælfric, *Colloquy*, ed. G. N. Garmonsway (London, 1947), pp. 20–21.

16 For discussion of this ritual, see Thomas D. Hill, 'The *Æcerbot* Charm and Its Christian User', *Anglo-Saxon England*, VI (1977), pp. 213–21; John D. Niles, 'The *Æcerbot* Ritual in Context', in *Old English Literature in Context*, ed. John D. Niles (Cambridge, 1980), pp. 44–56; Karen Louise Jolly, *Popular Religion in Late Saxon England: Elf Charms in Context* (London, 1996), pp. 6–11.

17 On this point see especially Niles, 'The *Æcerbot* Ritual'.

18 Richard Sermon, 'Wassail! The Origins of a Drinking Toast', *Third Stone*, XLVI (2003), pp. 15–19.

19 Ronald Hutton, *The Stations of the Sun: A History of the Ritual Year in Britain* (Oxford, 2001), pp. 45–50; Roud, *The English Year*, pp. 555–9.

20 Niles, 'The *Æcerbot* Ritual', pp. 47–9; Hutton, *Stations of the Sun*, pp. 124–33.

21 M. Bradford Bedingfield, *The Dramatic Liturgy of Anglo-Saxon England* (Woodbridge, 2002), pp. 50–72; Mary Clayton, *The Cult of the Virgin Mary in Anglo-Saxon England* (Cambridge, 2002), pp. 25–47.

22 Ælfric, *Catholic Homilies, The First Series*, p. 257.

23 William Stubbs, ed., *Memorials of Saint Dunstan, Archbishop of Canterbury* (London, 1874), p. 54.

24 Stubbs, *Memorials of Saint Dunstan*, p. 73.

4 THE COMING OF SPRING

1 Michael Swanton, ed., *Beowulf* (Manchester, 1997), pp. 108–13, lines 1557–650.

2 Ælfric, *De temporibus anni*, ed. Martin Blake (Cambridge, 2009), p. 86.

3 Bede, *The Reckoning of Time*, trans. Faith Wallis (Liverpool, 2004), p. 54; see Philip A. Shaw, *Pagan Goddesses in the Early Germanic World: Eostre, Hreda and the Cult of Matrons* (London, 2011), pp. 73–97.

4 Shaw, *Pagan Goddesses*, pp. 94–5. Ælfric, who spent his life in Wessex, uses this name; see for instance Ælfric, *De temporibus anni*, p. 84.

5 M. A. Courtney, *Cornish Feasts and Folk-Lore* (Penzance, 1890), p. 24.

6 'Lide, n.', https://oed.com, accessed 14 October 2021.

7 Ælfric, *De temporibus anni*, p. 94 (abbreviations expanded).

8 Peter Godman, ed., *Poetry of the Carolingian Renaissance* (London, 1985), pp. 144–9.

9 Bertram Colgrave, ed., *Felix's Life of Saint Guthlac* (Cambridge, 1985).

10 Bertram Colgrave, ed., *Two Lives of Saint Cuthbert* (Cambridge, 1985), pp. 188–91.

5 CHEESE AND ASHES

1 For a late use of the word with the 'spring' meaning, see the poem 'Lenten Is Come with Love to Toune', in R. T. Davies, ed., *Medieval English Lyrics: A Critical Anthology* (London, 1978), pp. 84–6.

2 M. Bradford Bedingfield, *The Dramatic Liturgy of Anglo-Saxon England* (Woodbridge, 2002), pp. 74–5.

3 Frederick Tupper Jr, 'Anglo-Saxon Dæg-Mæl', *PMLA*, X (1895), pp. 111–241 (pp. 217–18).

4 Tupper, 'Anglo-Saxon Dæg-Mæl', pp. 213–14.

5 R. T. Hampson, *Medii Ævi Kalendarium* (London, 1841), vol. I, pp. 149–50.

6 Ælfric, *Catholic Homilies, The Second Series: Text*, ed. Malcolm Godden (Oxford, 1979), pp. 49–50.

7 Ælfric, *Catholic Homilies, The First Series: Text*, ed. Peter Clemoes (Oxford, 1997), p. 265.

8 Ronald Hutton, *The Stations of the Sun: A History of the Ritual Year in Britain* (Oxford, 2001), pp. 151–68; Steve Roud, *The English Year* (London, 2008), pp. 62–85.

9 Tupper, 'Anglo-Saxon Dæg-Mæl', pp. 216–17.

10 Roud, *The English Year*, p. 62.

11 Ælfric, *Lives of Saints*, ed. Walter W. Skeat (London, 1881–1900), vol. I, p. 262.

12 Ælfric, *Catholic Homilies, The Second Series*, pp. 63–4 (punctuation added).

13 On treasure in Old English poetry, see Elizabeth M. Tyler, *Old English Poetics: The Aesthetics of the Familiar in Anglo-Saxon England* (York, 2006), pp. 9–100.

14 Michael Swanton, ed., *Beowulf* (Manchester, 1997), pp. 138–47, lines 2208–344.

15 Tyler, *Old English Poetics*, pp. 52–73.

16 Thomas J. Talley, *The Origins of the Liturgical Year* (Collegeville, MN, 1991), pp. 9–12; Paul F. Bradshaw and Lawrence A. Hoffman, eds, *Passover and Easter: Origin and History to Modern Times* (Notre Dame, IN, 1999); C. Philipp E. Nothaft, *Dating the Passion: The Life of Jesus and the Emergence of Scientific Chronology (200–1600)* (Leiden, 2012), pp. 35–56.

17 Talley, *Origins of the Liturgical Year*, pp. 81–99.

18 See for instance British Library, Cotton MS. Tiberius E IV, f. 36, digitized at www.bl.uk/manuscripts, accessed 14 October 2021.

19 Bede, *The Reckoning of Time*, trans. Faith Wallis (Liverpool, 2004), pp. 25–6.

20 Ælfric, *De temporibus anni*, ed. Martin Blake (Cambridge, 2009), pp. 78–81; Byrhtferth, *Enchiridion*, ed. Peter S. Baker and Michael Lapidge (Oxford, 1995), pp. 70–73.

21 Christine Rauer, ed., *The Old English Martyrology: Edition, Translation and Commentary* (Cambridge, 2013), pp. 73–5.

22 For an example from Anglo-Saxon England, see British Library, Cotton MS. Tiberius C VI, f. 7v, digitized at www.bl.uk/manuscripts, accessed 14 October 2021.

23 Bede, *Ecclesiastical History of the English People*, ed. Bertram Colgrave and R.A.B. Mynors (Oxford, 1969), pp. 414–21.

6 EASTER

1 Thomas J. Talley, *The Origins of the Liturgical Year* (Collegeville, MN, 1991), pp. 1–27; Bede, *The Reckoning of Time*, trans. Faith Wallis (Liverpool, 2004), pp. xxxiv–lxiii; Paul F. Bradshaw and Lawrence A. Hoffman, eds, *Passover and Easter: Origin and History to Modern Times* (Notre Dame, IN, 1999); C. Philipp E. Nothaft, *Dating the Passion: The Life of Jesus and the Emergence of Scientific Chronology (200–1600)* (Leiden, 2012).

2 On the Easter controversy and its context, see Richard Abels, 'The Council of Whitby: A Study in Early Anglo-Saxon Politics', *Journal of British Studies*, XXIII (1983), pp. 1–25; Patrick Wormald, *The Times of Bede: Studies in Early English Christian Society and Its Historian*, ed. Stephen Baxter (Oxford, 2006), pp. 207–28; Bede, *Reckoning of Time*, pp. lv–lxiii.

3 Bede, *Ecclesiastical History of the English People*, ed. Bertram Colgrave and R.A.B. Mynors (Oxford, 1969), pp. 296–7.

4 Bede, *Ecclesiastical History*, pp. 294–309.

5 On this idea, see Bradshaw and Hoffman, *Passover and Easter*.

6 Bede, *Reckoning of Time*, p. 54.

7 Jacob Grimm, *Teutonic Mythology*, trans. James Steven Stallybrass (London, 1880–88), vol. I, pp. 288–91; for a summary of other arguments, see Philip A. Shaw, *Pagan Goddesses in the Early Germanic World: Eostre, Hreda and the Cult of Matrons* (London, 2011), pp. 50–53.

8 R. I. Page, 'Anglo-Saxon Paganism: The Evidence of Bede', in *Pagans and Christians: The Interplay between Christian Latin and Traditional Germanic Cultures in Early Medieval Europe*, ed. T. Hofstra, L.A.J.R. Houwen and A. A. MacDonald (Groningen, 1995), pp. 99–129 (p. 125).

9 Shaw, *Pagan Goddesses*, pp. 49–71.

10 Steve Roud, *The English Year* (London, 2008), pp. 158–64; Ronald Hutton, *The Stations of the Sun: A History of the Ritual Year in Britain* (Oxford, 2001), pp. 198–203.

11 See, for instance, the use of *Eastre* in the Old English translation of Luke 22, as Christ and his disciples prepare for Passover; Benjamin Thorpe, ed., *The Anglo-Saxon Version of the Holy Gospels* (London, 1842), pp. 171–2.

12 Dorothy Whitelock, ed., *English Historical Documents, c. 500–1042* (London, 1996), p. 416.

13 Dom Thomas Symons, ed., *Regularis Concordia: Anglicae Nationis Monachorum Sanctimonialiumque; The Monastic Agreement of the Monks and Nuns of the English Nation* (London, 1953). On the liturgy of Palm Sunday and Holy Week, see M. Bradford Bedingfield, *The Dramatic Liturgy of Anglo-Saxon England* (Woodbridge, 2002), pp. 90–170.

14 Ælfric, *Catholic Homilies, The First Series: Text*, ed. Peter Clemoes (Oxford, 1997), p. 297.

15 Bedingfield, *Dramatic Liturgy*, p. 94; Hutton, *Stations of the Sun*, pp. 182–5.

16 Symons, *Regularis Concordia*, pp. 37–41.

17 British Library, Harley MS. 603, f. 66v, digitized at www.bl.uk/manuscripts, accessed 14 October 2021. On the 'royal Maundy', see Hutton, *Stations of the Sun*, pp. 185–7.

18 Symons, *Regularis Concordia*, pp. 36–7; A. J. MacGregor, *Fire and Light in the Western Triduum: Their Use at Tenebrae and at the Paschal Vigil* (Collegeville, MN, 1992).

19 Symons, *Regularis Concordia*, pp. 39, 47–8.

20 Frederick Tupper Jr, 'Anglo-Saxon Dæg-Mæl', *PMLA*, X (1895), pp. 111–241 (pp. 222–3).

21 Barbara Raw, *Anglo-Saxon Crucifixion Iconography and the Art of the Monastic Revival* (Cambridge, 1990).

22 See Inge B. Milfull, ed., *The Hymns of the Anglo-Saxon Church: A Study and Edition of the 'Durham Hymnal'* (Cambridge, 1996), pp. 274–8.

23 On the relationship between the poem and the Ruthwell Cross, see Éamonn Ó Carragáin, *Ritual and the Rood: Liturgical Images and the Old English Poems of the Dream of the Rood Tradition* (London, 2005).

24 For the development of the tradition, see Karl Tamburr, *The Harrowing of Hell in Medieval England* (Cambridge, 2007).

25 Symons, *Regularis Concordia*, pp. 49–50.

26 Eadmer of Canterbury, *Lives and Miracles of Saints Oda, Dunstan and Oswald*, ed. Andrew J. Turner and Bernard J. Muir (Oxford, 2006), p. 177.

27 Gale R. Owen-Crocker, *The Four Funerals in Beowulf and the Structure of the Poem* (Manchester, 2000), pp. 166–9; M. B. McNamee, 'Beowulf: An Allegory of Salvation?', *Journal of English and Germanic Philology*, LIX (1960), pp. 190–207.

7 BLOSSOMING SUMMER

1 Bede, *The Reckoning of Time*, trans. Faith Wallis (Liverpool, 2004), p. 54.

2 Ronald Hutton, *The Stations of the Sun: A History of the Ritual Year in Britain* (Oxford, 2001), pp. 226–61.

3 On the development of the legend, see Barbara Baert, *A Heritage of Holy Wood: The Legend of the True Cross in Text and Image*, trans. Lee Preedy (Leiden, 2004).

4 For discussion of some Anglo-Saxon examples, see Thomas N. Hall, 'The Cross as Green Tree in the *Vindicta Salvatoris* and the Green Rod of Moses in *Exodus*', *English Studies*, LXXII (1991), pp. 297–307.

5 Ælfric, *Catholic Homilies, The Second Series: Text*, ed. Malcolm Godden (Oxford, 1979), p. 136.

6 On knowledge of this hymn in Anglo-Saxon England, see Inge B. Milfull, ed., *The Hymns of the Anglo-Saxon Church: A Study and Edition of the 'Durham Hymnal'* (Cambridge, 1996), pp. 441–3.

7 Della Hooke, *Trees in Anglo-Saxon England: Literature, Lore and Landscape* (Woodbridge, 2010); Michael D. J. Bintley and Michael G. Shapland, eds, *Trees and Timber in the Anglo-Saxon World* (Oxford, 2014); Michael D. J. Bintley, *Trees in the Religions of Early Medieval England* (Woodbridge, 2013).

8 Hooke, *Trees in Anglo-Saxon England*, p. 59.

9 William of Malmesbury, *Saints' Lives: Lives of SS. Wulfstan, Dunstan, Patrick, Benignus and Indract*, ed. M. Winterbottom and R. M. Thomson (Oxford, 2002), pp. 94–7.

10 William of Malmesbury, *Saints' Lives*, pp. 16–21.

11 On the landscape descriptions in *The Phoenix* and the poem's sources,

see Helen Appleton, 'The Insular Landscape of the Old English Poem *The Phoenix*', *Neophilologus*, CI (2017), pp. 585–602.

8 FESTIVALS OF THE LAND AND SKY

1 Joyce Bazire and James E. Cross, eds, *Eleven Old English Rogationtide Homilies* (Toronto, 1982), p. 112.
2 M. Bradford Bedingfield, *The Dramatic Liturgy of Anglo-Saxon England* (Woodbridge, 2002), p. 194.
3 On Rogationtide in Anglo-Saxon England, see John Blair, *The Church in Anglo-Saxon Society* (Oxford, 2005), pp. 176 and 486–9; Helen Gittos, *Liturgy, Architecture, and Sacred Places in Anglo-Saxon England* (Oxford, 2013), pp. 134–8.
4 Bede, *Ecclesiastical History of the English People*, ed. Bertram Colgrave and R.A.B. Mynors (Oxford, 1969), pp. 74–7; see Bedingfield, *Dramatic Liturgy*, p. 200.
5 For Anglo-Saxon homilies for Rogationtide, see Bazire and Cross, *Eleven Old English Rogationtide Homilies*.
6 Ælfric, *Catholic Homilies, The First Series: Text*, ed. Peter Clemoes (Oxford, 1997), p. 317.
7 Ibid., pp. 338, 340–41; on its sources, see Ælfric, *Catholic Homilies: Introduction, Commentary and Glossary*, ed. Malcolm Godden (Oxford, 2000), pp. 159–66.
8 Christine Rauer, ed., *The Old English Martyrology: Edition, Translation and Commentary* (Cambridge, 2013), pp. 94–6; I have used my own translation here.
9 John Johnson, ed., *A Collection of the Laws and Canons of the Church of England* (Oxford, 1850–51), vol. I, p. 250.
10 Byrhtferth, *The Lives of St Oswald and St Ecgwine*, ed. Michael Lapidge (Oxford, 2009), pp. 132–5.
11 A. S. Napier, 'An Old English Vision of Leofric, Earl of Mercia', *Transactions of the Philological Society*, XXVI/2 (1908), pp. 180–88.
12 Ronald Hutton, *The Stations of the Sun: A History of the Ritual Year in Britain* (Oxford, 2001), pp. 277–87.
13 Steve Roud, *The English Year* (London, 2008), pp. 243–8.
14 Bazire and Cross, *Eleven Old English Rogationtide Homilies*, p. 31.
15 See for instance Bede, *Ecclesiastical History*, pp. 544–5.
16 Colin Chase, 'God's Presence through Grace as the Theme of Cynewulf's *Christ II* and the Relationship of This Theme to *Christ I* and *Christ III*', *Anglo-Saxon England*, III (1974), pp. 87–101.

17 British Library, Additional MS. 49598, f. 64v, digitized at www.bl.uk/
manuscripts, accessed 14 October 2021.

18 Hutton, *Stations of the Sun*, pp. 244–61.

19 Roud, *The English Year*, pp. 260–73.

20 Bede, *Ecclesiastical History*, pp. 166–7.

21 G. P. Cubbin, ed., *The Anglo-Saxon Chronicle MS. D* (Cambridge, 1996),
p. 83.

22 On the context of Edgar's coronation, see Jayne Carroll, '*Engla Waldend,
Rex Admirabilis*: Poetic Representations of King Edgar', *Review of
English Studies*, LVIII (2007), pp. 113–32.

23 See Katherine O'Brien O'Keeffe, ed., *The Anglo-Saxon Chronicle MS. C*
(Cambridge, 2001), p. 82; and Michael Swanton, trans., *The Anglo-Saxon
Chronicles* (London, 2000), p. 118.

9 MIDSUMMER

1 Bede, *The Reckoning of Time*, trans. Faith Wallis (Liverpool, 2004),
pp. 86–9.

2 Thomas J. Talley, *The Origins of the Liturgical Year* (Collegeville, MN,
1991), pp. 91–9.

3 Ælfric, *De temporibus anni*, ed. Martin Blake (Cambridge, 2009), p. 84.

4 Ibid., p. 88, and see the editor's note on p. 118.

5 Susan Irvine, ed., *The Anglo-Saxon Chronicle MS. E* (Cambridge, 2004),
p. 82.

6 Ælfric, *Catholic Homilies, The First Series: Text*, ed. Peter Clemoes
(Oxford, 1997), p. 383.

7 Anne Van Arsdall, *Medieval Herbal Remedies: The Old English
Herbarium and Anglo-Saxon Medicine* (New York, 2002), pp. 146, 210.

8 This text is from British Library, Cotton MS. Vitellius E XVIII, digitized
at www.bl.uk/manuscripts, accessed 14 October 2021.

9 Edward Pettit, ed., *Anglo-Saxon Remedies, Charms, and Prayers from
British Library MS. Harley 585: The Lacnunga* (Lewiston, NY, 2001),
vol. I, pp. 8–9; in this case the appointed date is the beginning of summer
on 9 May.

10 Karen Louise Jolly, 'Tapping the Power of the Cross: Who and for
Whom?', in *The Place of the Cross in Anglo-Saxon England*, ed. Catherine
E. Karkov, Sarah Larratt Keefer and Karen Louise Jolly (Woodbridge,
2006), pp. 58–79.

11 Steve Roud, *The English Year* (London, 2008), pp. 297–304.

12 John Mirk, *Mirk's Festial: A Collection of Homilies*, ed. Theodor Erbe
(London, 1905), vol. I, p. 183.

13 Ronald Hutton, *The Stations of the Sun: A History of the Ritual Year in Britain* (Oxford, 2001), pp. 311–21.

14 Goscelin, *Translatio S. Edithae*, in *Writing the Wilton Women: Goscelin's Legend of Edith and Liber confortatorius*, ed. Stephanie Hollis, with W. R. Barnes, Rebecca Hayward, Kathleen Loncar and Michael Wright (Turnhout, 2004), p. 92.

15 Roud, *The English Year*, pp. 304–5.

16 Donald Watts, *Dictionary of Plant Lore* (Amsterdam, 2007), pp. 339–42.

17 Roud, *The English Year*, pp. 300–301.

18 See Susan Irvine and Malcolm R. Godden, eds, *The Old English Boethius* (London, 2012), pp. 252–3.

19 Alaric Hall, 'The Images and Structure of *The Wife's Lament*', *Leeds Studies in English*, XXXIII (2002), pp. 1–29.

20 Sarah Semple, *Perceptions of the Prehistoric in Anglo-Saxon England: Religion, Ritual, and Rulership in the Landscape* (Oxford, 2013); John Blair, *Building Anglo-Saxon England* (Oxford, 2018), pp. 82–4.

21 Semple, *Perceptions of the Prehistoric*, pp. 143–92.

22 Bede, *Reckoning of Time*, p. 54.

23 Ælfric, *De temporibus anni*, p. 84.

24 Ælfric, *Catholic Homilies, First Series*, p. 293.

10 HARVEST

1 On the modern revival of harvest festivals, see Steve Roud, *The English Year* (London, 2008), pp. 376–87.

2 See Debby Banham and Rosamond Faith, *Anglo-Saxon Farms and Farming* (Oxford, 2014), pp. 20–33.

3 An often-cited source which appears to state this, William Somner, *Dictionarium Saxonico-Latino-Anglicum* (Oxford, 1659), offers a Latin explanation of Lammas (*festum primitiarum*) as a gloss to the use of the name in the *Anglo-Saxon Chronicle*, but the explanation does not appear in the *Chronicle*.

4 Máire MacNeill, *The Festival of Lughnasa: A Study of the Survival of the Celtic Festival of the Beginning of Harvest* (Oxford, 1962); Mark Williams, *Ireland's Immortals: A History of the Gods of Irish Myth* (Princeton, NJ, 2016), pp. 16–27; Ronald Hutton, *The Stations of the Sun: A History of the Ritual Year in Britain* (Oxford, 2001), pp. 327–31.

5 Christine Rauer, ed., *The Old English Martyrology: Edition, Translation and Commentary* (Cambridge, 2013), p. 150.

6 Malcolm R. Godden, ed., *The Old English History of the World: An Anglo-Saxon Rewriting of Orosius* (Cambridge, MA, 2016), pp. 342–3.

7　Michael Swanton, trans., *The Anglo-Saxon Chronicles* (London, 2000), p. 101.

8　See for instance Ælfric, *Catholic Homilies, The Second Series: Text*, ed. Malcolm Godden (Oxford, 1979), p. 222.

9　See László Sándor Chardonnens, ed., *Anglo-Saxon Prognostics, 900–1100: Study and Texts* (Leiden, 2007), p. 283.

10　Ibid., pp. 270–89.

11　Roud, *The English Year*, pp. 353–8.

12　This text is from British Library, Cotton MS. Vitellius E XVIII, digitized at www.bl.uk/manuscripts, accessed 14 October 2021.

13　Karen Louise Jolly, 'Tapping the Power of the Cross: Who and for Whom?', in *The Place of the Cross in Anglo-Saxon England*, ed. Catherine E. Karkov, Sarah Larratt Keefer and Karen Louise Jolly (Woodbridge, 2006), pp. 58–79.

14　See for instance Edward Pettit, ed., *Anglo-Saxon Remedies, Charms, and Prayers from British Library MS. Harley 585: The Lacnunga* (Lewiston, NY, 2001), vol. I, pp. 16–17 and 32–3.

15　G. N. Garmonsway and Jacqueline Simpson, *Beowulf and Its Analogues* (London, 1980), pp. 118–23; Alexander M. Bruce, *Scyld and Scef: Expanding the Analogues* (New York, 2002).

16　Scyld's story is told in lines 4–52 of *Beowulf*; see Michael Swanton, ed., *Beowulf* (Manchester, 1997), pp. 34–7.

17　Katherine Cross, *Heirs of the Vikings: History and Identity in Normandy and England, c. 950–c. 1015* (York, 2018), pp. 30–41; Roberta Frank, 'Skaldic Verse and the Date of *Beowulf*', in *The Dating of Beowulf*, ed. Colin Chase (Toronto, 1981), pp. 123–39; Eleanor Parker, *Dragon Lords: The History and Legends of Viking England* (London, 2018), pp. 32–4.

18　Bede, *The Reckoning of Time*, trans. Faith Wallis (Liverpool, 2004), p. 54.

19　Felix Lieberman, ed., *Die Gesetze der Angelsachsen* (Halle, 1903), vol. I, p. 12; Philip A. Shaw, *Pagan Goddesses in the Early Germanic World: Eostre, Hreda and the Cult of Matrons* (London, 2011), pp. 65–6.

20　'Our Lady day, n.', https://oed.com, accessed 14 October 2021. On these feasts in Anglo-Saxon England, see Mary Clayton, *The Cult of the Virgin Mary in Anglo-Saxon England* (Cambridge, 2002).

11 FALLOW AND FALL

1　Bede, *The Reckoning of Time*, trans. Faith Wallis (Liverpool, 2004), p. 54.

2　Ronald Hutton, *The Stations of the Sun: A History of the Ritual Year in Britain* (Oxford, 2001), pp. 332–47.

3　Thom Gobbitt, ed., 'Gerefa', *Early English Laws*, https://earlyenglishlaws.ac.uk, accessed 14 October 2021.

4 Richard Freeman Johnson, *Saint Michael the Archangel in Medieval English Legend* (Woodbridge, 2005).

5 See Richard Freeman Johnson, 'Archangel in the Margins: St Michael in the Homilies of Cambridge, Corpus Christi College 41', *Traditio*, LIII (1998), pp. 63–91.

6 Ælfric, *Grammatik und Glossar*, ed. Julius Zupitza (Berlin, 1880), p. 43.

7 Snorri Sturluson, *Edda: Skáldskaparmál*, ed. Anthony Faulkes (London, 1998), vol. I, p. 99.

8 Gobbitt, ed., 'Gerefa'.

9 Byrhtferth, *Enchiridion*, ed. Peter S. Baker and Michael Lapidge (Oxford, 1995), p. 78.

10 Bede, *Reckoning of Time*, p. 54.

11 J. J. Anderson, ed., *Sir Gawain and the Green Knight, Pearl, Cleanness, Patience* (London, 2005), p. 189.

12 For a translation of this poem and discussion of its context, see Mark Atherton, *The Battle of Maldon: War and Peace in Tenth-Century England* (London, 2021).

13 For discussion of the relationship between Old English and Old Norse wisdom poetry, see Carolyne Larrington, *A Store of Common Sense: Gnomic Theme and Style in Old Icelandic and Old English Wisdom Poetry* (Oxford, 1993).

14 Carolyne Larrington, trans., *The Poetic Edda* (Oxford, 1999), p. 6; Snorri Sturluson, *Edda*, trans. Anthony Faulkes (London, 1998), p. 13.

15 For example, see Larrington, *Poetic Edda*, pp. 179, 239; Michael D. J. Bintley, 'Life-Cycles of Men and Trees in *Sonatorrek*', *Opticon1826*, VI (2009), pp. 1–3.

16 Larrington, *Poetic Edda*, p. 21.

17 See Heather O'Donoghue, *From Asgard to Valhalla: The Remarkable History of the Norse Myths* (London, 2007), pp. 17–18.

18 Snorri, *Edda*, trans. Faulkes, p. 49.

19 Larrington, *Poetic Edda*, p. 47.

20 Eleanor Parker, *Dragon Lords: The History and Legends of Viking England* (London, 2018), pp. 115–19.

21 Frank Barlow, ed., *The Life of King Edward Who Rests at Westminster* (Oxford, 1992), pp. 116–21, 131–2.

12 THE MONTH OF BLOOD

1 Wilhelm Levison, *England and the Continent in the Eighth Century* (Oxford, 1946), pp. 159–60.

2 'All-Hallows, n.', https://oed.com, accessed 14 October 2021.

REFERENCES

3 Ronald Hutton, *The Stations of the Sun: A History of the Ritual Year in Britain* (Oxford, 2001), pp. 360–85.
4 Steve Roud, *The English Year* (London, 2008), pp. 439–45.
5 Ælfric, *Lives of Saints*, ed. Walter W. Skeat (London, 1881–1900), vol. II, p. 332.
6 Ibid., vol. I, p. 6.
7 Alistair Campbell, ed., *The Chronicle of Æthelweard* (London, 1962), pp. 32–3.
8 Patrick Wormald, 'Æthelweard (d. 998?)', *Oxford Dictionary of National Biography* (2004), https://doi.org/10.1093/ref:odnb/8918.
9 See Campbell, ed., *The Chronicle of Æthelweard*, pp. xii–xvi.
10 Eleanor Parker, *Dragon Lords: The History and Legends of Viking England* (London, 2018), pp. 50–57; for Cnut and Æthelnoth at Wilton, see William of Malmesbury, *Gesta Pontificum Anglorum*, ed. Michael Winterbottom and R. M. Thomson (Oxford, 2007), vol. I, pp. 298–301.
11 Emma Mason, 'Æthelnoth (d. 1038)', *Oxford Dictionary of National Biography* (2004), https://doi.org/10.1093/ref:odnb/8912.
12 Ælfric, *Catholic Homilies, The Second Series: Text*, ed. Malcolm Godden (Oxford, 1979), p. 289.
13 Bede, *The Reckoning of Time*, trans. Faith Wallis (Liverpool, 2004), p. 54.
14 For a recent overview, see Neil Price, *The Children of Ash and Elm: A History of the Vikings* (London, 2020), pp. 209–21.
15 Bede, *Ecclesiastical History of the English People*, ed. Bertram Colgrave and R.A.B. Mynors (Oxford, 1969), pp. 76–7.
16 On the cult of St Martin in Anglo-Saxon England, see Julia Barrow, 'Bishop Brictius – Saint Brice', in *Beretning fra seksogtyvende tværfaglige vikingesymposium*, ed. Niels Lund (Aarhus, 2007), pp. 68–88.
17 Bede, *Ecclesiastical History*, pp. 106–9.
18 Eleanor Searle, ed., *The Chronicle of Battle Abbey* (Oxford, 1980), pp. 32–9.
19 S. J. Ridyard, '*Condigna veneratio*: Post-Conquest Attitudes to the Saints of the Anglo-Saxons', *Anglo-Norman Studies*, IX (1986), pp. 179–206; P. A. Hayward, 'Translation-Narratives in Post-Conquest Hagiography and English Resistance to the Norman Conquest', *Anglo-Norman Studies*, XXI (1998), pp. 67–93.
20 See Tom Licence, ed., *Bury St Edmunds and the Norman Conquest* (Woodbridge, 2014).
21 See James Campbell, *Essays in Anglo-Saxon History* (London, 1986), pp. 209–28; Andrew Galloway, 'Writing History in England', in *The Cambridge History of Medieval English Literature*, ed. David Wallace (Cambridge, 1999), pp. 255–83; Martin Brett and D. A. Woodman, eds, *The Long Twelfth-Century View of the Anglo-Saxon Past* (London, 2016).

22 Elaine Treharne, 'Making Their Presence Felt: Readers of Ælfric, *c.* 1050–1350', in *A Companion to Ælfric*, ed. Hugh Magennis and Mary Swan (Boston, MA, 2009), pp. 399–422.

BIBLIOGRAPHY

FURTHER READING

Full texts and translations of the poems discussed in this book can be found in the following anthologies:

Bjork, Robert E., ed., *Old English Shorter Poems: Wisdom and Lyric* (Cambridge, MA, 2014): contains *Æcerbot* (*'Metrical Charm 1'*), *Deor*, *Maxims I*, *Maxims II*, *Solomon and Saturn*, *The Fortunes of Mortals*, *The Gifts of Mortals*, *The Husband's Message*, *The Old English Rune Poem*, *The Rhyming Poem*, *The Ruin*, *The Seafarer*, *The Wanderer*, *The Wife's Lament*

——, ed., *The Old English Poems of Cynewulf* (Cambridge, MA, 2013): contains *Christ II*, *Elene*, *Juliana*

Jones, Christopher A., ed., *Old English Shorter Poems: Religious and Didactic* (Cambridge, MA, 2012): contains *The Menologium*, *The Phoenix*, *Cædmon's Hymn*

Clayton, Mary, ed., *Old English Poems of Christ and His Saints* (Cambridge, MA, 2013): contains the *Advent Lyrics*, *Andreas*, *Guthlac A*, *The Descent into Hell*, *The Dream of the Rood* (*'The Vision of the Cross'*)

Other good anthologies of Old English literature in translation include S.A.J. Bradley, ed., *Anglo-Saxon Poetry* (London, 2003); Kevin Crossley-Holland, *The Anglo-Saxon World: An Anthology* (Oxford, 1999); and Simon Keynes and Michael Lapidge, ed., *Alfred the Great: Asser's Life of King Alfred and Other Contemporary Sources* (Harmondsworth, 1983). For accessible overviews of Anglo-Saxon history, see Henrietta Leyser, *A Short History of the Anglo-Saxons* (London, 2017) and John Blair, *The Anglo-Saxon Age: A Very Short Introduction*

(Oxford, 2000). Useful introductions to the Old English language include Mark Atherton, *Complete Old English: Teach Yourself* (London, 2010) and Peter Baker, *Introduction to Old English* (Chichester, 2012).

WORKS CITED

EDITIONS AND TRANSLATIONS OF MEDIEVAL TEXTS

Ælfric, *Catholic Homilies: Introduction, Commentary and Glossary*, ed. Malcolm Godden (Oxford, 2000)

—, *Catholic Homilies, The First Series: Text*, ed. Peter Clemoes (Oxford, 1997)

—, *Catholic Homilies, The Second Series: Text*, ed. Malcolm Godden (Oxford, 1979)

—, *Colloquy*, ed. G. N. Garmonsway (London, 1947)

—, *De temporibus anni*, ed. Martin Blake (Cambridge, 2009)

—, *Grammatik und Glossar*, ed. Julius Zupitza (Berlin, 1880)

—, *Lives of Saints*, ed. Walter W. Skeat (London, 1881–1900)

Anderson, J. J., ed., *Sir Gawain and the Green Knight, Pearl, Cleanness, Patience* (London, 2005)

Barlow, Frank, ed., *The Life of King Edward Who Rests at Westminster* (Oxford, 1992)

Bazire, Joyce, and James E. Cross, eds, *Eleven Old English Rogationtide Homilies* (Toronto, 1982)

Bede, *Ecclesiastical History of the English People*, ed. Bertram Colgrave and R.A.B. Mynors (Oxford, 1969)

—, *The Reckoning of Time*, trans. Faith Wallis (Liverpool, 2004)

Bischoff, Bernhard, and Michael Lapidge, eds, *Biblical Commentaries from the Canterbury School of Theodore and Hadrian* (Cambridge, 1994)

Byrhtferth, *Enchiridion*, ed. Peter S. Baker and Michael Lapidge (Oxford, 1995)

—, *The Lives of St Oswald and St Ecgwine*, ed. Michael Lapidge (Oxford, 2009)

Campbell, Alistair, ed., *The Chronicle of Æthelweard* (London, 1962)

Chardonnens, László Sándor, ed., *Anglo-Saxon Prognostics, 900–1100: Study and Texts* (Leiden, 2007)

Colgrave, Bertram, ed., *Felix's Life of Saint Guthlac* (Cambridge, 1985)

—, ed., *Two Lives of Saint Cuthbert* (Cambridge, 1985)

Cubbin, G. P., ed., *The Anglo-Saxon Chronicle MS. D* (Cambridge, 1996)

Davies, R. T., ed., *Medieval English Lyrics: A Critical Anthology* (London, 1978)

Eadmer of Canterbury, *Lives and Miracles of Saints Oda, Dunstan and Oswald*, ed. Andrew J. Turner and Bernard J. Muir (Oxford, 2006)

Garmonsway, G. N., and Jacqueline Simpson, *Beowulf and Its Analogues* (London, 1980)

Gobbitt, Thom, ed., 'Gerefa', *Early English Laws*, https://earlyenglishlaws. ac.uk, accessed 14 October 2021

Godden, Malcolm R., ed., *The Old English History of the World: An Anglo-Saxon Rewriting of Orosius* (Cambridge, MA, 2016)

Godman, Peter, ed., *Poetry of the Carolingian Renaissance* (London, 1985)

Goscelin, *Translatio S. Edithae*, in *Writing the Wilton Women: Goscelin's Legend of Edith and Liber confortatorius*, ed. Stephanie Hollis, with W. R. Barnes, Rebecca Hayward, Kathleen Loncar and Michael Wright (Turnhout, 2004)

Haddan, Arthur W., and William Stubbs, eds, *Councils and Ecclesiastical Documents Relating to Great Britain and Ireland* (Oxford, 1869–78)

Irvine, Susan, ed., *The Anglo-Saxon Chronicle MS. E* (Cambridge, 2004)

—, and Malcolm R. Godden, eds, *The Old English Boethius* (London, 2012)

Johnson, John, ed., *A Collection of the Laws and Canons of the Church of England* (Oxford, 1850–51)

Karasawa, Kazutomo, ed., *The Old English Metrical Calendar (Menologium)* (Cambridge, 2015)

Larrington, Carolyne, trans., *The Poetic Edda* (Oxford, 1999)

Lieberman, Felix, ed., *Die Gesetze der Angelsachsen* (Halle, 1903)

Liuzza, R. M., ed., *Anglo-Saxon Prognostics: An Edition and Translation of Texts from London, British Library, MS. Cotton Tiberius A III* (Cambridge, 2010)

Milfull, Inge B., ed., *The Hymns of the Anglo-Saxon Church: A Study and Edition of the 'Durham Hymnal'* (Cambridge, 1996)

Mirk, John, *Mirk's Festial: A Collection of Homilies*, ed. Theodor Erbe (London, 1905)

Napier, A. S., 'An Old English Vision of Leofric, Earl of Mercia', *Transactions of the Philological Society*, XXVI/2 (1908), pp. 180–88

O'Brien O'Keeffe, Katherine, ed., *The Anglo-Saxon Chronicle MS. C* (Cambridge, 2001)

Pettit, Edward, ed., *Anglo-Saxon Remedies, Charms, and Prayers from British Library MS. Harley 585: The Lacnunga* (Lewiston, NY, 2001)

Rauer, Christine, ed., *The Old English Martyrology: Edition, Translation and Commentary* (Cambridge, 2013)

Rushforth, Rebecca, ed., *Saints in English Kalendars before AD 1100* (London, 2008)

Searle, Eleanor, ed., *The Chronicle of Battle Abbey* (Oxford, 1980)

Snorri Sturluson, *Edda*, trans. Anthony Faulkes (London, 1998)

—, *Edda: Skáldskaparmál*, ed. Anthony Faulkes (London, 1998)

Stubbs, William, ed., *Memorials of Saint Dunstan, Archbishop of Canterbury* (London, 1874)

Swanton, Michael, trans., *The Anglo-Saxon Chronicles* (London, 2000)

—, ed., *Beowulf* (Manchester, 1997)

Symons, Dom Thomas, ed., *Regularis Concordia: Anglicae Nationis Monachorum Sanctimonialiumque; The Monastic Agreement of the Monks and Nuns of the English Nation* (London, 1953)

Thorpe, Benjamin, ed., *The Anglo-Saxon Version of the Holy Gospels* (London, 1842)

Van Arsdall, Anne, *Medieval Herbal Remedies: The Old English Herbarium and Anglo-Saxon Medicine* (New York, 2002)

Whitelock, Dorothy, ed., *English Historical Documents, c. 500–1042* (London, 1996)

William of Malmesbury, *Gesta Pontificum Anglorum*, ed. Michael Winterbottom and R. M. Thomson (Oxford, 2007)

—, *Saints' Lives: Lives of SS Wulfstan, Dunstan, Patrick, Benignus and Indract*, ed. M. Winterbottom and R. M. Thomson (Oxford, 2002)

SECONDARY SOURCES

Abels, Richard, 'The Council of Whitby: A Study in Early Anglo-Saxon Politics', *Journal of British Studies*, XXIII (1983), pp. 1–25

Anderson, Earl R., *Folk Taxonomies in Early English* (Madison, NJ, 2003)

Appleton, Helen, 'The Insular Landscape of the Old English Poem *The Phoenix*', *Neophilologus*, CI (2017), pp. 585–602

Atherton, Mark, *The Battle of Maldon: War and Peace in Tenth-Century England* (London, 2021)

Backhouse, Janet, D. H. Turner and Leslie Webster, eds, *The Golden Age of Anglo-Saxon Art, 966–1066* (London, 1984)

Baert, Barbara, *A Heritage of Holy Wood: The Legend of the True Cross in Text and Image*, trans. Lee Preedy (Leiden, 2004)

Banham, Debby, and Rosamond Faith, *Anglo-Saxon Farms and Farming* (Oxford, 2014)

Barrow, Julia, 'Bishop Brictius – Saint Brice', in *Beretning fra seksogtyvende tværfaglige vikingesymposium*, ed. Niels Lund (Aarhus, 2007), pp. 68–88

Bedingfield, M. Bradford, *The Dramatic Liturgy of Anglo-Saxon England* (Woodbridge, 2002)

Beechy, Tiffany, '*Eala Earendel*: Extraordinary Poetics in Old English', *Modern Philology*, CVIII (2010), pp. 1–19

Bintley, Michael D. J., 'Life-Cycles of Men and Trees in *Sonatorrek*', *Opticon1826*, VI (2009), pp. 1–3

—, *Trees in the Religions of Early Medieval England* (Woodbridge, 2013)

—, and Michael G. Shapland, eds, *Trees and Timber in the Anglo-Saxon World* (Oxford, 2014)

Blair, John, *Building Anglo-Saxon England* (Oxford, 2018)

—, *The Church in Anglo-Saxon Society* (Oxford, 2005)

Bradshaw, Paul F., and Lawrence A. Hoffman, eds, *Passover and Easter: Origin and History to Modern Times* (Notre Dame, IN, 1999)

Brett, Martin, and D. A. Woodman, eds, *The Long Twelfth-Century View of the Anglo-Saxon Past* (London, 2016)

British Library Digitised Manuscripts, www.bl.uk/manuscripts

Bruce, Alexander M., *Scyld and Scef: Expanding the Analogues* (New York, 2002)

Cameron, M. L., *Anglo-Saxon Medicine* (Cambridge, 1993)

Campbell, James, *Essays in Anglo-Saxon History* (London, 1986)

Carroll, Jayne, '*Engla Waldend, Rex Admirabilis*: Poetic Representations of King Edgar', *Review of English Studies*, LVIII (2007), pp. 113–32

Chase, Colin, 'God's Presence through Grace as the Theme of Cynewulf's *Christ II* and the Relationship of This Theme to *Christ I* and *Christ III*', *Anglo-Saxon England*, III (1974), pp. 87–101

Clayton, Mary, *The Cult of the Virgin Mary in Anglo-Saxon England* (Cambridge, 2002)

Courtney, M. A., *Cornish Feasts and Folk-Lore* (Penzance, 1890)

Cross, Katherine, *Heirs of the Vikings: History and Identity in Normandy and England, c. 950–c. 1015* (York, 2018)

Foot, Sarah, 'The Making of *Angelcynn*: English Identity before the Norman Conquest', *Transactions of the Royal Historical Society*, VI (1996), pp. 25–49

Frank, Roberta, 'Skaldic Verse and the Date of *Beowulf*', in *The Dating of Beowulf*, ed. Colin Chase (Toronto, 1981), pp. 123–39

Galloway, Andrew, 'Writing History in England', in *The Cambridge History of Medieval English Literature*, ed. David Wallace (Cambridge, 1999), pp. 255–83

Gittos, Helen, *Liturgy, Architecture, and Sacred Places in Anglo-Saxon England* (Oxford, 2013)

Grimm, Jacob, *Teutonic Mythology*, trans. James Steven Stallybrass (London, 1880–88)

Hall, Alaric, 'The Images and Structure of *The Wife's Lament*', *Leeds Studies in English*, XXXIII (2002), pp. 1–29

Hall, Thomas N., 'The Cross as Green Tree in the *Vindicta Salvatoris* and the Green Rod of Moses in *Exodus*', *English Studies*, LXXII (1991), pp. 297–307

Hampson, R. T., *Medii Ævi Kalendarium* (London, 1841)

Hayward, P. A., 'Translation-Narratives in Post-Conquest Hagiography and English Resistance to the Norman Conquest', *Anglo-Norman Studies*, XXI (1998), pp. 67–93

Hill, Thomas D., 'The *Æcerbot* Charm and Its Christian User', *Anglo-Saxon England*, VI (1977), pp. 213–21

Hooke, Della, *Trees in Anglo-Saxon England: Literature, Lore and Landscape* (Woodbridge, 2010)

Howe, Nicholas, *Writing the Map of Anglo-Saxon England: Essays in Cultural Geography* (New Haven, CT, 2008)

Hutton, Ronald, *The Stations of the Sun: A History of the Ritual Year in Britain* (Oxford, 2001)

Johnson, Richard Freeman, 'Archangel in the Margins: St Michael in the Homilies of Cambridge, Corpus Christi College 41', *Traditio*, LIII (1998), pp. 63–91

——, *Saint Michael the Archangel in Medieval English Legend* (Woodbridge, 2005)

Jolly, Karen Louise, 'Tapping the Power of the Cross: Who and for Whom?', in *The Place of the Cross in Anglo-Saxon England*, ed. Catherine E. Karkov, Sarah Larratt Keefer and Karen Louise Jolly (Woodbridge, 2006), pp. 58–79

——, *Popular Religion in Late Saxon England: Elf Charms in Context* (London, 1996)

Lacey, Mohamed Eric Rahman, 'Birds and Bird-Lore in the Literature of Anglo-Saxon England', PhD thesis, University College London, 2013

Langeslag, P. S., *Seasons in the Literatures of the Medieval North* (Cambridge, 2015)

Larrington, Carolyne, *A Store of Common Sense: Gnomic Theme and Style in Old Icelandic and Old English Wisdom Poetry* (Oxford, 1993)

Lee, Stuart, and Elizabeth Solopova, *The Keys of Middle-Earth: Discovering Medieval Literature through the Fiction of J.R.R. Tolkien* (Basingstoke, 2015)

Levison, Wilhelm, *England and the Continent in the Eighth Century* (Oxford, 1946)

Licence, Tom, ed., *Bury St Edmunds and the Norman Conquest* (Woodbridge, 2014)

MacGregor, A. J., *Fire and Light in the Western Triduum: Their Use at Tenebrae and at the Paschal Vigil* (Collegeville, MN, 1992)

McNamee, M. B., '*Beowulf*: An Allegory of Salvation?', *Journal of English and Germanic Philology*, LIX (1960), pp. 190–207

MacNeill, Máire, *The Festival of Lughnasa: A Study of the Survival of the Celtic Festival of the Beginning of Harvest* (Oxford, 1962)

Mason, Emma, 'Æthelnoth (d. 1038)', *Oxford Dictionary of National Biography* (2004), https://doi.org/10.1093/ref:odnb/8912

Meaney, Audrey L., 'Bede and Anglo-Saxon Paganism', *Parergon*, III (1985), pp. 1–29

Neville, Jennifer, *Representations of the Natural World in Old English Poetry* (Cambridge, 1999)

Niles, John D., 'The *Æcerbot* Ritual in Context', in *Old English Literature in Context*, ed. John D. Niles (Cambridge, 1980), pp. 44–56

Nothaft, C. Philipp E., *Dating the Passion: The Life of Jesus and the Emergence of Scientific Chronology (200–1600)* (Leiden, 2012)

Ó Carragáin, Éamonn, *Ritual and the Rood: Liturgical Images and the Old English Poems of the Dream of the Rood Tradition* (London, 2005)

O'Donoghue, Heather, *From Asgard to Valhalla: The Remarkable History of the Norse Myths* (London, 2007)

Owen-Crocker, Gale R., *The Four Funerals in Beowulf and the Structure of the Poem* (Manchester, 2000)

Page, R. I., 'Anglo-Saxon Paganism: The Evidence of Bede', in *Pagans and Christians: The Interplay between Christian Latin and Traditional Germanic Cultures in Early Medieval Europe*, ed. T. Hofstra, L.A.J.R. Houwen and A. A. MacDonald (Groningen, 1995), pp. 99–129

—, *An Introduction to English Runes* (Woodbridge, 1999)

Parker, Eleanor, *Dragon Lords: The History and Legends of Viking England* (London, 2018)

Poole, Robert, *Time's Alteration: Calendar Reform in Early Modern England* (London, 1998)

Price, Neil, *The Children of Ash and Elm: A History of the Vikings* (London, 2020)

Rankin, Susan, 'The Liturgical Background of the Old English Advent Lyrics: A Reappraisal', in *Learning and Literature in Anglo-Saxon England*, ed. Michael Lapidge and Helmut Gneuss (Cambridge, 1985), pp. 317–40

Raw, Barbara, *Anglo-Saxon Crucifixion Iconography and the Art of the Monastic Revival* (Cambridge, 1990)

Ridyard, S. J., '*Condigna veneratio*: Post-Conquest Attitudes to the Saints of the Anglo-Saxons', *Anglo-Norman Studies*, IX (1986), pp. 179–206

Roach, Levi, *Kingship and Consent in Anglo-Saxon England, 871–978: Assemblies and the State in the Early Middle Ages* (Cambridge, 2013)

Roud, Steve, *The English Year* (London, 2008)

Semple, Sarah, *Perceptions of the Prehistoric in Anglo-Saxon England: Religion, Ritual, and Rulership in the Landscape* (Oxford, 2013)

Sermon, Richard, 'Wassail! The Origins of a Drinking Toast', *Third Stone*, XLVI (2003), pp. 15–19

Shaw, Philip A., *Pagan Goddesses in the Early Germanic World: Eostre, Hreda and the Cult of Matrons* (London, 2011)

Somner, William, *Dictionarium Saxonico-Latino-Anglicum* (Oxford, 1659)

Stafford, Pauline, *After Alfred: Anglo-Saxon Chronicles and Chroniclers, 900–1150* (Oxford, 2020)

Talley, Thomas J., *The Origins of the Liturgical Year* (Collegeville, MN, 1991)

Tamburr, Karl, *The Harrowing of Hell in Medieval England* (Cambridge, 2007)

Treharne, Elaine, 'Making Their Presence Felt: Readers of Ælfric, *c.* 1050–1350', in *A Companion to Ælfric*, ed. Hugh Magennis and Mary Swan (Boston, MA, 2009), pp. 399–422

Tupper, Frederick Jr, 'Anglo-Saxon Dæg-Mæl', *PMLA*, X (1895), pp. 111–241

Turville-Petre, J. E., 'Hengest and Horsa', *Saga-Book of the Viking Society*, XIV (1953–7), pp. 273–90

Tyler, Elizabeth M., *Old English Poetics: The Aesthetics of the Familiar in Anglo-Saxon England* (York, 2006)

Watts, Donald, *Dictionary of Plant Lore* (Amsterdam, 2007)

Williams, Mark, *Ireland's Immortals: A History of the Gods of Irish Myth* (Princeton, NJ, 2016)

Wormald, Patrick, *The Times of Bede: Studies in Early English Christian Society and Its Historian*, ed. Stephen Baxter (Oxford, 2006)

——, 'Æthelweard (d. 998?)', *Oxford Dictionary of National Biography* (2004), https://doi.org/10.1093/ref:odnb/8918

ACKNOWLEDGEMENTS

I first became interested in the subject of this book through writing for my website, 'A Clerk of Oxford', and I'd like to acknowledge with gratitude all those readers over the years who have shared with me their thoughts, comments and enthusiasm for learning about the Anglo-Saxon year. Special thanks go to those who have supported me on Patreon; I could not have written this book without their encouragement. Two people to whom I owe a particular debt of gratitude are Tom Holland, who has been unfailingly kind and generous in his support for my work in this area, and Paul Lay, who by giving me the opportunity to write for *History Today* – on this and many other subjects – has helped me in ways for which I will always be thankful.

I want to end here, as I began, with an extract from one of the Old English translations associated with Alfred the Great, a version of St Augustine's *Soliloquies*. It's a beautiful meditation on change and constancy, death and the eternal – on the cycles of nature, but also on what lies beyond them.

You rule the year, and govern it through the turning of the four seasons, that is, spring and summer and harvest and winter. These change places, each with another, and turn so that each of them is again exactly what it was before, and where it was before; and likewise all heavenly bodies change places and turn in the same way, and the sea and rivers too. In this way all created things undergo change. But some change in another way, such that the same thing does not come again where it was before, or exactly as it was before, but another comes in its place; just so leaves on the trees, and fruits, grass, and plants and trees grow old and sere, and others come, grow green, and reach maturity, and ripen, and with that begin again to grow sere. And so do all beasts and birds, in such a way that it would take too long to reckon them all now. And indeed the bodies of men grow old, just as other created things grow old. But just as their lives are more precious than those of trees or other animals, so they will more worthily arise on Judgement Day, and then never again will the body come to an end or grow old.

INDEX